THE
SINGLE WOMAN–
MARRIED MAN
SYNDROME

THE
SINGLE WOMAN—
MARRIED MAN
SYNDROME

Richard Tuch, M.D.

Jason Aronson Inc.
Northvale, NJ

This book was set in 11 pt. New Aster by Alpha Graphics of Pittsfield, NH and printed and bound by Book-mart Press, Inc. of North Bergen, NJ.

Library of Congress Cataloging-in-Publication Data
Tuch, Richard.
    The single woman–married man syndrome / by Richard Tuch.
      p. cm.
    Includes index.
    ISBN 0-7657-0244-4
    1. Adultery—Psychological aspects. 2. Single women—Psychology.
  3. Husbands—Psychology. 4. Mistresses—Psychology. 5. Man–woman
  relationships. 6. Masochism. I. Title.
HQ806.T43 2000
306.73'6—dc21
99-43394

Printed in the United States of America on acid-free paper. For information and catalog write to Jason Aronson Inc., 230 Livingston Street, Northvale, NJ 07647-1726, or visit our website: www.aronson.com

To Sunnye, Alex, and Zachary
for making it all worthwhile

Contents

Acknowledgments

There are many people without whose help this book would not have been possible. I wish to thank Claudia Kohner, Gregory Wesley, and Susan Boylan, all of whom were instrumental in helping me research and edit the book. I am particularly indebted to those at Jason Aronson: Cindy Hyden, the former acquisitions editor whose useful advice helped me "over the transom"; Jason Aronson, whose enthusiasm and encouragement came just at the right time in my writing career; and Judy Cohen, my production editor, who helped gently guide the book to a successful completion. I want to thank Shirley Tuch Krieger and Arthur Ourieff, who provided me with useful feedback about the book. I am indebted to a cadre of outstanding teachers and supervisors at the Los Angeles Psychoanalytic Society and Institute who taught me most of what I know about psychoanalysis. I would also like to thank Joel Yager, who headed the department of Residency Education at U.C.L.A.'s Neuropsychiatric Institute, for having created an ideal psychiatric residency for my classmates and me. Teachers of note include: Edward Stainbrook, Mike Leavitt, Arthur Ourieff, Sid Fine, Leonard Gilman, Norm Atkins, Robert Stoller, Daniel Borenstein, Norm Tabachnick, Larry Warick, Ernie Masler, and Lars Lofgren. If I had failed to say it before, thank you all for your time and dedication. I would also like to acknowledge my debt to my long-lost intellectual soul mate, Glenn Siegel, and my longtime associate, Bruce Gainsley, for his years of caring support.

I want to reserve special thanks for the writers to whom I owe an intellectual debt, for their work is what made this book possible. These authors include: Otto Kernberg, Frank Pittman, Ethel Person, Karen Horney, John Gotteman, Laurel Richardson, Mary Anne Fitzpatrick, Emanuel Ghent, Shirley Glass, Lynne Hollander, and Salman Akhtar. I would additionally like to thank the following for having provided important case material: Leigh Cato, Morton Hunt, John Ross, and Andrew Morton. Many thanks also to Don Passman and Jerry Ament, who provided useful legal input, to Peter Gruenberg, M.D., who provided guidance regarding the ethical issues involved in bringing out this book, and to Baillie Vigon, for introducing me to the poetry of Judith Viorst. Thanks also to the folks at the American Psychoanalytic Association and the International Psycho-Analytic Association, who helped create the Psychoanalytic Electronic Press.

Finally, I would like to acknowledge my patients, who have taught me so much about the human condition, and my family, who had to deal for several months with my preoccupation with writing this book.

Introduction

The tempter or the tempted, who sins most?
William Shakespeare, *Measure for Measure*, II, ii, 163

One's initial reaction to a book about extramarital affairs is likely to be mixed. The topic may strike some as a trivial social issue unworthy of serious scientific consideration. Others may consider the subject too narrow to be of much interest to the average clinician, who encounters such issues only occasionally and who may not regard extramarital affairs as a clinical matter necessitating treatment. Still others may believe that the dynamics of extramarital affairs are apparent to most and that a book on the subject would only belabor the obvious. So why write a book about this subject, given these objections? Is this the type of subject about which serious scholarship can be conducted?

The subject of extramarital affairs is admittedly limited and narrow. Had the focus of my research remained confined to the subject of extramarital affairs, I would never have been motivated to write a book exclusively about this topic. Nor, I suspect, would many clinicians be interested in reading a book strictly about extramarital affairs. What I find appealing about this topic is that it offers entrée into the exploration of a host of other, related topics, all centered around the issue of relations between men and women: men's unique problems maintaining exclusive intimate attachments with women over time; women's unique inclinations to employ masochistic adaptations in their relations with men; married couples' varied styles of dealing with their differences; the relationship of power and control to the processes of domination, submission, and the act of surrendering; and the nature of the enterprise called "love."

As we begin to delve into the psychology behind such affairs, we encounter such issues as masochism, ambivalence, splitting, secrecy, vulnerability, and self-deception. The affair is our starting point, and our ultimate goal is an exploration of the dynamics of intimacy, commitment, and interpersonal control. As we would expect, some of the conclusions reached in this book will tend to support what many readers already suspect about such affairs. However, other conclusions are bound to prove surprising, in that they either are unexpected or run counter to what some may think to be the case.

My interest in writing this book grew out of my own clinical experience as both a psychoanalyst and general psychotherapist. I began to notice a marked similarity in the stories certain married men told me about the affairs they were having with single women. I likewise noticed remarkable similarities in the stories certain single women told me about the affairs they were conducting with married men. These patterns became so predictable that I found myself able to anticipate for my patients the next turn their relationships would take, and I began to wonder why I had not seen these patterns described in the literature as a recognizable syndrome.

The thesis of this book is that the behaviors, feelings, attitudes, and thoughts exhibited by certain types of married men involved in romantic relationships with certain types of single women are so recognizable and predictable as to constitute a genuine syndrome, which, for lack of a more elegant term, I have chosen to call the single woman–married man syndrome. It is critical that the reader understand that this book is about this special subset of extramarital affairs, which are distinguishable from other extramarital affairs on the basis of certain unique features. Although Chapter 6 discusses the issue of extramarital affairs, this book is not about extramarital affairs in general.

There are two dimensions of the single woman–married man syndrome that must be discussed before we embark on a complete description of the syndrome in Chapter 1. The single woman–married man syndrome differs from most other psychiatric syndromes in that other psychiatric syndromes refer to the behaviors, feelings, thoughts, and so on, of one person, whereas the single woman–married man syndrome refers specifically to the complementary motivations and behaviors of two individuals that happen to fit together like matching pieces of a jigsaw puzzle. The only other psychiatric conditions I can think of that are based on such pairings are those of sadomasochism and folie à deux, both of which share features in common with the single woman–married man syndrome. The second issue has to do with interpersonal power and the illusion that one can be controlled, or can control, the behaviors, feelings, or thoughts of another. In the single woman–married man syndrome, both parties come to feel as if they are being controlled by the actions of the other, and each, at different points during the relationship, ends up feeling as if he or she has been rendered powerless and is therefore incapable of acting. As we shall see, these dynamics become a central dimension of this syndrome.

INTERSUBJECTIVITY

The separate psychologies of single women and married men who become involved with one another are interrelated, the intrapsychic dynamics of one eliciting complementary dynamics in the other. The intersection of these two intrapsychic worlds constitutes what has come to be known as the *intersubjective field* (Atwood and Stolorow 1984). Once such an intersubjective field has been created, it becomes difficult to speak of individual psychologies apart from the context within which these psychologies have emerged. Each participant's behavior and subjectivity can be seen to be both a reaction to, and a stimulus for, the other's behavior and subjective responses.

Interactions between two individuals may or may not constitute an actual relationship. In the case of interactional patterns that do not amount to a relationship, one observes a limited form of intersubjectivity. But, in the case of the single woman–married man syndrome, as is the case with all interactional patterns worthy of being called relationships, intersubjectivity involves more than one person's subjectivity stimulating subjective reactions in the other. Relationships involve an intersubjectivity that includes the complementarity of subjective states, wherein certain needs of one participant are satisfied by the actions and subjective responses of the other, and vice versa.

The single woman–married man syndrome is a relationship between two parties who have entered into an unconscious contractual agreement to get certain of their needs met via specified types of interactions. According to this arrangement, nobody is anybody's victim. The man is not a scoundrel; the woman is not a ruthless, cunning home wrecker. The most that can be said is that each is the victim of the other's groping attempts to get something from the relationship that each hopes will fix, or make up for, some internal longing, or will prevent (defend against) an outcome about which each feels conflicted. This complementarity is in stark contrast to interactional dyads such as the rapist and his victim, the exhibitionist and the at-the-wrong-place-at-the-wrong-time onlooker, or the voyeur and his unwitting eyeful. When it comes to dyadic interactions such as these, one of the parties is not a willing participant, and the specific interactions that have occurred in no way serve any of the unwilling partner's needs. It is essential that we not confuse interactional patterns that are nonconsensual with those that clearly are. The rape victim was not "asking for it." But the same cannot be said for single women who pursue relationships with married men.

The single woman–married man syndrome constitutes an extreme form of intersubjectivity. Not only does one see the process of mutual influence over the feelings, thoughts, and behaviors of the other, one also sees two individuals who have become woven into one fabric, making it exceedingly hard for them to extricate themselves from the relationship. They regress to such an extent that they lose track of themselves as autonomous centers of initiative, capable of making up their own minds about what it is they want. This, in fact, is one of the exhilarating aspects of such an affair: the feeling of being swept away against one's better judgment and will. Ahhhhh . . . true love. But loss of an ability to make up one's mind also proves to be one of the most frustrating and disabling aspects of such affairs as will be described in this book.

This particular pattern of relating ultimately proves emotionally taxing for both parties. The deep pleasure of becoming lost in psychic and emotional union with the other ("falling in love," and then some) is counterbalanced with the prospect of losing a sense of one's autonomous identity in the process. These two processes pull the participants in two different directions, thus defining the relationship's character as one that alternately swings between ecstasy and agony. By the time the relationship is well under way, its participants often, but not invariably, show clear signs of psychopathology that beg for psychotherapeutic intervention. This is an uplifting entanglement that simultaneously tortures and imprisons.

Thinking in terms of dyadic patterns is not new to the field of psychology. In the 1960s Eric Berne's (1964) transactional analysis classified people in terms of the types of "games" they would engage others in. What Berne's theory lacked was a sophisticated look at the deeper, unconscious reasons why individuals engage in these "games." More recently, Kernberg (1991) offered a short list of such dyads commonly encountered in marriages: "the dependent, clinging, love-hungry woman and the narcissistic, indifferent, self-centered man; or the dominant, powerful, and controlling woman who feels frustrated by her insecure, childlike boy-man, who wants an adult man as a partner; or the 'sex hungry' man who cannot understand the limited sexual interest of his wife; and, of course, the guilty partner and the accusatory one in all of their varieties" (p. 67).

Interactional patterns that are co-determined by each of the participants involved are defined as much by the dyad as by the individual psychologies of those who make up that dyad. If people become involved with a new partner whose psychology is markedly different from that of the person with whom they had previously been involved, there is a chance that they will relate differently with the new person and, as a result, will become somewhat different in the new relationship. Sometimes leopards do change their spots. While such a thing as a core self undoubtedly exists, the selective emergence of different aspects of this self may prove context-dependent, specifically stimulated by the types of interactions one is having with the personalities with whom one is currently involved. What one individual brings out in another sometimes turns out to be quite different from what another individual elicits from that same individual. A man might look quite different to his mistress than to his wife.

Although I had originally been focused on the male psychology of these types of extramarital affairs when I began studying this syndrome, I found it impossible to ignore the woman's perspective given how integrally linked the experiences of single women and married men tend to be. Further, we also cannot ignore the third party, the wife, who must cope with her husband's unfaithfulness. Thus, we will look at the entire system from the perspective of all three parties.

THE DYNAMICS OF INTERPERSONAL POWER AND CONTROL

The second issue to consider is that of power and the illusion of interpersonal control. It is typical for both of the participants in this type of relationship to feel as if they are powerless, to feel as if the other wields tremendous control over them. This sense of powerlessness is most apparent in the woman, who complains that she has no power whatsoever over the man with whom she has become involved. She is forever waiting for him to free up time so that he can be with her. Eventually, she begins to believe that she needs him more than he needs her. Nothing could be further from the truth, but the married man is in no rush to correct this misperception, since there are clear advantages to the woman's thinking that this is so. If the woman dares to break off the relationship, it usually becomes readily apparent just how emotionally involved the man actually is. But she often is too afraid to make so bold a move. She may offer ultimatums and threaten to break off the relationship if the man does not leave his wife once and for all. But she typically does not carry through on her threats when the man inevitably fails to resolve the situation to her satisfaction. She struggles with the feeling that she is being neglected, but she feels as if her hands are tied. Were she to complain too loudly about how neglected she feels, the single woman fears that the married man would quickly tire of her as he had of his wife, and that that would spell the end of a relationship upon which she has come to depend. In these ways, and countless others, the woman becomes convinced that she is being controlled by the man.

Though she cannot imagine how the man could possibly feel controlled by her, there is little question about the fact that, at some point, he typically begins to feel as if he is not free to act as he sees fit. He fears that were he to break off the affair, she would retaliate. Out of a sense of desperation and utter powerlessness, the single woman often intimates that she has certain avenues available to her to keep the man involved, and telling the wife about the affair is number one on her list. The married man also fears the intensity of the single woman's determination and ire. Were he to suddenly withdraw, she might go berserk, as was portrayed in the movie *Fatal Attraction*. So the man feels controlled by covert, unspoken threats. Fear controls him, fear stimulated by the single woman's potential for unbridled rage born of her uncompromising determination to hold on to the relationship at all cost. And, if that were not enough, the man typically experiences intense ambivalence about the affair. He cannot decide whether to leave his wife for the single woman or return home. The intensity of his indecisiveness also leaves the man feeling powerless over the situation.

While it may appear to an onlooker as if the man engaged in an affair with a single woman maintains a superior position insofar as he seems to be calling all the shots, upon closer examination it cannot be said with any certainty whether he or the woman actually wields greater control over the relationship. It appears that the woman is submitting to or accepting the man's terms even though these terms are supposedly unacceptable to her. But a deeper analysis of the situation suggests that it is not so clear-cut.

It is not unusual to encounter individuals who have lost track of the fact that they are grown adults capable of making choices among the various options available to them. Such individuals may feel controlled from without, either by circumstances or by others. One frequently hears people accuse others of having "made" them do a particular thing. The notion of being "forced" to do something completely against one's will is an odd one, since it is a common enough subjective experience that, nevertheless, has no basis in reality. Even if there is a gun at one's head, one still has the choice to decide. Recognizing the fact that one is always making choices leads one to take responsibility for those choices, rather than acting as if one were being controlled by forces outside of oneself.

The situation becomes a little murkier when it comes to subjective experience. It is clear that one cannot be made to do something by another. But is it equally clear that one cannot be made to feel certain feelings by others? "You are making me feel guilty" is not the same as "You are trying to make me feel guilty." In the first instance, the subjective response would be guilt. In the second instance, the subjective response could be any of a host of different reactions from irritation and resentment to pity to bemusement. If the affect (guilt) fails to be aroused in its intended victim, if people who are trying to elicit guilt cannot locate a specific responsivity within the separate subjectivity of the person they are trying to influence, then they will fail in their attempt to produce a seamless, intersubjective connection along the lines they desire. In the case of the single woman–married man syndrome, each participant is quite able to locate in the other a response that makes it hard for the other to remain aware that he or she is an autonomous individual capable of independently choosing a particular path. Once one has lost track of the fact that one has choices, it is easy to lapse into believing that one is powerless in the face of the pressure brought to bear by the other.

Men are particularly sensitive to feeling as if they have been "made" to do things by the woman/women in their lives. Fearing they will be viewed, or will view themselves, as being "whipped" or "pushed around" by the one who "wears the pants in the family," men are left with a limited number of options: (1) they may become tyrants who intimidate; (2) they may employ passive-aggressive tactics by saying "Yes, dear," only to never follow through on what they had agreed to do; (3) they may seize every opportunity to openly resist their wife's controlling tyranny; or (4) they may become adept at engaging the wife as an equal as they come to the bargaining table to work out their differences. In this last instance, the man finds ways of making sure that agreeing with his wife does not take on the appearance of a humiliating defeat, that it is kept from looking like an act of capitulation or submission. Much more will be said about this topic in Chapters 5 and 10.

It is my contention that husbands who are unable to retain their sense of dignity as they attempt to work out the differences they have with their wives are more prone to have affairs. Affairs that arise for this reason are an expression of a man's rebellion against feeling as if he is being "made" to submit to his wife's demands. The affair serves to illustrate that the man is doing as he pleases rather than doing as he is told. Bold as he might seem, the married man's bravado is little more than a passive-aggressive maneuver insofar as it takes place behind the wife's back.

The affair has an additional advantage in that it places the man in what initially appears to be a powerful position vis-à-vis the single woman with whom he is having the affair. Unconsciously realizing that this is precisely what the man needs, given how powerless he feels at home, the single woman goes along with the portrayal of the affair as a relationship over which the man has greater control than she does. Permitting him this illusion is part of what the single woman offers in return for the man's continuing interest in, and involvement with, her. Later, the single woman will use her supposed inferior position, vis-à-vis the man, to her advantage. But for now, the man is none the wiser.

It is important that the reader not be misled into believing that what I have just presented satisfactorily explains why married men pursue single women. The dynamics I have just outlined represent only a small portion of what contributes to married men's motivations to have affairs with single women. Nothing as complex as extramarital affairs could ever be reduced to so simple a scenario as this.

DISCLAIMERS

Some readers may take me to task for believing that I am in a position to understand the single woman's plight, given the limitations of my gender and married status. Others might fault me for seeing things through psychoanalytic lenses, which undoubtedly biases me toward thinking along certain lines. Still others might note that my observations are culturally bound. Naturally, there is no way for me to completely transcend who I am, how I think, or the cultural milieu within which I live. I have tried to compensate for these limitations by learning from the experiences of women writers, and those of my women patients, in order to fill the gaps in my universe of experience. I have also attempted to balance my own psychoanalytically informed observations with the observations of researchers whose theoretic orientations are different from my own. I have included material from other eras. But I have not provided research that would free my conclusions from being culturally bound. I must make clear, however, that I am not arguing for the moral superiority of monogamy.

Being raised in modern American society, I assumed that monogamy and the idea that marriage is primarily based on the exchange of love, affection, and emotional intimacy are worldwide norms in most cultures. This, however, proves not to be universally so. Polygamous marriages, which often de-emphasize love and emotional intimacy, are officially sanctioned and openly practiced in many current-day cultures. Ford and Beach (reported in Hunt 1969) studied 185 societies and reported that "the pattern of lifelong monogamy, with fidelity a requisite, is a virtual anomaly: only 16 percent of the 185 had formal restrictions to a single mate, and of those, less than one third wholly disapproved of both pre-marital and extra-marital liaisons. Actual approval, rather than mere toleration, of extra-marital liaisons of specified types existed in 39 percent of the societies" (p. 18).

Many societies that accept or promote polygamy "do not emphasize intimate, social-economic bonds between partners" (Altman and Ginat 1996, p. 340). One example is that of the Bedouin culture of Israel in which husbands and wives "lead quite separate lives—men spend time with men and women spend time with women; a husband does not usually inform his wife about where he is going and when he will return; wives seldom participate in family decisions; and women and men do not shop or eat in restaurants together" (Altman and Ginat 1996, p. 340, quoting Marx 1987). And, among the Yoruba women of Niger, "only a small percentage . . . view marriage as ideally involving companionship, sexual satisfaction, and advice-giving between a husband and wife" (Altman and Ginat 1996, p. 342, quoting a study by Ware 1979). In still other cultures, young men and women are expected to accept the tradition of arranged marriages, which, over the course of time, may or may not grow into romantic love relationships characterized by emotional, as well as physical, intimacy.

The conclusions I reach in this book about the gender-specific psychologies of men and women are based on assumptions that are clearly not universal. I have accepted our culture's expectation of marriage as an institution that is ideally love-based and has emotional intimacy as its goal. Based on this norm, I have developed theories about female and male psychology that relate to the task of achieving and maintaining exclusive emotional intimacy with one individual over the course of time. Since this task is not universally held, some might think that my conclusions are not applicable to all cultures. It could be argued, however, that cultures that do not hold its members to this expectation are doing nothing more than institutionalizing a defense mechanism that stems from men's collective fear of involvement with women. It is hard to imagine a maternalistic society that would promote the practice of polygamy.

AN OVERVIEW OF THE BOOK

Chapter 1 describes the syndrome in detail. The following three chapters provide concrete examples, as found in literature, in clinical case presentations, and in first- and second-hand accounts, of the experiences of single women and married men who have been involved in such relationships. Once we have established a knowledge base about this phenomenon, we next move to an examination of the ways in which married couples attempt to work through their differences (Chapter 5), which, in part, helps explain why some men look elsewhere for love. Chapter 6 discusses extramarital affairs in general in order to illustrate how the single woman–married man syndrome fits into the larger picture of extramarital involvements. Chapters 7 and 8 offer speculation about the underlying psychological causes of the single woman–married man syndrome, and what this syndrome suggests about female and male psychology in general. Chapter 9 summarizes the treatment approaches for this syndrome. Finally, in Chapter 10, the book concludes with a discussion of the nature of love, including a review of Otto Kernberg's theories about the psychological prerequisites for falling in love and developing the capacity for mature love.

1

Introducing an Identifiable Syndrome

But Love is blind, and lovers cannot see
The pretty follies that themselves commit.
William Shakespeare, *Merchant of Venice*, II, vi, 36

The saga of the single woman and the married man is as old as it is common. It can be found on the front pages of our newspapers, in the lines of our novels, in the lyrics of country and western ballads. Most people either know somebody, or have been that somebody, who has been involved in a single woman–married man affair. And since most people think they know what such affairs are all about, many believe that there is little left to say that has not already been thought or said about the matter.

Lay theories about extramarital affairs are most often the product of a variety of different attitudes. People's attitudes about such affairs run the gamut from moralistic, to blame seeking, to dismissive, to prurient. For instance, there are those who tend to vilify one, if not both, of the parties involved, viewing them as morally corrupt home wreckers who are out to selfishly satisfy their own needs without regard for who gets hurt in the process. There are those who blame the man, seeing the extramarital relationship in terms of a male predator and his female prey. Some react to such affairs with a dismissive shrug, justifying them as a natural rebellion against the constraints of a society that demands unnatural monogamy. Finally, there are those who are voyeuristically, or vicariously, titillated by the naughtiness of others and want to hear whatever gossip is currently circulating.

Adopting any one of these four attitudes or stances limits one's ability to learn anything new about why single women and married men pursue one another. Judging the affair as wrong or bad closes the mind to a consideration of what might be at work, psychologically and emotionally, in the minds of the participants. A person who has adopted a moralistic stance will be suspicious of any attempts to determine the participants' motives, seeing such attempts as nothing more than a way to rationalize or excuse inexcusable behavior. A stance that is primarily concerned with determining who is to blame for the affair is likewise limiting even though it gives the appearance of being more open-minded than the moralistic stance in that it does not condemn the behavior but only seeks to determine who is using whom. Such a blaming attitude prevents one from seeing such affairs as resulting from the interdigitating needs of the two participants. Thinking of extramarital affairs as either the acting out of a biological-evolutionary imperative or an expression of man's innately polygamous tendencies is reductionistic in its dismissal of the personal motivations and meanings that draw the two parties together. Finally, an attitude of titillation shifts the mind into an entirely different realm, one that seeks gratification of one's voyeuristic tendencies and is unconcerned with what is going on in the minds of those engaged in the affair. The affair becomes fertile ground for voyeurs to project their own fantasies without regard for what it actually means to the participants.

The limitations imposed by these four commonly employed stances help explain the origin of some of the common stereotypes people have about extramarital affairs. Since most individuals are not intimately privy to more than a few such affairs in the course of their lives, the preconceived notions they form about such affairs may ultimately structure what they see; it is a case of expectation coloring perception. And while one might think that psychotherapists are in an ideal position to understand the psychology of extramarital affairs, they too struggle with conditions that limit their ability to make generalizations about what motivates single women and married men to couple. Very few therapists specialize in extramarital affairs. Accordingly, few have seen enough such cases to form a learned opinion about their dynamics. Therapists who see larger numbers of patients for relatively brief periods of time may have collected enough material to form hypotheses. But they may never be able to test these hypotheses because they may never get to know the unconscious of their patients well enough to discern the accuracy of their theories. On the other hand, psychoanalysts often have a chance to develop an in-depth understanding of the mental workings of a man or woman who has been engaged in an extramarital affair. These analysts may not, however, be exposed to enough such cases to be able to form meaningful generalizations.

In an effort to circumvent the limitations imposed by employing one of the four commonly encountered stances, I have adopted an empathic and inquisitive stance toward the phenomenon of single woman–married man affairs. Such a stance is defined by a disinclination to prejudge the material, at the outset, combined with an inclination to keep an open mind for as long as possible. No matter how hard we resist forming conclusions, eventually the need we all have to bring order to chaos and to organize the data results in our succumbing to the urge to make sense of what we have seen. The longer we maintain an empathic, inquisitive stance toward the material and resist the temptation to jump to conclusions, the more we are likely to learn about the phenomenon we are studying.

THE PSYCHOPATHOLOGY OF EVERYDAY AFFAIRS

Some may feel that extramarital affairs do not constitute a legitimate topic for psychological inquiry. They would argue that having an affair need not be the result of psychopathology. In fact, having such an affair might actually prove to be the sanest thing one can do, given the circumstances. It could be further argued that an individual's strict adherence to an antiquated moral code—one that dictates monogamy—represents a personal lack of courage, a caving in to peer pressure, a failure to personally decide for oneself whether it is necessary, or worthwhile, to remain forever faithful to one's spouse. Under such circumstances, a spouse who strays could conceivably do so without suffering some deep psychic disturbance.

Monogamy is an expectation Western society places on its married members. Accordingly, extramarital affairs could be considered to be more of a sociological issue than a psychological one. Failing to adhere to this societally dictated expectation may be no more complicated than one's either being rebellious, morally lax, or in basic disagreement with societal mores. It need not represent psychopathology, per se. If, however, such societal expectations become internalized, then remaining faithful to one's spouse becomes a way of being faithful to one's own moral code. Failing to live up to one's own code is likely to cause internal conflict that, if sufficiently severe, could give rise to psychological symptoms.

The theory I present in this book does not apply to all affairs between single women and married men. Rather, it applies to a subset of single women–married men relationships that are identifiable, on the basis of their highly characteristic features (behaviors, feelings, attitudes, and thoughts), and are predictable, with regard to their course and outcome. Given these dual aspects of identifiability and predictability, this particular type of relationship has earned the distinction to be considered a full-fledged syndrome. It justifies being referred to as a syndrome because it fits in with what that term connotes: a pattern formed by certain specific signs or symptoms that are found to occur together. This syndrome has never before been described in the literature. This is the very first time this behavior has been identified and proposed to constitute a syndrome.

Unlike other extramarital affairs, which may be neither emotionally upsetting nor reflective of psychological disturbances, the single woman–married man syndrome tends, at the very least, to be an emotionally upsetting experience, given how much its participants suffer on account of the emotional vicissitudes characteristic of such relationships. But the syndrome may go beyond being merely upsetting. It may come to constitute a bona fide psychological disturbance, one that reflects deep-seated conflicts that lead each of the participants to pursue such a relationship in the first place. Naturally, what I have to say is in the form of a hypothesis that will, in turn, need to be further tested before it can be considered valid. I will propose that the single woman–married man syndrome is a recognizable pattern of signs and symptoms that are often found whenever a subset of single women and married man "take up" with one another. The value in identifying this as a syndrome is that it permits clinicians to conduct meaningful discussions about it. It is so much easier to exchange observations about a condition when one knows that the discussants are in basic agreement that they are referring to the same clinical entity.

RECOGNIZABLE PATTERNS

From the moment infants open their eyes and begin to take in the world, they engage in the process of organizing seemingly disparate stimuli into coherent, recognizable patterns. Pattern recognition is essential in order for the mind to be freed up to contend with an expanding array of stimuli and situations, all of which infants come to terms with as they develop. Once infants come to expect a pattern, they can meet the world halfway, simultaneously organizing and perceiving it.

Some patterns are easily recognized and present no challenge to the viewer, such as the rising and setting of the sun and the lengthening and shortening of the days. Others take centuries to appreciate. Sometimes a special device or instrument is needed in order to perceive a previously unrecognized pattern. Sometimes a newly appreciated concept proves worthy insofar as it permits things to be seen that had previously gone unnoticed, as was the case with Freud's observations or Einstein's theories, which proved to be of great heuristic value.

Sometimes psychological patterns go unnoticed for quite some time because they are remarkably subtle or require special care and attention to observe. Sometimes they go unnoticed because commonsense lay opinion closes people's minds to the possibility that things may be much more complicated than they appear.

An example of a syndrome that went relatively unnoticed by the psychiatric and psychological communities for several decades is Asperger's syndrome (Asperger 1944), a psychological condition first described in 1944. Asperger observed a subtle behavioral pattern in certain children and adults who exhibit an impairment in their abilities to socialize, communicate, and use their imaginations. They are, to put it bluntly, socially inept. They "do not seem to possess the knack of entering and maintaining intimate two-way personal relationships. . . . Because of their idiosyncrasies, their egocentric bluntness and fragility, they find it difficult to live and work with others" (Frith 1991, p. 4). They seem to lack common sense and seem unable to "catch on" to social rules and patterns that others pick up instinctively.

Why had it taken so long for someone to recognize that this group of behaviors formed a pattern? One reason is that the condition is, in fact, relatively subtle in its clinical presentation.

Another reason is that until the 1980s—decades after Asperger published his observations and theory—the field of psychology had no appreciation of the underlying psychological system that goes haywire in such patients. Only after psychologists came to understand the stages by which children develop a sense of what goes on in the minds of others (referred to as "theory of mind") were they able to understand Asperger's syndrome as a disorder in which children fail to develop this ability. Not until there is sufficient scientific understanding of the underlying thread that draws data together into a coherent whole will certain patterns become recognizable. One final reason why it took decades before the psychological and psychiatric community accepted Asperger's syndrome as a legitimate condition is that these individuals provoked strong negative reactions in others, which led to judgmental attitudes that these individuals were "weird" or "naughty." Individuals suffering from Asperger's syndrome had previously been seen by most as "simply obnoxious brats" who "did not fit in anywhere and were troublesome because they lacked any respect for authority. They made their parents' lives miserable and drove their teachers to despair. So unappealing were these strange boys that other children and adults were drawn to ridicule them" (Frith 1991, p. 7). It was these strong emotional reactions, provoked by these children's behaviors, that made a sympathetic understanding of them nearly impossible, thereby interfering with the recognition that these children were suffering from an identifiable psychological condition.

Extramarital affairs are another type of behavior that is prone to provoke strong reactions that tend to blind people to a dispassionate inquiry into the psychodynamics of the behavior. Furthermore, affairs tend to be a highly private matter. When the existence of an affair is shared with a confidant, it is made clear that the information is not to be broadcast. These factors make it unlikely that any one individual would be privy to enough affairs to be able to begin to recognize patterns. An inclination to lump all affairs together, as if they were all about the same thing, also muddies the waters, thus making it difficult to draw meaningful conclusions. The fact that those who are engaged in affairs are often oblivious to the underlying psychological issues that are driving such behavior also contributes to the general misunderstanding about such affairs.

CLINICAL EXPERIENCE

In the course of their careers, most therapists are likely to encounter either married men who have become intimately involved with single women and/or single women who have become involved with married men. Sometimes such relationships present as incidental to the chief reason the patient seeks treatment. At other times, patients specifically come to treatment because they have found it hard, if not impossible, to cope with the ups and downs of so mercurial a relationship as these affairs tend to be. Treating such cases can prove taxing for therapists, who find themselves struggling to find ways to help their patients cope with a problem that many in our field consider akin to an addiction. Central to the treatment of such patients are two questions: (1) Why do certain women remain wholeheartedly committed to relationships that obviously have no future? and (2) Why do certain married men find it impossible to remain wholeheartedly emotionally and intimately committed to their wives?

Why has the single woman–married man syndrome gone undescribed in the literature until now? Given the assumption that some therapists must have caught on to this pattern, it is curious that none of them has presented a description in the literature of the single woman–married man syndrome. There are two likely explanations for this oversight. While all clinical material is highly confidential and in need of adequate safeguards to protect the identity of the subjects being discussed, when it comes to patients who may still be actively pursuing extramarital affairs, the issue of confidentiality usually precludes the reporting of such cases altogether. For instance, while John Ross

(1996) has reported the case of a man who had had an affair with a single woman (to be described in Chapter 3), Ross only felt comfortable describing the case in detail because it had been twelve years since the patient had been involved with the single woman, the patient's wife already knew of the affair, and the patient was no longer inclined to become extramaritally involved. But when it comes to the treatment of men or women who are actively engaged in extramarital affairs, secrecy is a central feature of the affair, and the obligation of secrecy spills over into the patient's therapy. The second reason this syndrome has not been described in the literature is the fact that while one sporadically encounters individual case reports of such affairs in the literature, there have been almost no published series of cases that illustrate a pattern that transcends the specifics of any given individual case. In this book I will fill in the gap by doing just that. For reasons of confidentiality, I will primarily rely on a review of the literature to make my case. When I cite my own cases, I will do so in the form of vignettes that make identification of the particular individual impossible. When seemingly legitimate names are used in the presentation of a case, this is only done in order to be faithful to the original source. It is my assumption that these names are always pseudonyms.

What I am about to present is a composite portrait of what can happen when a single woman and a married man become romantically involved. Naturally, couplings between single women and married men can take a very different path from that seen in the single woman–married man syndrome. Sometimes an unhappily married man finds a single woman with whom he falls in love and he subsequently goes on to marry her. Usually, an outside observer has little trouble distinguishing such cases from those in which the man never seems to take steps toward making an "honest" woman of the girlfriend with whom he is having an affair. Sometimes, single women and married men have a one night stand or a brief affair, which is the typical dalliance of philanderers, though philanderers sometimes become caught up in single woman–married man syndrome–type affairs even though they thought they had taken every precaution to prevent that from happening. It is important to make clear that when I speak of the single woman–married man syndrome, I am speaking about a very specific kind of relationship, one in which a single woman and a married man conduct a relatively long-standing, clandestine, emotionally involving, yet unresolvable relationship with one another.

THE SYNDROME

Typically, women and men who become involved in the single woman–married man syndrome are remarkably uninsightful about the underlying dynamics that have driven them to become involved with one another. To a woman currently in pursuit of a married man, the suggestion that she may *not*, in fact, want the only thing she has been living for will strike her as absurd. A woman in this position tends not to give much thought to the role that unavailability plays in her attraction to the married men. She considers it an unfortunate, and regrettable, coincidence that the man with whom she has fallen in love just happens to be married. It is hard for such a woman to imagine that she wants her life to be this way, especially given the frustration and heartache she has suffered putting up with the situation. Even when women have a pattern of dating married men, they still find it hard to see that there may be something psychological about their belief that the only men worth pursuing just happen to already be taken.

The married men who engage in these types of extramarital affairs tend to be just as unconscious about what motivates their behavior as are the women they pursue. Such men often reason that man was not made to be monogamous. Thinking of making love to the same woman for the rest of their lives strikes them as incomprehensible. Anyway, they conclude, every married man has affairs, but only some admit it. Such men typically lack insight into what drives them to have extramarital affairs. Such men are like George Roundy, the promiscuous hairdresser played by Warren Beatty in the movie *Shampoo*. When confronted by the husband of one of his lovers and asked for an accounting of his behavior, George shrugs and offers the innocent sounding explanation: "I just love women!" As one might expect, the women and men who exhibit the signs and symptoms of the single woman–married man syndrome can be quite difficult to treat, given how unpsychologically minded they tend to be, at least when it comes to a consideration of this aspect of their behavior.

The Single Woman

Let us begin with a discussion of the psychology of women who become involved with married men. What do such women have in common? There are any number of reasons single women show interest in becoming involved with men who are not, strictly speaking, available. However, it is important to note that many such women share certain things in common. Women involved in this syndrome tend to exhibit remarkably similar behaviors, attitudes, feelings, and beliefs.

Affairs that are conducted clandestinely place tremendous constraints on the couple with regard to where they can go, how often they can meet, and what others must be told about their periodic disappearances. Sneaking around seems to be part of the affair's attraction. The couple is engaged in some sort of naughty, forbidden act that must be kept from being discovered. Danger heightens the excitement.

The single woman almost always comes second. She has no claim on the man's time. She must always try to be on her best behavior since, she reasons, no man would want to leave his wife for yet another "nag." So most of the time she puts up with what little she gets and tries to play at being the "understanding" woman, in contrast to the wife who the man complains is lacking in that area.

The single woman is also afforded no status. She is forbidden by the vow of secrecy from even being publicly granted the title of "mistress." She secretly knows that she has won the affections of another woman's man, but she must not announce as much or proudly parade her victory. That is part of the agreement. In so many different ways, the single woman gets so little back for what she gives.

By virtue of the relationship's sequestration, it remains uncontaminated for quite some time by the types of everyday disagreements, resentments, and misunderstandings that typically arise in a married couple's day-to-day life. The single woman tends to be on her best behavior. In addition, the single woman sees to it that she is available whenever he is available, and that her complete, undivided attention is focused on him when they are together. As a result, the man rarely has to suffer the frustration of wanting her when she is unavailable. The extramarital affair is unreal in these respects and, as such, it is very much a fairy tale. No marriage can compete with so perfect an arrangement as this. The affair seems too good to be true. And so it is.

Conflict and resentment do ultimately make their way into the extramarital affair, but they typically focus exclusively on one matter: if and when the man is going to leave his wife. Most single women who remain involved for extended periods with married men do so with the expectation that one day the man will be theirs. Sometimes the man has promised as much. The woman tries to be patient, hoping she will ultimately be rewarded for her patience. After a time, however, she grows impatient and begins to try to pin the man down as to when he thinks he might leave the wife. This is often when the problems begin.

The man may believe he has every intention of leaving his wife, someday. After all, why wouldn't he? The relationship he has with his mistress is so much better than the one he has with his wife in almost every respect. But when push comes to shove, he balks. He offers excuse after excuse to explain why the time is not right to make the change. Soon the single woman catches on. The time is *never* right: the holidays are almost here, pressures at work are too great, and so on. The woman may resort to giving ultimatums: he had better leave the wife by such-and-such a date or she will leave him once and for all. In response, the man either reacts angrily to the pressure he is being put under or he redoubles his efforts to try to decide whom he would rather be with, his wife or his lover. Either way, the uprising soon settles down—if only for a short time.

If the married man attempts to decide with whom he ultimately prefers to be, he soon finds himself psychologically and emotionally unequipped to answer that question. In part, this is because he does not know his own mind. Ambivalence reigns, and decision making is rendered impossible. Even if the man exhibits complete decisiveness in other areas of his life, interpersonal conflict resolution is not his long suit. That is partly why he got himself into such a jam in the first place. Rather than confronting and coming to terms with the discord generated in his marriage, he turned his back and looked elsewhere for comfort and sexual gratification.

If the single woman threatens to call it quits by a certain date unless she sees the man is making definitive progress toward leaving his wife, typically that date comes and goes without either partner taking any action whatsoever. The single woman ends up staying, for she, like he, is in over her head. The relationship is one she can neither live with nor live without, no matter how frustrating it seems to be. Thus begins the next cycle in a series of endless cycles that seem to go nowhere.

The single woman never seems to give up hope. She resumes her long-suffering position of waiting patiently for the right time to come for her and her lover to be one. Maybe she has "bought" the man's explanations as to why he cannot leave his wife at this juncture. Maybe she has come to some understanding about just how difficult it is for the man to decide. Maybe she realizes she

just cannot bear to give up on something to which she has devoted this much time and energy. Though she threatens to leave,
she can never carry out the threat. She is too much in need of the
relationship.

Being patient offers the woman the advantage of having a
claim on the role of "victim." She is the one who has put her
life on hold. "I've given you the best years of my life" becomes a
legitimate accusation-lament. If nothing thus far has worked,
maybe a healthy dose of guilt will get the man off his duff. Doubt
may creep into her mind as to whether the man ever intends to
make her his wife, but subtle reassurances or a period of increased devotion on the man's part quell these concerns.

The frustrations of such a relationship were well portrayed
in the English movie *Sliding Doors* (Howitt 1997). The man in the
middle, Gerry, is involved in a long-term, committed relationship
with Helen. Meanwhile, he has been "cheating" with his girlfriend
Lydia. But he is unable to decide whom he really wants to be with,
which is driving Lydia a bit batty. At one point in the movie, Gerry
confronts Lydia about her having acted in a way that threatens
to blow their cover with Helen. He addresses Lydia in a conde-
scending way, demanding to know: "Are you completely insane?
What are you trying to do?" To which Lydia fires back viciously:
"Don't you know, Gerry, I'm trying to be your girlfriend. That's
what I'm trying to do. I'm standing on the platform at 'Limbo
Central' with my heart and soul packed in my suitcase waiting
for the Gerry fucking Express to roll in and tell me that my ticket
is valid and that I may board the train. Only the station announcer
keeps coming on telling me that the train has been delayed as the
driver has suffered a major panic attack at Indecision City, please
await further announcements. That's what I'm trying to do, you
wanker!"

Single women involved with married men exhibit blind hope
about the prospects of ultimately marrying an already married
man. As months go by without the man making any serious effort to dissolve the marriage, one would expect the single woman

to begin to wonder if she is ever going to get her man. But this is not what happens. For quite some time the woman does not exhibit any doubt about where the relationship is headed. In the end, the woman reasons, love will win out. For now, it is just a matter of waiting.

The Married Man

Let us turn now to what motivates married men to seek out single women. Every man, from time to time, does his share of "window shopping." The idea that a man becomes so smitten by his wife as to never notice or be aroused by another woman ever again is a romantic myth held by some women. Believing in such a myth leads women to become devastated at the mere thought of their husband ever showing any interest in other women. "Why aren't I enough?" is the lament usually expressed. Empathy for such feelings leads married men to be discreet about their interests. A thoughtful man does not parade his lustful interests before his wife's eyes. His eyes may glance but his head must not turn.

At times, some men more than note the attractive women who pass by. They let certain images register and later give such women a second thought. They entertain the possibility and imagine what it would be like to have a sexual encounter with the woman. They feel tempted and imagine arousing scenarios. But they take it no further. Oftentimes an inclination to think twice about a prospect proves symptomatic of a transient problem in the marriage, or a prolonged separation from the wife.

Then there are men who go "all the way." Some men do it just once, and are immediately seized with remorse and guilt. The affair generates a crisis in their lives. Some seek relief by admitting their wayward ways to their wives. Others struggle with the meaning of their actions so as to learn from their mistakes. They are shaken by having jeopardized a relationship that means everything to them, and they vow to never let such a thing happen again.

And then there are the philanderers. While they do not publicize their proclivities, they privately believe there is nothing wrong with having extramarital affairs. After all, they reason, man was not made to be monogamous. Thinking of making love to the same woman for the rest of their lives strikes them as incomprehensible. Such men typically lack insight into what drives them to be promiscuous and may never become entangled in an affair of the single woman–married man type. But others may.

Sometimes married men find themselves "caught up" in a relationship they had never intended to remain engaged in for any length of time. This can happen with philanderers who were "playing around" and got more than they had bargained for. But it can also happen just once in a married man's life, as will be illustrated in the case of Edwin Gottesman in Chapter 3. The relationship proves unusually satisfying, especially in comparison to what the man has in his marriage, so it becomes hard for the man to break it off. The amount of time and energy the single woman dedicates to the pursuit of her man and the single-minded devotion she demonstrates toward him become an ego-inflating aphrodisiac for the man. The man reasons that he must "really be something" if this women is willing to go to such lengths to be with him, especially considering how little she gets back in return. The arithmetic says it all: He has two women, she has half of a man. Some stud! But what the man does not know, and must remain unaware of in order for him to go on feeling the way he does about their relationship, is that the single woman is only half interested in him. The other half of her is in hot pursuit of Daddy (or Mommy, in Dad's clothing). And it is that second half that generates the lion's share of the woman's drive.

In other ways the affair provides something with which the marriage cannot possibly compete. For quite some time the affair remains relatively sheltered from the everyday conflicts and squabbles that are an inevitable product of negotiating a life together. The anger and resentment that such conflicts sometimes generate do not occur early in the course of the affair. The single woman has yet to win her man, so she bends over backward and aims to please. As a result, the man is treated to better sex than he can remember having had in some time. For a while, the couple is engaged in extramarital bliss.

Things Turn Ugly

After a period of time, the woman's determination to "land" the man, combined with her growing sense of frustration over the man's failure to make a good-faith effort to move toward leaving his wife, often drives the woman to extremes. When this happens, things often turn ugly. The single woman's determination to get her man translates into all kinds of uncomfortable and frightening experiences for the man. She feels justified doing whatever it takes to bring the affair to a successful resolution and will stop at nothing to get what she wants. She may begin to stalk the man, which causes both of them to wonder if they are headed for a "fatal attraction." She may call him at home, something she knows she is never to do. Blackmail enters in; she threatens to "tell all." Such behavior smacks of desperation. Once a single woman has established a relationship with a married man, she holds on to it and stops at nothing to prevent its dissolution.

The single woman complains about how much she has given and how little she gets in return, and she portrays herself as a victim of a man who has been lying to her all along when he claimed that he intended to leave his wife for her. The man may initially feel that he is guilty as charged and may act as if he is willing to make it up to her. But he is quick to remind the woman that it has been hard for him to juggle two relationships, that he has gone out of his way to please her, and that she is being unreasonable and ungrateful, given all of his efforts.

Before long the man begins to feel as if *he* is the victim of the woman's criticisms, manipulations, threats, ultimatums, and tirades. He complains that he would have left her long ago had it not been for her threats to tell his wife were he to do so. As each partner vies for the position of victim, it occurs to neither that both are victims of each other's desperate need to use the other to restore themselves, and to find some way to feel good about themselves.

What may prove the worst of it for the man is that the woman no longer appreciates him to the absolute and unconditional degree she once had, which is an ego-deflating experience for him. "What happened to the guy you thought the world of, huh? What did such a nice guy do to deserve all of this?" While she had formerly regarded him as her knight in shining armor, she now views him as little more than a despicable, selfish cad who had been lying to her all along about his intentions. The man finds it hard to tolerate his descent from the ideal man to nothing more than a "creep."

The man ultimately begins to feel as if he wants nothing more than to get as far away from the woman as fast as he can. When the woman senses that her man is fed up and is moving toward the door, she abruptly ceases berating him, at least for a time. She is contrite and apologizes for her outbursts. What had gotten into her? she wonders. How could she have treated the man she loves in such a despicable way. She resumes her loving ways, which stops the man short of actually ending the relationship. So ends round one in what are sure to be endless cycles of ecstasy and agony. The saga of the single woman and the married man is a match made in heaven . . . and hell.

In summary, such liaisons typically prove unusually gratifying in the beginning. But after a time they dissolve into something that is unmistakably self-destructive for both parties. But this is something that is much more apparent to outside observers than to the main players engaged in the drama. After a while it becomes hard to tell who is victimizing whom. It would be more accurate to say that both are the victims of their own unsatisfied needs, which draw each like moths to the flame. Typically there is more going on unconsciously than either partner is aware of, and that makes the situation hard for either to break off or to understand. For both, the link takes on addictive-like qualities.

FEMALE PSYCHOLOGY AND THE BITTERSWEET APPEAL OF UNREQUITED LOVE

Women involved in a clandestine relationship never feel much satisfaction, so they are always living for the future. Unrequited relationships are among the most intense, compelling, and frustrating of all human experiences. And if there is anything harder to deal with than unrequited love, it is *partially* requited love, where one is permitted a taste of what it might be like to have it all, only to have the promise of more dangled as a tease just out of one's reach.

While it appears as if many single women caught up in relationships with married men want nothing more in life than to be married to the man they have waited for all those years, it is fair to ask whether this *is* what such single women ultimately want. The fact that such women have put their heart and soul into winning the man need not rule out the possibility that what attracted them to married men in the first place, and what keeps them so interested in them, is the man's unavailability. Might a married man lose some of his appeal once he is free and available?

A married physician in his mid-fifties had been intimately involved with his nurse, Ms. K., for over four years. During the course of their stormy affair, Dr. O. had gone back and forth about whether to leave his wife of thirty years, with whom he had raised four children, all of whom were now away either in college or graduate school. After his wife came upon letters that made it clear just what had been happening, Dr. O. moved out and his wife filed for divorce. Dr. O. was now completely free to spend time with Ms. K. Though he had taken an apartment, he increasingly spent nights at Ms. K.'s place. Everything seemed to be going in the direction that Ms. K. had for so long only dreamed about.

One night, as the couple took a mid-summer, late-night, top-down drive in Dr. O.'s convertible, savoring their newly won freedom to travel about without the constraints of secrecy, Dr. O. spoke of how close and intimate the moment felt to him. At first, Ms. K. agreed. Then, suddenly and unexpectedly, Ms. K. flew into a rage as she found herself remembering how, eighteen months before, Dr. O. had taken just such a drive with his now-estranged wife the night he bought the car in which they were driving. The image of Dr. O. and his soon-to-be-ex spending an intimate moment together prevented Ms. K. from being able to appreciate what she and Dr. O. were now experiencing together at that moment.

Dr. O., who was in therapy, felt stunned and befuddled by Ms. K.'s behavior. An exploration of his reactions led him to realize how the intrusion of such thoughts had utterly destroyed the intimacy that Ms. K. had been ostensibly craving for months. But, when Dr. O. later confronted her and asked her to reflect about why such thoughts would come to her mind at such a moment, Ms. K. offered nothing more than rationalizations to explain her reactions.

Could it be that Ms. K. was more conflicted about being intimate with Dr. O. than she had ever imagined? Might not the prospect of finally, once and for all, having Dr. O. to herself be more than Ms. K. could bear? These are some of the questions we will now take up and explore.

Needing to be involved with a man who remains unavailable satisfies certain of the woman's unconscious needs. As much as the unmarried woman claims to want greater involvement with her lover, she is also frightened of the heightened intimacy that would result were he to be hers. Furthermore, there is the matter of unconscious guilt over stealing another woman's husband, which relates to guilt over having wanted to be favored by father over mother. This unconscious guilt results in the woman's feeling the need to be punished, and what better punishment than to never get what she believes she desperately wants. Another reason a woman may feel she does not deserve more than what little she gets from the married man is that she had been treated by her childhood caregivers as someone who was unworthy of reward. Internalizing such attitudes results in anticipating similar treatment from her present-day relationships. Such are the origins of masochism.

So what is it about unavailable men that so attracts some women? Competing with another woman for a man's affections offers multiple rewards. If one prevails, one is then in a relationship that promises to satisfy a host of needs—needs for intimacy, to be loved and to have someone to love, security, and so on. But beyond these rewards is the sense one has of having bested another, of having been so alluring, so appealing, and so worth leaving another woman or an entire family for. The narcissistic gratification of not just having won a man's heart, but having won that man's heart when it had been locked up, committed, and given to another is heady stuff. Such an achievement is likely to make a woman feel special—as special as a young girl might feel were she to get her father to consistently show more interest in her than he does in his own wife! Such a conquest could help bolster a young woman's self-esteem, which, at least in part, is what drives women to pursue married men.

Unrequited love is the basis of Freud's concept of the Oedipus complex. He took the ancient concept of unrequited love and located its roots in the original childhood triangle of mother, father, and child. Getting some, but not all, of Daddy's love is something with which every girl has to contend. It is often difficult to tell which aspect of the unrequited experience is harder for girls to tolerate and which is more likely to prove damaging to a girl's sense of herself—the experience of having her deepest wishes frustrated, or the belief that, were it not for some personal failing, she could have gotten everything she had wanted. Some girls believe that all it takes to ultimately prevail is to further perfect themselves in some specified way. This belief leads girls to feel that it is premature to try to come to terms with the fact that they have failed to get what they desperately wanted. The ball game is not over yet. There are other things that could be tried that might snatch victory from defeat. And if the ball game ends, and adulthood intervenes, there are other games, other men, with whom this can be played out. It's not over 'til it's over. God help the man who steps up to the plate.

Some girls find ways to come to terms with the degree of disappointment and hurt that accompanies the realization that they will never have Daddy all to themselves. For these girls, feeling validated does not hinge completely on proving that they, alone, are the most precious thing in their father's life, even though they may flourish for a time in the glow of this illusion. And when the time comes to accept the ways in which that is not so, they are able to come to terms with the fact that they never were, and never will be, their father's "one and only." For these women, the loss of this dream does not imply anything about their worthiness as women. There will be other men. But not all women are lucky enough to resolve things in so satisfactory a manner. Some women find it impossible to accept the situation for what it is. They cannot stop thinking: "If only I had done this better, or done that better, things could have turned out differently, and I would now feel complete satisfaction." If such women persist in thinking that their failure to win Daddy over had only to do with some inadequacy or personal failing on their part, this belief can go on to become the basis of a core sense of inferiority. Becoming involved later in life with yet another married man offers the woman a second shot at rectifying all that had been lost the first time around with her father.

Feeling disappointed in what one got from one's father during childhood is what most therapists would expect to find in the backgrounds of single women who have affairs with married men. It turns out that there are at least two other types of father–daughter relationships that contribute to the single woman–married man syndrome. Sometimes daughters have poor relationships with their mothers. When they ultimately turn their attention to their fathers, they may be looking to them for both maternal support and paternal love. But since it is usually hard for a father to completely compensate for what was lacking in the mother–daughter relationship, such girls tend to grow up to be women who remain fixated on their fathers. The other type of pattern that may contribute to the woman's involvement in the single woman–married man syndrome is the father acting seductively toward her, thus intensifying the daughter's desires for closeness along with her own conflicts about such desires.

Let us review what single women bring to the mix. Single women are typically in a position to be able to dedicate themselves completely to the pursuit of the man. They have no significant others placing demands on their time, so they are in a position to drop everything whenever the man whistles. They are willing to give the relationship their all, since success promises to undo childhood frustrations and traumas. And they are willing, for a time, to accept what little they get in return from the man. They accept the "crumbs" that drop from the table because they are not sure they deserve much more than that. The masochism they exhibit is, in part, the wish to be punished for the sin of having gone beyond merely coveting their neighbor's husband. It is also a manifestation of their belief that mistreatment is a condition they must accept as an inevitable by-product of being loved by a man. They wish the man would disprove this belief, but the only way he can do that is to marry her, and this he is unprepared to do.

MALE PSYCHOLOGY: NEEDING TWO WHEN ONE WON'T DO

Why is it that married men choose single women with whom to have affairs? The answer might seem obvious: because they are the ones who are available. But while there is undeniable truth in that answer, it fails to account for the complexities presented above. To begin with, the single woman I have described responds to the interest shown her by a married man by developing a do-or-die determination to win the man over. Because the man is oblivious to the underlying childhood issues that are driving the woman, he accepts at face value the woman's passionate, selfless love and devotion as having *just* to do with him. Considering the fact that the woman's intense love occurs in the context of her getting so little back in return from the man, it is easy to understand how the man could feel intensely validated.

But there is more to the story. Sometimes a man feels that things have changed between himself and his wife. The passion just isn't there anymore. Sex has become mechanical and routine. Things at home seem dull and boring. The relationship has ceased to validate his sense of worth as a man and a person. Some men may figure that this is the inevitable fate of a long-term marriage. Others may believe that the relationship has gotten to this point because angers and resentments have gone unacknowledged and unaddressed, and have accordingly taken their toll on the couple's ability or desire to be intimate. Sometimes the man is in touch with this, sometimes not. Sometimes he blames the wife's behavior or personality: She is too controlling, or not affectionate or supportive enough. "My wife doesn't understand me." But there are also times when no specific complaint is registered by the man. It seems to be a situation of needing two when one won't do.

Sometimes men who seek out affairs with single women feel they need more than what their wife, or any one woman, can offer. Sex with their wife might be fine, but they still find it impossible to remain deeply and monogamously committed to one woman. The origins of such difficulties most likely reside in the man's childhood, in the way certain situations were handled, or mishandled, by him or his parents. If a boy feels overly frustrated by his mother's intermittent departures from what he sees as her primary role as someone whose chief function is to be on call to satisfy his every whim without delay, he may grow up to be a man who is highly conflicted about ever letting another woman become so important that she could end up deeply disappointing him as his mother once had. I am not distinguishing between instances when the child was excessively needy or the mother failed to be adequately responsive to his needs. Whichever the case, if childhood frustrations generate a degree of rage the child fears could destroy his relationship with those upon whom he depends, he may split off such feelings for the good of the relationship. In general, splitting is motivated by the unconscious belief that were certain mental elements to be permitted to come together, something terrible would happen.

If, for instance, people are threatened by feeling both love and hate toward someone they are emotionally dependent upon, they will attempt to "split off," or compartmentalize, one of these two feelings. They will then be in touch with only one of these two feelings, the other feeling undergoing repression. This may result in a reaction formation (excessively loving another in order to obscure the underlying hate) or a displacement (directing love or hate toward an entirely different relationship, even though that feeling rightfully belongs to the present relationship). If a man grows increasingly resentful of his wife and cannot openly hate her, if only for a time, splitting may result. Under such circumstances, marriage may cease to be the favored venue for love. Home becomes where one experiences conflict and resentment. Meanwhile, love has split.

There are any number of different ways that men may split their feelings, their memories of interactions with others, their views of women, even their senses of themselves. Love and hate are just the most obvious set of feelings that may become split. Affection and lustful passion may also become split in ways that can prove disastrous to an ongoing relationship. This leads to what has been referred to as the "whore–madonna" complex. Freud (1912) put it aptly: "Where they love they do not desire and where they desire they cannot love" (p. 183). Such men can only be "turned on" by women they look down on. The whore-madonna split results in men's developing two classes of women: devalued women toward whom they feel sexual desire, and idealized women toward whom they feel deep affection and feelings of caring concern. Unable to experience both feelings toward the same woman, a man finds it impossible to remain deeply involved with, and committed to, one woman over the course of time.

Sometimes splitting even occurs within the core of one's personality, which can result in a person experiencing himself as an unintegrated personality. Such individuals tend to bring out selective aspects of themselves depending on the circumstance they are in. Were such a person to feel the need to permit himself greater expression within a relationship, he may opt to take up a second relationship rather than risk bringing more of himself into the first relationship.

What happens if the single woman catches on to the fact that the man has compartmentalized his feelings and seems only interested in carrying on a sexual relationship with her? If she confronts him by asking him whether he has interest in her as a person, and if, in response, he thinks to himself, No, I'm only interested in using you sexually, then what is he going to say? Unless he is a complete cad, it seems unlikely that he would be comfortable with the idea that he is nothing but a user. To create a more palatable self-image, the man might engage in a little self-deceit, which would then lead him to think of himself as caring more for the woman than he actually does. Once he has convinced himself that his motives are pure, he would accordingly be able to interact with the woman as if he loved her, thus becoming confused as to his true motives.*

Things become even more complicated when you consider the fact that the man has split off his sexual feelings from his affectionate feelings because he is frightened by the prospect of loving the woman he desires. Depending on just one woman to satisfy both of these needs is something about which such a man remains conflicted. Yet, here he is telling himself, and telling the woman, that he desires her both as a sex object and as an object of his loving affections. God help the woman who becomes entangled in such a web.

---

*While this scenario seems to parallel an instance that was alleged to have taken place between Monica Lewinsky and President Clinton, as will be presented in Chapter 2, the vignette described here has no direct bearing on their circumstance. To think otherwise is to indulge in idle speculation.

In fact, such a man is not using the woman just as a sexual object. But that is not to say that he is not using her. Yes, he loves the sex. But even more than the sex, he loves the way the woman's interest in him makes him feel about himself. But does he love *her*, apart from how she is able to make him feel about himself?

Such a man relies on the woman's single-minded dedication and devotion to prop up his self-esteem. But he may not be aware, or may find it hard to acknowledge, that he needs her in this way. He may be inclined, therefore, to think of his interest in her as being strictly sexual. It is safer that way. When the woman asks him to clarify whether he loves her, if he does not immediately resort to self-deceit as described above, he may realize that he is completely confused about how he feels, what he wants, and why he continues in the relationship, especially given how hellish it has become. At some level he knows that all of him does not truly love all of her, so he is reluctant to take the relationship to the next stage. What he has not yet grasped, however, is how the intensity of her love for him has more to do with her unresolved feelings about her father than it has to do with him. In other words, she is using him every bit as much as he is using her. Such a realization is likely to spell the beginning of the end of his ability to continue to experience her love, or the relationship, in the same way.

In addition to the narcissistic gratification that such affairs afford married men, and their ability to use such affairs as a vehicle to effect splits in their psyches, there are two additional psychological aspects that warrant attention: passive-aggressiveness and dependency. An affair can serve as the man's way of secretly rebelling against a wife whom he considers controlling. In true passive-aggressive style, an affair can be a man's way of thumbing his nose at his wife behind her back. *He* knows what he is getting away with. *He* knows that he is really the one in control. He will permit her the illusion of feeling as if he is firmly in her grasp, and she will be none the wiser because she remains in the dark about what her husband is actually up to. But what the man had not counted on is the single woman being just as passive-aggressive as is he. When two passive-aggressive individuals form a relationship, the dynamics of that relationship take on a particular cast.

Having to depend on another person is something that does not come easily for many men. By having an affair, the man is momentarily able to create the illusion that it is the other two, his mistress and his wife, who need him, depend on him, and are fighting over him, while he gets his pick. This is one way the man has of coming to terms with a time when just the opposite had occurred, that he had been one of at least two, counting his father and siblings, competing for the affections of his mother. If this had proven to be a particularly difficult situation for him, as an adult he may feel the need to turn things around, to get to be the one for whom others are competing.

SUMMARY

What I have presented is a composite portrait of what can happen when a single woman and a married man become romantically involved. Naturally, couplings between single women and married men can take very different paths, such as when an affair proceeds in a reasonable fashion toward the couple's marrying. And if a woman does not enter the affair haunted by the types of issues I have outlined above, an affair between her and a married man will not look anything like what I have described. It is important to once again state that I am speaking about a very specific kind of relationship when I refer to this syndrome.

The single woman–married man syndrome is defined by the following features: The woman has typically never been married and is usually unencumbered by the demands of children. Most often, she is much younger than the man and is in less of a position to command power, due either to her lack of experience or her lower socioeconomic status relative to that of the man. She remains firmly committed to the man over time and pursues the relationship with a vengeance. She strikes others as obsessive, as addicted to the married man. She is unreasonably hopeful about the relationship's prospects, in spite of mounting evidence to the contrary and the advice of friends and relatives who advise her to cut her losses and move on. She experiences intense frustration mixed with blind hope, bordering on naiveté, and she tends to idealize the man. She is so caught up in the relationship that she exhibits little ability to reflect on the meaning of her actions—to understand why she would want to pursue a married man and what keeps her involved in so frustrating a situation. She typically remains focused on the man's motives, rather than on her own, and tries to figure out what is going on in his head rather than in hers. She tends not to be particularly psychologically minded, which leads her to blame the man and to take no personal responsibility for having gotten herself into a situation that gradually sours. Over the course of her relationship with the married man, the single woman experiences a gradual diminution in the degree of power she has vis-à-vis the man. In her mind, feeling victimized justifies her going to any length to hold on to the relationship. Ultimately, she resorts to desperate behaviors in an effort to regain a sense of power. And, in the end, what she believes she wholeheartedly wants often proves not to be the case when she is ultimately in a position to have it.

With regard to the man's behavior, the syndrome is defined by (1) the maintenance of an extramarital relationship with a single woman over a protracted period of time; (2) the tendency not to seek psychological help until the girlfriend offers an ultimatum or the wife discovers the affair; (3) the tendency to view the wife as a decent person, maybe a bit too practical and cut-and-dry for the husband's taste; (4) the inability to resolve the question of whether he wants to remain married to his wife; (5) the inability to extricate himself from the extramarital relationship even when he has come to believe that it is wisest to do so, (6) the inability to decide about the fate of one relationship independent of any consideration regarding the fate of the other relationship, leading to obsessive indecisiveness with regard to which of the women he should be with; (7) the inability to deal openly and directly with any hostility toward the wife or girl-friend, with a concomitant tendency to employ passive-aggres-sive techniques of dealing with confrontations with the women in his life; (8) the tendency to experience himself as selflessly try-ing to please both women simultaneously; (9) the tendency to feel guilty about what he is putting these two women through; and (10) the tendency to feel intensely validated and affirmed by the girlfriend, who remains intensely interested in the married man in spite of the fact that she gets so little back in return.

The relationship defined by this syndrome runs a predict-able course toward an almost certain outcome. The relationship is tumultuous, characterized by intense highs and equally intense lows. It tends to alternate between times when it is extremely exciting for both parties, to times when things turn ugly as each drags the other through hell. Though each suffers greatly on ac-count of the relationship, neither seems psychologically able to call it quits. The affair is one neither can live with or without. In this way it resembles an addiction. On the surface it may appear as if the man has the upper hand in the relationship, but a deeper analysis reveals the ways in which the woman covertly exerts control over certain aspects of the relationship. Each partner vies for the position of victim. The affair is not primarily about sex. It has much more to do with the way each partner hopes for the relationship to cure some unresolved narcissistic needs. The single woman–married man syndrome almost never ends in marriage. If the man ends up divorced, he almost certainly will not marry the woman with whom he had been having the affair.

The single woman–married man syndrome is a purely de-scriptive entity insofar as it delineates particular types of behav-iors exhibited by certain single women who become romantically involved with married men and those of certain married men who become involved with single women. Hence, this syndrome is nei-ther a disease nor a disorder. Rather, it is a grouping of behav-iors (thoughts, feelings, beliefs, attitudes, hopes, intentions, and so on) that can be observed to occur together under very special conditions. These behaviors form a recognizable and predictable pattern. This syndrome may be associated with a variety of different developmental backgrounds and personal psychologies. It may be caused by a woman's having become involved with a married man in the absence of any antecedent "causative" psychological conditions that would predispose her to become involved with the married man in the first place (in other words, the syndrome can be the *effect* of the relationship). Or, alternatively, a woman may be psychologically predisposed to this syndrome on account of her particular psychology (e.g., may be masochistically inclined). The same can be said for the married man. The fact that a given individual's behavior satisfies the syndrome's criterion (justifying the conclusion that his or her behavior illustrates the syndrome) does not prove that he or she shares underlying psychologies with others who behave in similar ways.

The next three chapters discuss the phenomenology of the single woman–married man syndrome. Chapters 2 and 3 look at the affair from the perspective of the single woman and the married man, respectively. Chapter 4 describes both the types of marriages that may contribute to husbands' pursuing extramarital affairs and the types of reactions wives may have upon learning about such affairs.

I

TALES OF INFIDELITY: THE DATA DOCUMENTING THE PHENOMENON

2

From the Single Woman's Perspective: Looking for Love in All the Wrong Places

*These fellows of infinite tongue, that can rhyme themselves
into ladies' favors, they do always reason themselves out again.*
William Shakespeare, Henry V, V, ii, 160

In the beginning months of 1998, the American people witnessed the unfolding of a scandal that involved the forty-second president of the United States and a 21-year-old White House employee with whom he was alleged to have had an affair. In certain ways, there was nothing particularly remarkable about the story of a powerful man's involvement in an extramarital affair. Many presidents and world leaders, over the centuries, have had mistresses. But in the past, the public and the press overlooked their leaders' indiscretions, treating them as delicate matters that are best left unmentioned. This was not, however, to be the case with the affair between Bill Clinton and Monica Lewinsky.

The president's extramarital affair with Ms. Lewinsky raised two central questions in the minds of the American public—

questions commonly asked about affairs between single women and married men. The first focused on the matter of who was ultimately responsible for the affair. Was Ms. Lewinsky a naive victim of an older man who ought to have known better than to take advantage of "so innocent a thing"? After all, when the affair first began she was barely 21. Or had she gone off to Washington ready to have a sexual encounter with the president, and had accordingly walked into the affair with her eyes open? Some pictured her as a temptress dangling an irresistible morsel under the nose of her hapless prey. In the report by Kenneth Starr, the independent counsel who investigated the affair (1998), Monica complains that the people who surrounded the president "were wary of his weaknesses. . . . They didn't want to look at him and think that he could be responsible for anything, so it had to be all my fault. . . . I was stalking him or I was making advances towards him" (p. 56). Fifteen months after the story of the affair first broke, a Time/CNN poll asked the public whether they considered Ms. Lewinsky to be an opportunist or a victim, and seven times as many respondents answered the former rather than the latter (Cloud 1999).

The second question that the American public wondered about—again, one often posed about affairs between single women and married men—was what motivated the president and Ms. Lewinsky to carry on as they had. Was the president a self-destructive sex addict? Was Ms. Lewinsky an insatiable woman, determined to win the affections of other women's men, who would stop at nothing to get what she wanted? Was Monica a "bad girl"? Was Clinton a predatory male? What in God's name was Clinton thinking? How could he have risked losing all he had worked so hard to achieve? And why had Monica not realized that their relationship was inevitably doomed before it even began? After all, she had been through it once before with another married man.

Some might think it odd to pick Monica Lewinsky's story as one that exemplifies the single woman's involvement with a married man, given the unique nature of her affair. But while

Monica's affair with the president was in some respects larger than life, it was also pedestrian. Since her story illustrates so many of the features of extramarital relations between single women and married men, it is well suited for this purpose.

The account of Ms. Lewinsky's life that follows should not be thought to represent my psychoanalysis of her character or that of President Clinton. I have no first-hand information and thus can say nothing definitive about either of their motives. What follows are Monica's ideas and those of her friends and relatives, as seen primarily through the eyes of Special Prosecutor Kenneth Starr and his staff and Andrew Morton, who wrote Monica's official biography, *Monica's Story*. Whether President Clinton in fact acted as Monica Lewinsky claims he did or said the things she quotes him as saying will probably never be known.

I have tried to limit myself to a presentation of Monica's self-reported behaviors, feelings, and attitudes, carefully avoiding speculating about the internal mental workings of either Monica Lewinsky or President Clinton. Such speculation would be unfair to both of them. Furthermore, it could lead readers into mistakenly believing that I am in a position to know what was going on in their heads, which is obviously not the case.

The information presented in this chapter is limited to what has already been made public. This may lead some to anticipate that my presentation will amount to little more than yesterday's news. However, the material has been selected and organized to illustrate two main points that have previously gone unemphasized. The first is the question of the single woman's experience—what it is like for the woman to be in such a relationship over the course of time. The *Starr Report* and the Morton book give one a sense of how Ms. Lewinsky had experienced and interpreted her relationship with the president. Reading the Starr report is like browsing through a young girl's diary in that many of the passages quoted in the report are e-mail messages she composed yet never sent to the intended addressee, Bill Clinton. The second point I wish to illustrate is just how easy it is for a young woman to slip into a state of powerlessness relative to the married man. We will see, as her story proceeds, how Ms. Lewinsky, a self-proclaimed control freak (Morton 1999), gradually lost any sense of being able to influence or control the relationship in which she found herself.

MONICA'S DAD

Morton (1999) suggests that two main factors contributed to Monica's proclivity to pursue relationships with married men: (1) she felt socially snubbed when she was growing up, because she was a chubby girl in appearance-conscious Beverly Hills; and (2) she felt rejected by her father, an emotionally undemonstrative man whose approval Monica felt she could never win. These two factors seemed to have taken a toll on Monica's self-esteem.

Her father, Dr. Bernard Lewinsky, is described as a hard-working physician who was apt to return home after a busy day feeling "tired and irascible" (Morton 1999, p. 26). She and her father frequently fought, often resulting in Monica's running from the dinner table in tears. This pattern may well have contributed to Monica's later feeling: "I want to be in love and enjoy the perfect relationship, yet I only believe the relationship is 'real' if a man gets mad at me" (p. 28). Dr. Lewinsky tended to be critical, and Monica took his criticisms to heart. He also tended to be autocratic and stern, particularly in comparison to his wife, with whom Monica had a particularly affectionate relationship. Though Monica, in her mother's view, had always yearned to be "Daddy's little girl," her father was not the type to say, "Come and sit on my knee, you pretty girl," (p. 26). As an adolescent, Monica wrote a story about how a witch cast a spell on her father, causing him to be indifferent to her. In the story, the spell was broken and the father was free to love her as she always wished he might.

When Monica was 14 her parents separated. In conversations about the pending divorce, her mother let slip the fact that the divorce was precipitated in part by the father's extramarital affair with his nurse. Thereafter, Monica blamed her father exclusively for the divorce and refused to see him on weekends when he had visitation rights.

ENTER, MARRIED MAN NO. 1

After her parents divorced, Monica attended Beverly Hills High School and became very involved in the drama department, which served as a second family for her. It was there that she met a 25-year-old drama technician named Andy Bleiler, who was already engaged to marry a divorced mother eight years his senior.

After graduating from high school in 1991, Monica volunteered her time and services to her alma mater's drama department. It was then that Andy Bleiler turned his attentions to her, as he had done with many of the students he had worked with. He began to flirt with Monica and, after one school performance, the two stayed after and "made out." Thus began a romance that was to last five years, well into Monica's affair with the president.

Bleiler, who was eight years older than Monica, flirted with her throughout that summer of 1991. Then, in the fall, he married Kate Nason, the older woman to whom he had been engaged. Early the next year, Bleiler continued to flirt with Monica, and the two spent afternoons together in local motels, talking and making out. Though Bleiler was married, Monica felt gratified that a man was paying such attention to her: "It was great because he thought I was so sexy and, I mean, for a fat girl, for a guy to find you really attractive, it was really rewarding for me" (Morton 1999, p. 39). When Monica retrospectively reflected on the relationship, she felt that it was the result of a lack of self-worth, of thinking she did not deserve any better.

As 1992 went on, Monica began to fall in love with Andy Bleiler. By year's end, soon after Bleiler's wife became pregnant,

Monica had sexual intercourse with him for the first time. Though Monica and Andy split up early the next year, before long the relationship was back in full swing, only weeks after it had ended. Thus began the on-again-off-again pattern that was to characterize their relationship.

Their affair was a tumultuous one. Monica would swing from anger and hurt to forgiveness and reconciliation. Andy was forever breaking off the affair, saying he felt too guilty about being unfaithful to his wife. But he would return to Monica, teaching her a lesson that she was later to apply to her relationship with Bill Clinton: "I came to learn with married men that they feel guilty, say they want to stop it and then succumb to temptation anyway. So they always come back" (p. 41).

Monica found her relationship with Andy hard to tolerate. Even so, it was difficult for her to stay away from him. Her mother concluded that Monica's attachment to Andy was like an addiction or an obsession. Monica decided to leave California to go to college, partly to get away from Andy. She chose to attend Lewis and Clark College in Oregon, hoping to make a fresh start. However, she could not resist calling Andy when she felt lonely. And, when she returned to Los Angeles for Thanksgiving and spring break of 1993–1994, the two arranged to meet.

Shortly after their spring meeting Andy told Monica he was thinking of moving to Portland since it was expensive raising children in Los Angeles. Monica greeted the news with a mixture of eagerness and dread (Morton 1999), fearing that she might not have the resolve to resist rekindling their affair. That summer Andy came to Oregon to scout out the area, leaving his wife and children behind in Los Angeles. For the first time, he told Monica that he was in love with her and that she was a wonderful person about whom he cared a great deal. But his behavior was inconsistent, because at other times he would completely ignore her.

When Kate and the children joined Andy in Oregon in the fall of 1994, Monica and Andy once again broke up. But they maintained a friendship that included Andy's wife and children, for whom Monica would baby-sit. By year's end, Monica and Andy were back together again. When she subsequently attempted to break off the relationship he reacted by "pleading, begging, and beseeching her" (p. 48) to remain his friend. By Monica's account, Andy said he could not live without her.

The relationship continued through 1995. At one point, Monica obtained official Lewis and Clark College stationery and forged notes from the shop foreman of the theater department, David Bliss, outlining times when Bliss would supposedly need Andy's help, thus helping Andy establish an alibi so that he could see Monica without incurring his wife's suspicion. One of these letters was returned to Bliss, who figured Monica had written them, since she had been to see him on several occasions asking whether there would be any work for her "cousin" Andy Bleiler. Bliss confronted Monica, and Monica protected Andy, who had gone along with the ruse, by lying—saying that Andy was oblivious to what she was up to. This presaged a time when she would lie to protect another man she loved, Bill Clinton. She told Bliss that the Bleilers were financially strapped, and she feared that Andy would leave the area if there were no sign of pending work. In a letter of apology, Monica said to Bliss, "In all honesty, I never imagined that doing what I thought would be a kind, helpful thing for one of my closest friends would turn out to be one of the biggest nightmares of my life thus far" (The Pioneer Log 1999)

Monica concluded that the only way she would get over Andy was, once again, by leaving town. Her mother, Marcia Lewis, had grown increasingly concerned about Monica's inability to extricate herself from what appeared to be a decidedly unhealthy relationship. She suggested to Monica that she consider coming to work in Washington, D.C., where Marcia and Marcia's sister, Debra Finerman, had moved. Through her mother's connections, Monica was able to obtain a White House internship. Thus began the next chapter in Monica's life.

ENTER, MARRIED MAN NO. 2

In August 1995, shortly after moving to Washington, Monica had an opportunity to meet President Clinton as she was standing in a roped-off crowd at an official gathering of interns at the White House. She reports that when he spotted her, he gave her "the full Bill Clinton. . . . It was this look, it's the way he flirts with women. When it was time to shake my hand, the smile disappeared, the rest of the crowd disappeared and we shared an intense but brief sexual exchange. He undressed me with his eyes" (Morton 1999, p. 58). The president later would tell Monica that he remembered that moment vividly and had figured that one day he would be kissing her.

The following day, the White House interns were invited to a surprise forty-ninth birthday party for the president on the South Lawn of the White House. Monica felt flattered and excited to be receiving so much of the president's attention (Morton 1999), considering that he was looking at her as much as he was. She had another chance to shake hands with him and wish him a happy birthday. She remembers vividly that "he looked deep into my eyes and I was hooked" (p. 58).

Caught by the spell of what she had experienced over the course of the preceding two days, Monica nurtured a fantasy that she would soon be hearing from Secret Service men, who would arrange for a clandestine meeting with the president, just as the Secret Service had done for President Kennedy whenever he felt like "company." Monica had clearly been bitten by the bug! She spoke to her mother and aunt about the president's flirtations, and both considered her newfound interest a "welcome respite" from her obsession with Andy Bleiler (p. 60).

In October 1995, Monica returned briefly to Portland to visit with Andy, who informed her that he felt guilty about their affair and wanted to focus on his family. Monica returned to Washington feeling devastated and depressed, and would not see Andy for another year.

In November 1995, Monica was offered a job working in the correspondence section in the Office of Legislative Affairs at the White House. On her first day at work, November 15, the president stopped by Monica's office what seemed to her to be an inordinate number of times. Later that day, he dropped in on an office party she was attending, and spent a lot of time looking and smiling at her. When she knew that only he was watching, Monica seized an opportunity to expose her thong underwear to the presidential eye, a daring move that was "rewarded with an appreciative look as the President walked past" (p. 63).

Later that evening, Monica walked past an open office and noticed that Clinton was standing in the office alone. He motioned to her to come in, and he began making small talk with her, asking her where she had gone to school. Feeling nervous, Monica blurted out that she had a big crush on him. Each acknowledged the fact that there had been chemistry between them and that they were mutually attracted to one another (Starr 1998). Clinton invited her into the back office where he held her tightly and told her that she was beautiful and that she lit up a room, all of which made Monica feel "incredibly special" (Morton 1999, p. 64). Then he kissed her, and by her account, did so with feeling. Later that same night she and the president had yet another chance to be physically intimate as the two found a private place to fondle each other and kiss. It was at this time that Monica performed oral sex on the president, which left her feeling that she and Bill Clinton were "sexual soulmates" who "clicked on an incredible level" (p. 65).

Monica was prone to assume "that any man who took the slightest interest in her did so out of pity or because there was no one else available" (p. 64), so she came away from these encounters figuring that the president's regular White House girlfriend was away; otherwise he would not have given her a second thought. Based on this assumption, she took the incident for what she thought it was worth and tried hard not to hang her hopes on what she had just experienced.

When she and the president saw each other the next day, he initially ignored her, but when she feigned indifference toward him, he grew more interested in her, so much so, in fact, that it was noticeable to others. Another intern commented to Monica that it appeared to her as if the president had a crush on her.

The following day, November 17, she and the president had another occasion to talk. Monica was working late and Clinton spotted her and invited her into the Oval Office. She told him she imagined that he didn't even remember her name, but this proved not to be true (Morton 1999). He told her that he liked her smile and her energy (Starr 1998). They proceeded to the bathroom where they "fooled around" some more. It was then that the president told her he was usually around on weekends and suggested she could come by to see him then (Starr 1998). Monica left feeling that she had another man who was interested in her now, so she no longer had to pine for Andy Bleiler.

A third sexual encounter occurred on December 31, 1995. Again, Monica acted as if the president had forgotten her name, basing this belief on the fact that he had called her "Kiddo" whenever they would pass in the halls. Monica introduced herself to the president, who responded sheepishly about appearing to have forgotten her name. He told her that he had remembered it; he also said he had intended to call her, but he had lost the piece of paper upon which she had written her number. And since her number was unlisted, Monica wrote it down again, but warned him that this was the last time she would provide it for him.

On January 7, 1996, Monica was taken off guard when the president called her at home. Mistaking his voice for that of a college friend, she responded casually and made small talk, until she suddenly realized who it was on the other end of the line. As they spoke Clinton mentioned in passing that he was about to head off to work. Picking up on the hint, Monica asked if he would like company. The president said, "That would be great" (Morton 1999, p. 68).

During this encounter, the first to take place in the Oval Office, Monica Lewinsky and President Clinton were physically intimate for about half an hour. This was followed by their chatting for a long time—he sitting at his desk, and she sitting in a chair to the right of the desk. But while the two conversed for quite some time, it appears that their conversation did not go in the direction of his getting to know Monica any better, given what she had to say to him the next time they met two weeks later.

After this encounter Clinton and Monica engaged in phone sex on a couple of occasions. He promised he would call her and arrange for them to meet in person again, but Monica was disappointed and felt insecure when he failed to follow through. On January 21, two weeks after their first prearranged encounter, the president spotted Monica in the White House corridors and beckoned her. But Monica stood firm and demanded answers to her questions and reassurances for her doubts before things went any further. The president would later liken this "feisty, argumentative" girl (Morton 1999, p. 83) to his own mother, Virginia Kelley, who had died the year before of breast cancer: "You are full of piss and vinegar, just like her" (p. 83), he told Monica.

Monica confronted the president about how he had ignored her. She complained that she had no sense of how he actually felt about her; and she insisted that if they were to have a relationship, there had to be a little give and take (Morton 1999). Clinton responded by defusing the situation, changing the subject, and using his charm, complimenting her on how her beret framed her "cute little face" (p. 71) so well. He shared some of his feelings about what it was like to be the commander-in-chief of an army that was fighting in Bosnia, with American soldiers being killed. Then the president added: "It's very lonely and people don't understand that" (p. 71).

His sharing such feelings made Monica feel closer to him. But she did not let up and confronted him again: "I asked him why he doesn't ask me any questions about myself, and . . . is this just about sex . . . or do you have some interest in trying to get to know me as a person?" (Starr 1998, p. 51). The president acted shocked, and wondered how she could think such a thing. With tears in his eyes, he told her, "I don't ever want you to feel that way. That's not what this is" (Morton 1999, p. 72). He reassured Monica, telling her, in her words, that he "cherishes the time that he had with me" (Starr 1998, p. 17). Monica reportedly considered what Clinton said "a little bit odd" given the fact that "he didn't really even know me yet" (Starr 1998, p. 51).

It was after this point that Monica came to feel their "friendship started to blossom" (Starr 1998, p. 52). On February 4, the two had their first of many lengthy conversations, which Monica speculates was in response to her having previously questioned the president about his intentions toward her (Starr 1998). Over time, both Clinton and Monica spoke to one another about their childhoods. "[W]e spent hours on the phone talking. . . . we talked about everything under the sun" (Starr 1998, p. 35). The president called her at the office or at home every three to four days.

As their relationship developed, it was characterized by tremendous amounts of flattery on Clinton's part. He played the role of the consummate charmer. He complimented Monica on her beauty, her energy, and her mind. Knowing how sensitive she was about her weight, he was careful to always comment on how she seemed to have lost weight, or noting how slender she looked. After one prearranged encounter, Clinton called to tell her, just minutes after they had parted, that he really enjoyed seeing her and thought she was a "neat" person. He told Monica that she made him "feel twenty-five again" (Morton 1999, p. 72), and that he wished they could spend more time together.

In turn, Monica idealized the man with whom she was fast becoming infatuated, telling him that he was "like rays of sunshine that made plants grow faster and made colors more vibrant" (Morton 1999, p. 70). But while she saw the president as a "sensitive, loving, tender person, a needy man who was not getting the kind of love and nurturing he deserved," she had what she referred to as a "double way" (p. 70) of looking at him insofar as she could not dismiss the idea that he was a philanderer who was prone to have a different woman every day.

Over time, Monica grew attached to the president and told him that she had fallen in love with him. She was under the impression that he loved her back, though she never quotes him as having said as much. The two were physically affectionate. They often hugged or held hands. They exchanged expressions of affection; he called her "Sweetie," "Baby," or "Dear," while she addressed him as "Handsome" (Starr 1998, p. 34).

Not long after they had begun seeing one another, Clinton got cold feet. After their February 4th encounter, fifteen days went by without Monica hearing from him. When he finally did call, on February 19, she could tell from his tone of voice that things had changed. She asked whether she could visit him. Clinton hesitated, then answered that he did not know how long he would be there. It was then that Monica decided, for the first and only time, to pay an uninvited call on the president.

Taken off guard by her unexpected appearance, he told Monica that he liked her as a person, but no longer felt right about their intimate relationship. Echoing the words Andy Bleiler had spoken, Clinton told her he felt guilty about the affair and did not want to hurt his wife and child. He told her he would have to put a stop to their involvement for the sake of his marriage, but that they could remain friends (Starr 1998). Monica left the Oval Office feeling devastated and bitter.

Once again feigning lack of interest, Monica made sure thereafter to walk the other way whenever the president was nearby, which, predictably, precipitated further calls from him. Six weeks after breaking off their relationship, Clinton was once again in full pursuit, thus replaying the experience that Monica had had with Andy Bleiler. But it was not long before external forces intervened and placed a considerable impediment in the path of the affair. Evelyn Lieberman, the Deputy Chief of Staff for Operations at the White House, became concerned about what people might think of Monica's apparent closeness with the president, so she decided to transfer Monica to the Pentagon.

Monica was devastated. She worried that this would spell the end of her relationship with the president. When she told Clinton about the transfer he, too, appeared upset by the news of her imminent departure. He complained to her: "Why do they have to take you away from me? I trust you" (Starr 1998, p. 58). But as upset as he might have been, he did nothing to interfere with the transfer. What he did do, according to Monica, was promise her that if he won reelection in November, he would bring her back to the White House (Starr 1998). Monica told the president that she was in love with him, and he answered by saying that meant a lot to him.

Monica hated her job at the Pentagon, making her separation from Clinton that much harder to bear. She comforted herself by thinking about how she would soon be returning to the White House once the election was over and the coast was clear for the two of them to resume their affair. She ticked off the days to the election on a calendar as her way of tolerating their separation. Unknown to her, the president had a calendar of his own, upon which he kept track of how long he had been good by resisting sexual temptation (Morton 1999).

During the first few months after she was transferred, the president called her every four to seven days. Monica came to believe that he missed her as much as she missed him. Sometimes he would call several times a day, if, for instance, their calls had been interrupted by official business. At times the president seemed to turn to Monica for comfort and consolation, such as when his close friend Admiral Jeremy "Mike" Boorda committed suicide and Clinton called Monica, telling her "I wish you were here to give me a big hug" (Morton 1999, p. 87).

But as the November election approached, his calls became less frequent and Monica grew increasingly frustrated. She sent him many cards and letters and attended public gatherings, hoping that they might catch glimpses of one another. But she never got a chance to see him privately. From this point forward, their relationship would be sustained in other ways, including the president's wearing the ties, pins, or sunglasses Monica had bought for him.

MONICA LOSES HER GRIP

Though Monica had shown herself to be feisty in her early confrontations with the president and had exhibited chutzpah by dropping in on him uninvited, she ceased to be able to maintain her initial strength. She took to sitting by the phone waiting for him to call, afraid to leave her room lest she miss him. She reasoned that if Clinton called and was unable to reach her he might lose interest and seek the company of another woman. Monica often fell asleep waiting for him to call, awakening later, looking at the clock, and crying because he had yet to contact her. She experienced such hoping and waiting as torturous.

The power balance in the relationship was turning more and more in favor of the president. It was he who was now calling the shots. Monica made excuses for him, saying, "It wasn't his fault, he never had any idea how much pain I was in. I was such a glutton for punishment—it's scary not being clear-headed enough or having the strength to get out of an emotional situation" (Morton 1999, p. 137).

Gradually, Monica was reduced to having to settle for mere "crumbs" that fell from the president's table. She became hypersensitive to whatever he had to say, and, as Andrew Morton (1999) observed, she "attached enormous importance to the president's smallest utterance" (p. 118). Morton speculates that Clinton had no inkling of the extent to which Monica read meaning into whatever he said, thus "building up her hopes on the flimsiest of foundations" (p. 118). The president's interest could lift her up, just as his ignoring her, or his not following through on a promise, could plunge her into the pits of despair. A friend of Monica's noticed that if Monica had failed to hear from Clinton for several days "she became insane and crazy" (p. 89).

When Monica felt frustrated over not seeing the president, she arranged for "chance meetings," and Clinton acted as if he never understood that she had actually staged these meetings. It was her penchant for popping up everywhere that earned her the reputation of being a stalker, a label Monica took exception to, justifying her actions as the only way she could maintain a relationship with someone who unconsciously wanted continued involvement with her but who was in no position to be pursuing her publicly. Monica believed she was someone who could be easily forgotten were she not constantly to remind the president of her continued existence.

In September 1996, during a phone conversation, Monica pressed the question of when the president and she would sexually consummate their relationship. Clinton was firm, making it clear that was not going to happen (Starr 1998, p. 63). Monica was greatly disappointed and angry with the president, who snapped back, "If you don't want me to call you anymore, just say so" (Morton 1999, pp. 89–90), thus putting Monica in her place. Increasingly, things were much more on Clinton's terms than on Monica's.

During this period, Monica dated a number of men, most of whom were much older than she. It appears as if she used dating in part to redress the imbalance in her relationship with the president by teasing him about having competition. She failed to mention, however, that while she was seeing other men, her heart remained his. Though she would be invited to sleep over when out on dates, she was careful to be back home by midnight on the off chance that Clinton might call.

Over the course of time, as Morton sums it up, "the less Monica socialized, the lonelier she became and the more she focused on the affair" (p. 90). As had been the case with Andy Bleiler, Monica was once again falling into an obsessive relationship with an unavailable man. Even though most of her closest friends and relatives expressed concern about her continuing to pursue a relationship with the president, there was one person prodding her on, encouraging her to "go for it." This was Linda Tripp, the woman who would eventually betray her friendship with Monica by taping their private conversations. She initially knew nothing of what had actually gone on between Monica and the president, but she intuited that Monica was the type that

Clinton would find irresistible. Linda's encouragement sustained and fueled Monica's hopes, which, in the final analysis, only served to prolong Monica's agony.

Monica had expected to receive a call from the president on election night, but grew despairing when it never came. After the election she readied herself for her return to the White House. Then she sat and waited . . . and waited . . . and waited. When she failed to hear from Clinton, she threw things about her apartment and cried uncontrollably. She later wrote him an unsent letter: "I was so sure that the weekend after the election you would call me to come visit and you would kiss me passionately and tell me you couldn't wait to have me back. You'd ask me where I wanted to work and say something akin to 'Consider it done' and it would be. Instead I didn't hear from you for weeks and subsequently your phone calls became less frequent" (Starr 1998, pp. 64–65).

Monica confided in Tripp, saying, "Look Linda, I'm going to tell you this and I hope you don't tell anyone. I already had an affair with him and it's over. Just leave it alone—it's not going to happen" (Morton 1999, p. 98).

It was not until December 2, when Monica had all but lost her last shred of hope of ever hearing from the president, that he ultimately called. The two caught up on the details of each other's lives, and then Clinton told her "I wish I was there and I could put my arms around you" (Morton 1999, p. 100). Monica remembers him as being very sweet and tender as he told her how much he had missed her.

It was at this point that Monica returned to Oregon to visit Andy Bleiler, who seemed uncharacteristically anxious to see her. It was during this trip that she slept with Andy for the last time. She left Portland feeling warm and romantic toward him, but realized that the relationship was over and that he no longer held power over her. He told her he valued her as a friend, and apologized for his behavior during the affair.

The president's relationship with Monica resumed shortly after her return to Washington. He maintained phone contact in

January and February, but they did not see one another until February 28, 1997. Monica had launched an all-out campaign to get rehired at the White House and it appeared as if her much-hoped-for job might materialize. The president was very encouraging about this matter, thus fueling her hope.

Shortly after Valentine's Day, 1997, the president again expressed his wish to end the affair, and to do so in a way that would not hurt Monica. But true to form, this conversation ultimately ended not with a final parting but with the two having phone sex and with him promising to call her again. Over the course of time, the relationship proved to be the same on-again-off-again fare that she had previously experienced with Bleiler. Morton summed it up in this way: "He would tell her it was over and then shortly afterwards would call her or even see her, his every action, however casual, perhaps unintentionally renewing her belief that they did, after all, have a future together" (1999, p. 103).

On February 28 Monica Lewinsky and President Clinton had a chance to be alone together for the first time in ten months. Monica was invited to attend a radio address that the president was giving. When they finally were alone, he presented Monica with some gifts, but he also expressed his concern that the two might become addicted to one another. The two then were physically intimate. Monica told him how much it would mean to her were he to let himself go and permit himself complete orgasmic pleasure when she performed oral sex on him. According to Monica, Clinton replied, "I don't want to disappoint you" (Starr 1998, p. 71). With that, the president permitted himself, for the first time in the fifteen months they had been sexually involved, to ejaculate in her presence. As fate would have it, a small amount of semen stained Monica's blue dress, which later served as irrefutable proof of the extent to which the intimate relationship between the president and Monica had gone.

Now, more than ever, Monica was sure that she and Clinton had a future together. She saw his hesitation as much like Andy Bleiler's. Monica told him that their relationship "nurtured the little girl in her," that he "made her life seem complete" (Morton 1999, p. 107). By this point, Monica was thinking about marriage, about living the rest of her life as the president's wife. But while she seemed to be in seventh heaven, Clinton was later to testify before the grand jury that he did not feel the same: "I was sick after it was over [referring to the sexual encounter when he had ejaculated], and I . . . was pleased at that time that it had been nearly a year since any inappropriate contact had occurred with Ms. Lewinsky. I promised myself it wasn't going to happen again" (Starr 1998, p. 71).

A week later, on May 24, 1997, the president and Monica once again met in the Oval Office. He told her that he felt tormented about the affair and wanted to end it and that he considered her a great person and hoped they would remain friends, and he still wanted her in his life (Starr 1998, p. 75). Though she was devastated, Monica clutched on to the president's pledge that he could, in his words, "be helpful [to her] in ways [she had] not imagined." Though she left the Oval Office wondering to herself "how could he have messed with me so cruelly" (Morton 1999, p. 115), she nevertheless still believed that he wanted to take care of her. But from that point forward, the two would never be sexually intimate again. Their eighteen-month affair was over.

Paradoxically, it was at this time that Clinton chose to be more revealing with her than he had ever been before. In Monica's words, the president explained to her that

> for all his life . . . he had lived a secret existence, a life filled with lies and subterfuge. As a little boy he had lied to his parents, and, even though he was a smart kid and knew the consequences of his actions, he had maintained that hidden life, safe in the knowledge than no one knew about it, knew the true Bill Clinton. . . . [He] became increasingly appalled at himself, at his capacity not only for deceiving others, but also for self-deception. [Morton 1999, pp. 113–114]

IT'S NOT OVER TILL IT'S OVER

Even though the sexual aspect of their relationship was over, the two continued to speak, often at length, and occasionally at a great emotional pitch. They also exchanged gifts on special occasions. Monica remained singularly focused on her plan to regain employment at the White House, and she continued to hope that the president's rejection would not prove to be final. If only she could get back to the White House, maybe she could rekindle the flame he had tried to extinguish.

President Clinton initially appeared to be going to bat for Monica by pressing to have her rehired as a White House staffer, but no job materialized. Monica wrote that she had been beyond patient waiting for the job she felt had been promised her (Starr 1998). It was becoming increasingly clear to her that she was not going to be returning to the White House, and she began to believe he was leading her on.

On June 29, Monica wrote a note to the president pleading for his attention after not having heard from him in over five weeks. "Please do not do this to me. I feel disposable, used and insignificant" (Starr 1998, p. 77). This letter was followed, in short order, by another, which finally got the president's attention. On July 3, Monica wrote a "peevish Dear Sir" (Starr 1998, p. 78) letter to him in which she made a veiled threat to disclose the nature of their relationship to her parents if she could not return to work at the White House.

Clinton responded swiftly to Monica's letter. He summoned her to meet him the following day, scolded her for having threatened him, and lectured her about her having addressed him in the manner that she had. He reminded her that he was trying to help her and suggested that she was ungrateful. Monica fired back, enumerating the ways he had failed to come through for her as he had promised to do. She complained that while Clinton claimed he wanted to be her friend, he was not acting like one. Then she burst into tears, which caused the president to melt. He then became, in Monica's words, "the most affectionate with me he'd ever been" (Starr 1998, p. 79). He hugged her and stroked her hair and pleaded with her to stop crying. He complimented her and lamented the fact that he could not spend more time with her. Monica suggested that maybe it would be possible for them to spend more time together after he left office, to which the president answered, "I don't know, I might be alone in three years" (Starr 1998, p. 79). Monica joked about how they would make a good team, to which the president replied, "Well, what are we going to do when I'm 75 and have to pee 25 times a day?" (Starr 1998, pp. 79–80).

Monica came away from the meeting "emotionally stunned" and concluded, "I just knew he was in love with me" (Starr 1998, p. 80). But while she felt encouraged about her relationship with the president, she was never able, from that point forward, to rekindle what the two had previously had. On August 16, 1997, she visited Clinton bearing birthday gifts, and tried to engage him sexually, but he rebuffed her. She grew angry, the two fought, and he ordered her to lower her voice. She told one friend regarding the president: "In some ways I hope I never hear from him again because he'll just lead me on because he doesn't have the balls to tell me the truth" (Starr 1998, pp. 84–85).

Throughout the latter part of 1997, Monica continued to pursue employment at the White House. She made numerous calls and sent many notes to both the president and Betty Currie, the president's personal secretary, most of which went unanswered. In a letter to Clinton, drafted but never sent, Monica demonstrated an awareness that she had become "consumed with this disappointment, frustration and anger" (Morton 1999, p. 147). She wrote: "You want me out of your life. I guess the signs have been made clear for awhile—not wanting to see me and rarely calling. I used to think it was you putting up walls" (Starr 1998, p. 98).

Monica kept contacting Ms. Currie in the hope of talking to Clinton about her job prospects. But Ms. Currie kept putting her off. At times Monica would go to the southwest gate of the White House, contact Ms. Currie and beg that the president see her.

Ms. Currie told Monica, "You really worry me when you are like this" (Morton 1999, p. 129). When Monica's requests were turned down, she would become increasingly angry and frustrated. She grew more and more desperate in her attempts to see the president. In her frustration she frequently grew hysterical. Sometimes she would get to the point of feeling that she had had enough, that she could not take it anymore. Monica remembers: "I was angry, I was frustrated, I was out of my mind. I was such a moron —I should have walked away from it all much sooner" (p. 129).

Monica drafted yet another letter to Clinton that went unsent. In that letter she said that other women who had been treated by men as she had been treated by the president would reason this way: "He doesn't call me, he doesn't want to see me—screw it." But she goes on to admit that, unlike them, "I can't let go." She was holding on to what little she had left of a relationship with him when, in her words, "any normal person" in her shoes "would have walked away" (Starr 1998, p. 87).

Monica now sought an apology from the president and an acknowledgment that he had "fucked up my life" (Starr 1998, p. 87). She let loose at Ms. Currie with yet another one of her tirades, saying that she had had enough of Ms. Currie and Clinton's stringing her along. On October 10, the president responded by calling Monica at 2:30 in the morning. The two launched into a screaming match that lasted ninety minutes. Clinton became so angry that Monica envisioned him turning purple. It was during this conversation that he told her, "If I had known the kind of person you really are, I wouldn't have gotten involved with you" (Morton 1999, p. 137). He reminded her that she had promised to quit the relationship if he ever got to the point of feeling he wanted to "stop doing this" (Starr 1998, p. 88). Then Clinton added, "If I had known it was going to be this much trouble, I would have stopped it in the first place" (Starr 1998, p. 88).

Coming to the ultimate realization that nothing more would occur romantically between them, Monica wrote a good-bye note to the president and brought the note to the southwest gate the next day, along with a Christmas gift for him. Though Ms. Currie had told Monica that he was meeting with lawyers, the secret service officer on duty told her that he was, in fact, meeting with Eleanor Mondale, a friend of Clinton's who was a CBS-TV reporter who Monica suspected had caught the president's eye. Learning this, Monica became infuriated. She went to a pay phone, called Ms. Currie, and delivered an angry diatribe attacking her and the president.

Monica then returned to the White House to talk to Clinton about this incident, and he responded, telling her, in Monica's words, that "he had never been treated as poorly by anyone else as I treated him" (Starr 1998, p. 36). Then he reminded Monica that "he spent more time with [her] than anyone else in the world, aside from his family, friends and staff" (Starr 1998, p. 36). "How dare you make such a scene!" the president reportedly said to her (Morton 1999, p. 151). He then chastised her for having spoken to Ms. Currie as she had, saying, "You had no right to talk to anyone like that." And then he added: "I don't understand—this has become your everything. You told me when this affair started that when it was over you would not give me any trouble" (Morton 1999, p. 151).

Monica summed up her experience with the president when she wrote to him regarding their relationship. "For the life of me I can't understand how you can be so kind and so cruel to me. When I think of all the times you have filled my heart and soul with sunshine, and then think of all the times you made me cry for hours and want to die, I feel nauseous" (Morton 1999, p. 152). Clearly, the affair between Monica Lewinsky and President Bill Clinton was a match made in heaven . . . and hell.

DISCUSSION

Monica Lewinsky's relationship with President Clinton exhibits many of the hallmarks of the single woman–married man syndrome. There are characteristics in Monica's behavior that are representative of how single women act in relationships with married men. Monica's relationship with her father was, by her own account and that of her mother, unsatisfying. He was emotionally undemonstrative, the type of father who leaves a daughter hungering for more. The story she had written during adolescence about a father who is magically freed of his indifference toward his daughter says it all. Single women who pursue relationships with married men quite often have unsatisfactory relationships with their fathers and tend to date men who are considerably older than themselves.

By all accounts, Monica thought little of herself, much like other single women who pursue relationships with married men. She was self-conscious about her weight and reasoned that no man would be interested in her unless it was out of pity. She described herself as lacking self-worth and figured, in retrospect, that she had accepted what little she was able to get from Andy Bleiler and President Clinton because she did not deserve any better.

Relations between single women and married men typically become emotionally labile after a period of time, and Monica's relationships with Andy Bleiler and President Clinton were no exceptions. Raised voices, screaming matches, and emotional scenes became commonplace. Andy Bleiler would "cry like a baby" (Morton 1999, p. 48) and threaten suicide, Clinton would "turn purple with anger" (Morton 1999, p. 137), and Monica would become livid, thus causing the otherwise unflappable Ms. Currie to tremble as she herself became caught up in the maelstrom.

As is common in relationships between single women and married men, Monica and the president each ended up feeling like the victim of the other. When she was transferred to the Pentagon, Monica felt that she had obediently left the White House without causing a fuss the way other women might. She considered herself to be "beyond patient" (Starr 1998, p. 77) as she waited, month after month, to be rehired at the White House. When she ultimately blew her stack, she talked and acted as if her style of expressing anger was completely justified. For his part, the president considered Monica ungrateful for all he had done for her, and said that no one had ever treated him as shabbily as she had.

Relationships between single women and married men are highly ambivalent. Monica greeted the news that Andy Bleiler was moving to Portland with "eagerness and dread," and she was split about how she viewed the president, seeing him as kind and loving but also little more than a philanderer. The behaviors of Andy Bleiler and President Clinton seem to have been more blatantly ambivalent; each man repeatedly initiated breakups that were followed in short order by reconciliations.

Like other single women who are seeing married men, Monica and Clinton evidently had ways of privately signaling one another that they were still involved on some level. For instance, the president seemed to go out of his way to wear the ties Monica gave him when he knew she would see him wearing them. And Monica came to think of the chair that was positioned just to the right of his desk as "her chair." By adopting that position as "hers," she staked out a place for herself in Clinton's life.

As much as single women tend to hold on to these private signs that their relationship with the married man is ongoing, relations between single women and married men ultimately prove to be a tease. This was particularly true when it came to Monica's relationship with President Clinton. The president would break off their relationship, only to act in ways that subsequently suggested that they might indeed have a future together. He evidently went so far as to muse about the possibility that he might be alone and hence available after serving his second term in office, which obviously stimulated Monica's hope that they might be together one day.

The logistics of Monica's relationship with President Clinton, much like all affairs that conform to the single woman–married man syndrome, were characterized by her ultimately having to pursue him, since he was not completely free to pursue her. While his being in the public eye compounded their need for secrecy, the logistics of their relationship were quite similar to what most single women experience when dating married men. Monica familiarized herself with both President Clinton and Mrs. Clinton's schedules in order to optimize her chances of getting to see him. She had to engineer "chance meetings" whereby they could see each other in public and exchange knowing glances. This led her to be described as a stalker, a label that may seem applicable to most single women in Monica's shoes, who feel that the burden of responsibility for maintaining the relationship falls to them, given the man's lack of freedom.

The power imbalance that gradually develops in most single woman–married man relationships that conform to the syndrome is particularly well illustrated in Monica's relationship with the president. She initially came across as "pushy" (Starr 1998, p. 75) and "full of piss and vinegar" (Morton 1999, p. 83). She had the audacity to expose herself to him the first chance the two were alone, to confront him with questions about his intentions toward her, and to pay him an uninvited call. How such a seemingly strong woman could regress to the point of feeling almost completely powerless in her relationship with the president is a point worth pondering.

For all her bravado, Monica Lewinsky was not the self-assured woman she appeared to be. By her own admission, she was full of self-doubts. When she had gained the president's attention she describes herself as having been "hooked" (Morton 1999, p. 58). Part of what contributed to Monica's obsession with Clinton, as her aunt put it, was the fact that he made her feel "incredibly special" (p. 64). Monica was too emotionally involved with the president, and had romanticized the relationship to such a degree, that it became hard for her to see it for what it was. Only toward the end was she able to open her eyes to the obvious signs that ought to have clued her early on that it had no future.

Another factor that contributed to the eventual imbalance of power is that over the course of their relationship together, Monica regressed by virtue of her social withdrawal, which led her to focus more and more on her relationship with the president. Though she permitted herself to date, she was never truly available to other men. She had Clinton on her mind, and would turn down opportunities to sleep over on the off chance that he would pick that night to call. This regression led her to use desperate measures to achieve her goals. She had tantrums, was reduced to making threats, would even lie if the need arose, all in an effort to hold on to a relationship she felt she could not live without.

Finally there is President Clinton's behavior. We cannot know with any certainty how close Monica's account of his actions is to reality. She formed her own conclusions and conveyed them to Kenneth Starr's investigation team and to the journalist Andrew Morton. They wrote the story as it seemed to them, and now I am conveying my version of their version (or her version) of the president's behavior. There are certain things Clinton was purported to have said and done that are strikingly similar to what other married men involved with single women say and do. The three things that stand out are the president's disclosure that (1) he lived his life in such a way that no one really got to know the real Bill Clinton, (2) he had lied so much that even he was no longer sure what was true; in other words, he was prone to self-deception; and (3) he thought of himself as someone who primarily wished to please others, or was inclined to act in ways that would support such a view of himself, whatever the truth may be.

3

From the Married Man's Perspective: Getting More Than He Bargained For

But if thy love were ever like to mine,—
As sure I think that did never man love so—
How many actions most ridiculous
Hast thou been drawn to by fantasy? . . .
If thou rememb'rest not the slightest folly
That ever love did make thee run into,
Thou hast not lov'd.

William Shakespeare, *As You Like It*, II, iv, 32

The experience of a married man involved in an extramarital affair that conforms to the single woman–married man syndrome differs from that of his lover. This chapter presents two cases that describe this syndrome from the married man's perspective. In the first, the extramarital affair is the first the man has ever had. In the second, the man had dabbled in affairs from time to time, but none ever meant anything to him until he met this particular woman.

The first example is taken from a book entitled *The Affair: A Portrait of Extramarital Love in Contemporary America*, which contains the research of freelance writer Morton Hunt (1969). In his book, Hunt describes four affairs in detail, one of which serves as a particularly good example of the single woman–married man syndrome. Hunt meticulously chronicles this affair over the course of time, providing a wealth of phenomenologic data for us to study. The second example is taken from a chapter of a book entitled *Intimacy and Infidelity: Separation-Individuation Perspectives* (Akhtar and Kramer 1996). The chapter is written by John Ross (1996), a training and supervising psychoanalyst at the Columbia University Center for Psychoanalytic Training and Research. Ross's case material provides us with a lot less information about the phenomenology of extramarital affairs and a lot more information about this particular man's developmental background, along with theoretical speculation about the relationship between his background, his difficulties finding satisfaction in marriage, and his tendency to go outside his marriage for the satisfaction of his needs.

These cases illustrate the two basic patterns by which a married man comes to be involved with a single woman. In Hunt's case of Edwin Gottesman and Jennifer Scott, it was Edwin's first experience with infidelity. So he was surprised to find himself dating a young, single woman. In John Ross's case of Irv Schoenfeld and Ann, Irv only became emotionally involved with a single woman after having "played around" with lots of other women. He had never planned on becoming emotionally involved with any woman until Ann came along. In spite of his intentions, Irv ended up getting more than he bargained for when he fell for Ann.

EDWIN GOTTESMAN AND JENNIFER SCOTT

When he first met Jennifer Scott, Edwin Gottesman was a 37-year-old, happily married, well-to-do father of two, and Jennifer was a 22-year-old, single, down-on-her-luck secretary. They met in the fall of 1965 when Edwin traveled to Philadelphia to pay a visit to her employer, Mr. Hartman, a real estate agent who had helped him complete a shopping-center deal. Edwin had scarcely noticed Jennifer as he passed through the shabby real estate office en route to Hartman's desk. Only when Hartman referred to Jennifer's ineptness as the reason he had failed to move as quickly on the project as Edwin wished him to did Edwin pay her a second thought.

Hartman explained that he was hesitant to fire Jennifer. She was depressed over the recent breaking-off of her engagement, and was too deep in debt to be able to pay for a much-needed operation. In fact, Hartman added, she had gone so far as to entertain suicide or "selling herself to some rich old man" (Hunt 1969, p. 71) as desperate solutions to her plight.

Upon hearing her hard-luck story, Edwin immediately felt sorry for her. She was a skinny girl, and her posture spoke of either "weariness or dejection" (p. 71). He thought about how different her life might be were someone to "take her in hand" (p. 71). As he and Hartman left the office on their way to dinner, Edwin impulsively invited Jennifer along, thinking that she looked lonely and in need of a decent meal.

Though he had at first thought of her as "a nice kid with lots of problems" (p. 72), his attitude toward her changed as the evening wore on. After the threesome wrapped up their business discussion, Edwin reported finding himself "talking very freely and proudly about my house and my children and my art collection; I could see she was impressed by me, and I played up to her because I liked the way it made me feel" (p. 72). After dinner Edwin offered Jennifer a cab ride back to her place since they were both headed in the same direction. By the end of the evening, Edwin had gone from seeing Jennifer as someone unworthy of notice to thinking of her as pretty.

The next morning Edwin called Hartman's office to run some ideas past him. When Jennifer answered the phone, she seemed "warm and friendly, almost personal . . . and it made me feel very good, very set up" (p. 72).

After hanging up, Edwin found himself struggling with the urge to call Jennifer back to invite her out to dinner. Three times he dialed her number, and three times he hung up. He asked himself, "What kind of *narrishkeit* [nonsense] is this . . . me, a married man with a wonderful wife and two fine children—what business have I got inviting a tough-luck girl fifteen years younger than me to dinner? . . . I walked over and looked at myself in the mirror in my room: 'You fool,' I said, 'stop that nonsense!' But then I said, 'No, not a fool—a coward.' And that did it: I phoned again, and asked her to dinner" (p. 72).

As Edwin sat waiting for Jennifer at the bar, he felt "excited and a trifle wicked" (p. 72). She seemed quite cheerful when she arrived, and before long the two were speaking candidly about their respective childhoods, laughing as they compared what they had gone through as children. Such were the beginnings of the affair, an affair that was to last the better part of a year and that would prove to both revitalize and wreak havoc on Edwin's life.

Throughout the fall and winter months, Edwin traveled weekly from his home in Washington, D.C., to Philadelphia to rendezvous with Jennifer. They would go to dinner, nightclubs, and movies. He considered her "good company" in part because she took such an active interest in his business dealings. He notes: "Usually I'm very stingy with my time, but something about her made me feel differently. I was able to give her things—good dinners, good talk, little presents, a taste of the bigger world—and meanwhile she made me feel younger and more interesting than I had ever felt in my life. . . . I felt marvelous, I felt handsome" (p. 73).

Edwin felt no great sexual desire for Jennifer, and after three months of dating, the two had yet to be sexually intimate. But he worried that were he to pursue a sexual relationship with her, she might not find him attractive. Maybe his sexual advances would just serve to ruin a good thing.

Then an opportunity arose for Jennifer to accompany Edwin on a three-day business trip to Puerto Rico. When Edwin's wife, Betsy, first heard about the trip, she expressed an interest in going, but Edwin dissuaded her, arguing persuasively that their new maid had not been on the job long enough to be trusted alone with the kids. His argument prevailed, and Edwin was free to whisk Jennifer away on a romantic holiday. Anticipating their time away, Edwin found himself wondering whether those he passed on the street as they hurried off to work felt "as alive" and "as cheerfully immoral as he" (p. 75).

The trip to Puerto Rico started out like a sensuous dream, but in the end it proved to be more than Edwin could handle. The two were guests on a 72-foot yacht owned by a business associate who tended to enjoy pursuing extramarital affairs. Sitting on the boat's deck, holding hands with Jennifer, Edwin was "almost overcome by the wonder of it all, by the spectacle of a handsomer, younger, and wittier Edwin enjoying a life he had never imagined possible for him. Oddly enough it all seemed absolutely right and natural" (p. 123). On the evening of their arrival, the two were sexually intimate for the first time. Conditions seemed right for Edwin to proceed, and so he did—even though he had not felt particularly driven to pursue Jennifer sexually. What amazed Edwin was how natural, easy, and comfortable the lovemaking with Jennifer turned out to be. It made him feel "like a real man of the world. . . . She wasn't nearly as good at it as Betsy . . . but it made me feel marvelous anyhow; I was delighted by the idea of what I was doing more than by the thing itself. That night I was completely in tune with the world and with myself" (p. 124).

Some time that first evening, Edwin was seized with the urge to call home to see if everything was all right. Though he initially dismissed the urge, telling himself that everything was okay, he could not put to rest his apprehension that something might be happening at home that only he could take care of. The next morning, while Jennifer lay sleeping, Edwin sneaked away and phoned Betsy. Betsy sounded "querulous, testy, and even a trifle suspicious" (p. 132), or so it seemed to Edwin. After completing the call, Edwin realized that, rather than feeling relieved, he felt even less at ease than he had felt before calling. Later that same day, after being distracted by a morning of business dealings, a nagging feeling again crept back into Edwin's mind. Shortly before dinner, and just after he and Jennifer had made love, Betsy called to apologize for having sounded "cranky" (p. 132). She said she had been feeling weepy and had been missing Edwin, and she seemed anxious for him to return home. Edwin reports

> "I got a very strange feeling that I'd better get home fast or something terrible was going to happen. But what? A fire? Burglars? An automobile accident? My father having a stroke? My children—my little mensch, Buddy, my little rosy-face, Sue—coming down with something terrible? Betsy having an affair with someone, or finding out about me and taking sleeping pills to end it all? Ridiculous ideas came and went in my mind; none of them made any sense, but I couldn't get rid of them. Someday, if I have the time, I should go to a shrink and find out about that and a lot of other things that are mysteries to me." [p. 133]

Edwin was barely able to eat dinner, and slept miserably all night. By morning, he decided to beat a hasty retreat home. He told his host that he was being called back to Washington and would need to be leaving on the next flight. He told Jennifer that only one seat was available, so she would have to fly back by herself the following day on their original reservation. But, before leaving, he overheard Jennifer remark to the host's girlfriend: "What kind of fool am I to get mixed up with a man like this? He takes me away for a three-day stay, and the minute his wife calls he goes running home, and leaves me on my own, fifteen hundred miles from home" (p. 133).

Once he was safely back at home with his wife and kids, Edwin enjoyed feeling the inner warmth that he was "doing the right thing" (p. 178). But that feeling did not last. At 5 A.M. the next morning, Edwin awakened with Jennifer on his mind. He found himself struggling with the urge to continue pursuing a relationship with her.

Edwin considered his marriage "intimate, emotionally secure, and the very center of his life and work" (p. 177). He considered it a happy one, though life with Betsy was "pleasant rather than passionate, regulated rather than romantic" (p. 177). Though Betsy was "calm and reserved all day long," she tended to get "very excited and active in bed" (p. 177). Yet, around Betsy, Edwin was incapable of being the "impulsive, carefree, impetuous, gallant, passionate lover" (p. 177) that he could be with Jennifer. Edwin considered Betsy "too cool, well-mannered and proper" to elicit from him the sort of behavior he had dreamed of, but had never attempted, until meeting Jennifer.

Edwin and Jennifer were an improbable pairing. They could not have been less alike. Edwin, the child of Jewish immigrants, had never before been out with a "shiksa" (p. 179). He was a middle-aged man who lived in a big house, collected art, wore expensive, custom-tailored suits, and made great sums of money. She, on the other hand, wore bargain basement clothes and applied her makeup in ways that cheapened her look—causing one woman with whom Edwin was doing business to comment on how Jennifer looked like a French whore. Jennifer grew up in a bleak, working-class neighborhood with parents who fought continually until divorce brought an end to their incessant squabbling. As a teenager, Jennifer ran away from home twice, only to be brought back by the police. Then she dropped out of high school and lived semi-communally with a group of artists and models in downtown Philadelphia. She returned home long enough to finish high school, after which she held different jobs as a secretary—work she did not like. Her real aspiration was to be a photographer or an artist's model.

When Edwin compared Jennifer to Betsy, Jennifer was no match. "On most counts, Betsy was much superior. Jennifer could never have run my home properly, brought up my children decently, or even handled a dinner party for my friends and associates" (p. 179). In every respect—looks, education, social poise, moral values, skills as a homemaker and mother, and so on— Betsy was superior to Jennifer.

> "Yet I wanted [Jennifer], I ached for her. I couldn't un- derstand at that time what it was; I only knew there was something immensely important about the way I felt about her. Was it the age thing? I found it very flattering that a girl of twenty-two wanted me—but I told myself that that shouldn't matter so much. . . . Was it her looks? To me she was beautiful, but I knew that others might not think so. Her brains? To me she seemed very bright and understanding, but I could see that other people might not agree. Her personality? To me she was free and natural, but I was certain that a lot of people would call her lazy and sloppy. But when I got all through try- ing to score her off and get rid of her, I said to myself, 'Schmuck, stop trying to be so sensible! The truth is, with that girl you lived a little—and that's worth every- thing'." [p. 179]

Edwin set out in earnest to make up for his having run out on Jennifer in Puerto Rico. On successive days, he sent Jennifer flowers, perfume, and a volume of love lyrics. Then, he called her. Though she was initially cool to him, she seemed to warm up when Edwin mentioned how she had been on his mind every morning when he awakened. She agreed to meet him for lunch. They met in a large Polynesian restaurant, where they rekindled their romance. And, after the second round of drinks, they were closer and more loving than they had been before. After lunch they made their way back to Jennifer's apartment for an after- noon of fireside wine drinking and lovemaking. Edwin reports,

> "I was completely happy. It was an escape from every- thing that weighed down on me: it was another world. We talked and sipped wine and necked, and then we

went to bed and made love; afterwards, I was feeling so overflowing that I told her that she meant more to me than I would have believed that anyone could. She said that I meant a great deal to her, which was why she had felt terrible when she thought I was gone for good." [p. 180]

Their afternoon together left Edwin feeling a bit smug and superior to those he met at a party that he and Betsy attended that evening back in Washington. He found himself wondering, "What did any of them know about life and love?" (p. 180).

For the next two months, Edwin visited Jennifer weekly, and the two would talk by phone three to four times a week. He took pleasure in buying things for Jennifer that she seemed to need— a phone for her apartment, a wool coat with a mink collar. Then, when Jennifer's boss fired her, Edwin suggested that she move to Washington so that they could see one another more often. He set her up in an apartment, got her a job, and subsidized her rent. Now they were meeting three to four times weekly.

Edwin was no longer concentrating on work and his income suffered accordingly. And yet, he considered it all worthwhile given how valuable he considered his time with Jennifer. After a couple of months on the job, Jennifer's new boss fired her, explaining that "she wasn't cut out for secretarial work" (p. 181). Edwin reached deeper into his pockets in order to support Jennifer.

Edwin summed it up:

"All this was costing me plenty—what I wasn't earning, plus what I was spending on her. . . . All these things gave me very mixed feelings. I did them because I wanted to, and because it made me feel wonderful to do things for her—but at the same time I felt annoyed and uneasy at doing them. It was a violation of my upbringing. I had always been very conservative and frugal until I met her. I spent money on my house and furniture, but that was different, that was permanent and my own home; but with Jennifer I became a big spender out-side of my home, and it made me feel very good and very disturbed, both at the same time.

"But I couldn't stop myself, and I didn't even want to. This wasn't just a roll in the hay, it was a very important thing to me; it seemed like the biggest thing that had ever happened to me. Our sexual relationship had gotten quite good, but it was never the most important thing; the most important was the whole way I felt about being with her and doing all these crazy marvelous things with her. If we got a nutty idea in our heads to rent a little plane and have a pilot fly us up to Connecticut to have lunch with an old girlfriend of hers, we would do it—and if I had to cancel a business meeting because of it, I would tell myself I was having an experience to remember, and that was worth more than money. That's the way it was.

"For a man like me, the whole thing was crazy, absolutely crazy. I had the best wife you could want, and a good life, and I had been making a hundred thousand a year [which amounted to much more in the pre-inflationary days of the mid-1960s], and here I was letting my business fall apart and making only a half or a third that much and ignoring my kids and my wife and taking more and more chances, and letting more and more people in on what I was doing. And what did I think would come of it all? I didn't think. I couldn't imagine myself ever asking Betsy for a divorce, but I couldn't see things going on like this indefinitely either. Jennifer said she loved me—we used that word, by this time—and she'd be happy just to see me a few times a week; she'd settle for that, she didn't have any future plans. I half believed her, because I wanted to, and said it was fine with me.

"Which was nonsense, but you can convince your-self of anything, for a little while. Something had to give, and soon. A man like me couldn't be so much in love with a girl like Jennifer without wrecking his home and destroying his career. But I wouldn't look at the facts; I felt I was living the best and most exciting life possible, and I didn't ask myself any questions because I didn't have any answers." [pp. 182–183]

By this point, Edwin was beginning to realize just how unworkable his relationship with Jennifer was. The two began having very emotional arguments. After Jennifer bought Edwin an exorbitantly priced smoking jacket and Dunhill pipe, Edwin chastised her for having spent so much money. If she had bought less extravagant gifts, Edwin told her, she would have been able to pay off some of her debt, rather than relying almost exclusively on him to bankroll her life. In response, Jennifer threw the gifts down onto the floor and charged Edwin with "reckoning the cost of their relationship in dollars, and worst of all, of being stingy" (p. 198). This last charge threw Edwin into a rage. In Hunt's words, "He snapped back—astonished at his own words—that she was either a vicious bitch or a stupid child; this felt so good that he began pacing the floor enumerating his acts of generosity, counting them off on his pudgy fingers. After a while, Jennifer put her hands over her ears, and Edwin stormed out, slamming the door and walked the streets in a fury for half an hour" (p. 198). But before long Edwin was back, making up, unable to stay away.

A second episode followed shortly thereafter that only tended to compound matters. After Jennifer's apartment was broken into by burglars, she complained bitterly about how she preferred her apartment in Philadelphia, felt lonely in Washington, and wished she were at home living near friends and family. She complained about how she had given up everything to be with Edwin and about how little time they actually got to spend with one another, "just enough time for him to get laid," Jennifer added. "I began to feel sick," Edwin remembers. "I didn't have the heart to even answer her. I got up while she was still raging at me, and walked out the door, thinking 'this time it is for real. This closes the books, this ends the most foolish chapter of my life.' And I felt sure I would never go back, and I was relieved. I had found out what kind of person I was mixed up with, and I knew I would be better off without her" (p. 199).

The next day, Edwin received a phone call from the superintendent of Jennifer's apartment building informing him that Jennifer had left town for an indefinite period of time.

> "When I heard that, I could hardly talk for minutes. I realized I'd been kidding myself: I'd really been expecting to go back to her as soon as she got around to apologizing. I rushed over to the apartment in a panic . . . and ran around the apartment, looking for clues. . . . I collected [some] papers and the address book, and went back to my office. . . . [I] closed my door and started calling New Jersey and New York numbers from the pieces of paper and from her book. I said I was Detective Simpson of the felony squad, and I was looking for Miss Scott in connection with the burglary of her apartment. I'm amazed when I think of it now; I had never done anything like that before in my life." [p. 199]

After making fifteen unsuccessful calls, Edwin decided to call Jennifer's mother in New Jersey. She told Edwin that Jennifer was en route home, and she would have her call him when she arrived. "I nearly went out of my mind, waiting all afternoon" (p. 200). He called back, reached Jennifer, and the two cried and told each other how much they missed one another. Edwin begged Jennifer to return, telling her he needed her, but Jennifer insisted on staying with her mother for a week. A few days later when Edwin called again, Jennifer's mother delivered the bad news that Jennifer had flown to Rome without leaving a forwarding address.

> "For two days I was immobilized, and didn't do anything except call her mother every few hours to see if

she had heard from Jennifer. She hadn't. I couldn't take care of my business at all, I couldn't eat, I couldn't sleep. . . . The third day, I started making long-distance calls. For days I played the detective, telephoning people and asking questions—I began with her sisters and her brother, I went on to her father, her former boyfriends, her former employers, I told a hundred lies—I had no shame about anything. No shame, did I say? Sometimes I even told the *truth*!" [p. 201]

Edwin pieced together what he learned. Clearly, Jennifer had been planning this getaway behind his back for some time. She had had a passport for three months. She bought a one-way ticket to Rome. Edwin kept trying to reach her. "Finally, I thought to call the consulate in Rome, and said I was her lawyer and had to reach her on a matter of great urgency. They told me she had gone to Spain. I lost heart; I quit trying. I was half dead, a zombie" (p. 201).

A week later Edwin received a letter from Madrid. Jennifer apologized for running off, and wrote of how much she loved him and how she would be returning to him "as soon as she got things straightened out in her own mind" (p. 201). Posing as a pharmacist who was in desperate need of contacting Jennifer about her having been given a wrong medication, Edwin succeeded in getting through to Jennifer in spite of a 6-hour delay on calls to Madrid. "I told her she was destroying me, I had to have her back at once. She cried and said she would come home in three or four days. I was so happy that I was blubbering like a child" (p. 201). The one hitch was that Jennifer needed four hundred dollars to pay off her debts, and she needed a ticket home. Edwin sent Jennifer what she said she needed. "Then I waited and waited—and five days later I got a cable from Casablanca saying that she'd been delayed but would be in touch with me soon. That's the way it went for well over a month. She told me one story after another" (p. 201).

After a month, Edwin found Jennifer a new apartment in Georgetown that was much nicer than the one she had been living in. She told Edwin that she would have returned earlier but had again gotten herself into debt and was embarrassed to tell him so. "So I sent her more money and three days later met her at the airport with my heart in my throat. It was all tears and forgiveness, and old times again. I made myself believe everything she told me, despite all the evidence to the contrary. I drove her to her new apartment, and when she saw it, she was out of her mind with joy and kissed me a hundred times" (p. 202).

But not all was well in paradise. Increasingly, Edwin felt used by Jennifer. She needed dental work so Edwin paid for her to see a dentist. She told the dentist, who, in turn, told Edwin, that the dentist should spare no expense and give her the best treatment available since her "rich boyfriend was paying for everything" (p. 202). When Edwin confronted her with what the dentist had said, Jennifer called the dentist a liar. Edwin backed down and sent her to another dentist.

In ensuing weeks, similar situations left Edwin feeling sick.

"I could see that I was involved with someone who was a liar, a spendthrift, unfaithful, greedy, lazy—but when she hung around my neck and clung to me, or when we went out someplace together and I had that big showy girl on my arm, I didn't care. I'd talk to her on the phone ten times a day, I'd see her almost every afternoon or evening. I hardly saw my wife or children, I was ignoring my business shamefully, I was spending eight hundred, a thousand, twelve hundred a month on her. I was like a man in a poker game who's been losing and losing, and insists on playing for higher stakes because he has to win it all back. . . .

"As time went on, I could see myself becoming less and less a husband and a father. I tried not to think about it because I was having so exciting a time with Jennifer, but somewhere inside me I felt it was very wrong. . . . Sometimes, when Jennifer and I had a fight and weren't seeing each other, I'd come home after the kids were in bed, and Betsy would fix me a drink and sit and chat awhile before dinner, and I'd feel like smacking my forehead and saying to myself, '*Putz!* For a slut like that, you take chances of ruining your marriage to this wonderful woman? I *knew* better—but knowing didn't matter." [pp. 203, 228–229]

The relationship between Edwin and Jennifer became rockier and rockier. Jennifer became more and more demanding, and the two quarreled incessantly about money, about her not working, and about the men she would see on the nights that Edwin remained home. The relationship gyrated between times when they were closer than ever to times when they would quarrel and then not see or speak to one another for days at a time.

Edwin began to wonder whether marrying Jennifer might lessen these tensions. Jennifer, too, had marriage on her mind and proposed it to Edwin as the only way to improve their relationship. Edwin admitted that he had been thinking the same thing for months, which made Jennifer's face light up with happiness. "I knew she was trouble, I knew she was a mess—but I wanted her, and when things were going well between us, I made myself believe that it could be like that all the time" (p. 229).

Edwin went so far as to set up an appointment with a divorce attorney. But, at the last minute, he canceled the appointment. Still, he would go back and forth in his mind as to what to do.

At times, Edwin reasoned that neither his family, his property, nor his business made him feel as happy as Jennifer did. He would trump up charges against Betsy, magnifying certain petty resentments he had toward her in order to make his involvement with Jennifer seem right. "I liked having something to be annoyed at, but a few days later I realized what I was doing, and I was ashamed of myself" (p. 229).

As things worsened between Edwin and Jennifer, the relationship went into its agonal death throes. Every time Edwin decided to leave Jennifer once and for all, either he would cave in, unable to hold to his resolve, or Jennifer would call him up, pleading for him to help her out of a jam that she had gotten herself into, thus necessitating another reunion. This ushered in a period of Jennifer's disappearances. Each time Jennifer would vanish for periods of time, as she had done when she ran off to Europe, it became easier and easier for Edwin to tolerate. They went through cycles of "final" partings followed by reconciliations. The relationship did not have one ending; rather, it had many. Edwin cut back on the amount of money he gave Jennifer, began spending more time at home, and was more attentive to his work. Pulling away from Jennifer was the result of Edwin's growing realization that their relationship was utterly untenable—combined with his reappreciation for all he had risked losing with his wife and children.

Edwin and Jennifer played out one final scene—one precipitated by Jennifer's sudden, unannounced move to New York City. Edwin ran up to see her, and the two had lunch together, during which Jennifer told Edwin that he was obviously not going to marry her so she had to get on with her life. After all, reasoned Jennifer, why should she waste the best years of her life on him? Edwin responded by saying that he still cared about her and still wanted her. He then reminded her that "it wasn't his fault if they were so different they could never make a go of it" (p. 231). And then, Edwin added, "If she had thought otherwise, she had been kidding herself" (p. 231).

Hunt writes about the conclusion of the relationship:

> Jennifer called him a bastard, got up violently, knocked over her coffee, and fled from the restaurant; Edwin threw money on the table and rushed out after her. He ran half a block . . . [and] begged her not to end it this way after they had loved each other so dearly. She relented and they went into a bar, drank, held hands, cried a little, and came to the same conclusion, this time calmly and sorrowfully. Then she asked him if, as a favor, he could lend her two thousand dollars to get started in New York. Edwin was disgusted and said so

plainly. Again she rushed out. This time he paid the check at his leisure, and took a cab back to the office, telling himself for perhaps the tenth or twelfth time in as many months that this was the end. And this time it was. [pp. 231–232]

Discussion

Edwin Gottesman's affair with Jennifer Scott illustrates many of the features of the single woman–married man syndrome. The relationship began as an ego-inflating and narcissistically gratifying experience for Edwin. In fact, much of what appealed to Edwin about the affair was its ability to bring out a side of himself he had never known. He began to experience himself as a different person. He attributed this completely to Jennifer, who stimulated the impulsive, carefree, gallant side of him that his wife could not. He enjoyed discovering this entirely new, previously hidden side of himself. It made him feel alive. The affair was not about sex. Far from it. It was about something much more exciting and rejuvenating. Furthermore, Jennifer was able to gratify Edwin's narcissism in ways his wife seemed unable to do. Jennifer appeared to be interested in hearing about his business dealings. Jennifer made him feel younger, more interesting, and more handsome.

Edwin's relationship with Jennifer was so emotional that he found it difficult to think, which illustrates three other features of the single woman–married man syndrome: (1) a tendency to deceive oneself into believing whatever one wants to believe, (2) a tendency to act irrationally, and (3) a tendency to lack insight about why one is engaged in the affair. Only after the affair's "spell" had been broken was Edwin able to retrospectively see how he had convinced himself that certain things were so by carefully ignoring the glaring facts and by never asking himself questions for which he had no answers. As Edwin put it, "I knew better—but knowing didn't matter" (Hunt 1969, p. 229). Self-deception, irrationality, and lack of insight about the unconscious processes driving the affair kept him from seeing how destructive this affair had become and how much he risked losing.

Edwin would take inventories of what he had at home with his wife and kids. On paper, life with Jennifer did not hold a candle to the wonderful family life he had at home. Yet such things ceased to matter for a time. He loved the person he felt he had become with Jennifer, and he blamed his staid wife for having failed to elicit this other, more alive and exciting dimension of his personality. This is yet another classic feature of the single woman–married man syndrome. Though he had always considered himself to be happily married, Edwin found himself becoming annoyed at his wife. He would magnify certain petty resentments so as to feel better about what he had going with Jennifer. This illustrates Pittman's (1989) observation: "Romantics get into intense affairs, and turn a comfortable marriage into a prison from which they must escape so that they can sacrifice for love" (p. 202).

Edwin and Jennifer's relationship was romantic in every sense of the word, which is typical of affairs that constitute the single woman–married man syndrome. Edwin experienced romance as he never had before. He was blinded by love, which prevented him from taking a good, hard look at Jennifer. He permitted himself to view her in soft focus, a focus that was flattering to her, thus returning the favor of her having idealized him. Only later was Edwin able to see the extent to which he had idealized Jennifer by seeing her as being smarter and more attractive than others saw her. Edwin had to admit, when he thought about it, that he was more excited by the idea of what was happening to him than by the thing itself. The relationship became a vehicle that permitted him to throw caution to the wind, to feel free of the daily burdens that weighed him down. He was in love with love.

Edwin imagined that others could not possibly feel as alive as he did, and he felt smugly superior to those in his social circle who, he reasoned, knew nothing of life and love. Ethel Person (1988) describes this aspect of romantic love: "The lovers savor the secret knowledge that is theirs. In their experience, never has there been such rapture, such transport, such transcendency and bliss. . . . The lovers believe their friends could never understand, for they alone (or in company with perhaps a few legendary couples from the past) have been initiated into the divine mysteries of true love" (p. 13).

The trajectory of the relationship between Edwin and Jennifer also fits the single woman–married man syndrome. With time, things turned ugly. Edwin got to the point of feeling that he had completely lost control. When Jennifer would leave, he would become desperate and would act in ways that were completely uncharacteristic of him. He become obsessed with getting her back and would do whatever it took to accomplish that goal. The ego-inflating and narcissistically fueling aspects of the relationship gave it an addictive-like quality, which is another characteristic component of the syndrome. Hunt (1969) concludes:

> Edwin's growing disillusionment with Jennifer might of itself have led to the end of the affair except for the strength of his need—which it so well gratified—to see himself as romantic, virile, free-spending, and beneficent. Alarmed about the relationship but unable to relinquish it, he was much like an addict who hates his own need for the drug, knows its comforts to be ephemeral and ultimately destructive, but whose craving makes him say and do anything to obtain his temporary quietus. [p. 228]

When Edwin and Jennifer began to fight, the fights were furious. As romantically passionate as his affair with Jennifer could sometimes be, their arguing was equally intense. After a while their relationship began to gyrate out of control. They would break it off, only to make up shortly thereafter. She complained that he did not see her enough. She had become socially isolated, was lonely without her friends, and felt she had given up too much of her life for Edwin and had gotten too little back in return. Ultimately, she came to feel that the relationship was just about sex, and that she meant nothing to Edwin apart from her ability to sexually service him. In turn, Edwin complained about feeling used by her. As is typically the case with the single woman–married man syndrome, each party ends up feeling as if he or she has gotten the short end of the stick. Slowly Edwin awakened from his romantic idealizations to recognize Jennifer for who she was, to finally see the kind of person he had become mixed up with, echoing what Monica Lewinsky credits President Clinton with having said to her in the waning days of their relationship.

THE CASE OF IRV SCHOENFELD AND ANN

Irv Schoenfeld sought treatment with Dr. Ross twelve years after he had terminated an affair with a woman named Ann. Though he had made a conscious decision to remain with Leah, his wife of more than forty years, he still wondered why he had not left her for Ann, the woman he considered to be his soul mate. Had it been guilt, he wondered, that brought him back to Leah?

When Irv Schoenfeld was in the throes of his affair with Ann, he had no interest in reflecting on it. It was only years later, when he looked at the relationship in retrospect, that he was able to engage in an analysis of what it had been all about. Dr. Ross (1996) writes that Schoenfeld was one of five men he treated, four in psychoanalysis and one in psychotherapy, who exhibited the same pattern. Each had married his childhood sweetheart, and each had begun an affair well into the marriage. Three of these men were having affairs at the time they were in treatment. The other two, including Schoenfeld, were looking back on the affair after it had ended. None of the men, in Ross's estimation, deserved to be considered philanderers. Quite the contrary. He saw them as acting out a moral masochistic adaptation derived from a superego pathology that was the result of having had to submit as children to their sadistic and narcissistic fathers.

Irv Schoenfeld came to see Dr. Ross at the behest of his wife, who was concerned about her husband's inability to slow down, to sit still for even a moment. He was forever "running off to jungles, islands, and mountains" (Ross 1996, p. 118), all in the spirit of "adventure and discovery" (p. 118), while his wife remained at home unwilling to participate or take interest in the types of things that excited him. In a broad sense, this was the patient's biggest complaint about his wife. She would never read any of the novels or listen to any of the operas that he found so dear. She would never marvel at his accomplishments or participate in the celebration of his many honors and awards. He complained that "he got so little from her, so little intimacy and empathy" (p. 115), and he considered her cold. Over time, they had drifted apart like ships passing in the night.

Mr. Schoenfeld seemed to employ manic defenses. He was macho, the bold adventurer upon whom others often depended. It was he who was forever dutifully taking care of everyone else. Just as he had been there for his parents and siblings to rely on, in the end he dutifully returned to his lifetime companion rather than abandoning her. He saw himself as having provided for his family more than he had ever seen anybody care for others before. He had, in Ross's estimation, a "lifelong disavowal of his undeniable dependency" (p. 119). With regard to his wife, "he took care of her, made love to her, supported her career even when he felt that his wife never shared his joie de vivre and his infinite enthusiasms" (p. 119). But he was not comfortable when it came to leaning on others to satisfy his needs, in spite of his complaints about how little he got from his wife. In fact, it was not until he had been in therapy that he became able to let himself receive pleasure by lying back and having his wife bring him to orgasm by orally stimulating him. Previously, in spite of his defenses, he had his own ways of getting his dependency needs met. He would frequently injure himself, or take sick, leading him back into the nursing arms of his wife.

Aside from his virtues as a tireless provider and caregiver, and his own strivings to be "an essentially good man," aspiring to "decency and high-mindedness" (p. 117), Mr. Schoenfeld was no boy scout. Prior to his involvement with Ann, which had begun shortly after losing his father to bladder cancer, he had conducted half a dozen peccadilloes, all of which seemed to satisfy the part of him that his wife would not, or could not, satisfy. He more or less justified these affairs as "a response to and retaliation for Leah's less boldfaced betrayals of the heart" (p. 117). These were "lovers who gave his enthusiasm back to him in the form of their own, invigorating him with their love of him, of his accomplishments, and of life itself" (p. 118). These affairs provided him an opportunity for "intercourse with his fellow adventurers, women who extended their arms to him from the cultivated world he had greeted wide-eyed as a young man with the promise of intoxication and aspiration" (p. 120). But Ann somehow seemed different, though Ross never makes clear what it was about her that got Schoenfeld to become more deeply involved with her than with any other woman with whom he had had affairs. Maybe it was the combination of her capacity for multiple orgasms and the fact that she shared an interest in the cultural pursuits that had no appeal to Leah.

Schoenfeld was born to coarse "peasant parents" who had immigrated to America from Europe. He had grown up in a dirty tenement, and he took pride in being a self-made man: "an internationally acclaimed scientist, academic, and foundation administrator" (p. 114). His parents evidently hated one another and would frequently yell at each other in their foreign tongue. The patient experienced them as completely out of sync with his emotional needs. The patient's brother, Stan, had been frail from birth and had accordingly garnered a greater share of the parents' attention than had the patient. So, too, had the patient's sister, who had always been emotionally troubled.

At the outset of therapy, the patient exhibited a split in the way he regarded his parents. He hated his mother for having ignored his emotional needs and intellectual sensitivities, and he accordingly saw her as "all bad." By contrast, he idealized his father as "all good," though Ross never makes clear why the patient felt so positive toward his father.

Schoenfeld was 17 and Leah was 16 when they first met. She came from a middle-class family that the patient had admired from afar. Ross speculates that the patient had married young to escape his unbearable home life and to make a life for himself. Six years after marrying, the couple had a house and four children.

Ross's initial formulation was that Schoenfeld's affairs represented his attempts to "escape the hold of his withholding wife" (p. 118), an acting out of the patient's emotional reaction to his wife's cool style, her "compulsion to deprive him of any narcissistic satisfaction" (p. 118), which made her appear much like the patient's mother. As Ross saw it, the patient was "forever trying to free himself from the unnurturing and emasculating arms of his preoedipal mother" (p. 118). This formulation hinges on a perception of the wife as a phallic, controlling, castrating mother from whom the patient must escape for his own good.

In the course of the analysis, material surfaced that forced Ross to reconsider his initial impressions. In the process of working through his feelings about his father, Mr. Schoenfeld began to recall how much he had felt ignored by the father he had idealized all along: "A father who never noticed, much less cared for, his boy—a father who never knew what his son was studying, much less how spectacular his grades were; a father who never managed to see him play ball, much less hit one of his many home runs, bringing him 'home but with nobody there'" (pp. 119–120).

Ross speculates that having experienced such a father would have a definite effect on the development of a son's superego. This is an illustration of the point Otto Kernberg (1977) makes with regard to the development of a mature superego as one of the prerequisites to an adult's ability to experience mature love, a topic to be discussed in Chapter 10. As Kernberg sees it, a boy must go from experiencing the father as a "primitive, controlling, and sadistic male who represents the fantasied jealous and restrictive father of the early oedipal period" to identifying with the "generous father who no longer operates by means of repressive laws against the sons" (pp. 91–92). Such a father welcomes the son's competitive strivings rather than reacting to them as if they were a rebellious threat needing to be squelched.

Ross's ultimate formulation is that the patient's wife became the recipient of the projection of the patient's primitive superego functioning onto her, which led him to experience her as if she were a cold, demanding, no-nonsense figure who wanted nothing more than to deprive him of any satisfactions he desired. The patient describes it thusly: "I made Leah my father, or my ideal father, but she could be just as diffident as he. She could make me feel like that naked little boy, a plucked chicken waiting to have its kidneys cut, a little boy kicked helpless out of my room to make way for my brother. Only with Leah it was our son" (p. 121). Ross offers the following: "By transforming his wife into a father figure who demands duty and performance and imposes her notions and values on his way of thinking" (p. 127), the husband creates a primitive ego ideal that he tries to live up to, yet has no hope of ever succeeding in doing so.

I believe Ross erred by dismissing his original formulation in favor of one that views the patient's experiencing his wife as if she were his father. The wife may have a natural, innate valence for being transformed by the husband into a figure that demands duty and performance, given certain of her personality traits. In fact, that may have much to do with why Mr. Schoenfeld had married her in the first place. Furthermore, I consider it an error either to assume that it is strictly the wife's fault for being undemonstrative and ungiving, or to think exclusively in terms of the man's being unrealistic in his expectations that his wife play the part of someone who is there to constantly bolster his self-esteem.

Discussion

The case of Irv Schoenfeld illustrates different aspects of the single woman–married man syndrome than the case of Edwin Gottesman. Irv Schoenfeld liked thinking of himself as someone who selflessly served others, as the tireless caregiver who provided for their needs, even though he typically got little back in return. He was much in need of a woman who could constantly admire him, and he resented his wife's refusal to adopt that role and serve that function. On the surface he seemed to endure this situation masochistically, yet his resentment toward her drove him to retaliate against her by having a series of affairs. Rather than happening upon the affair, as had Edwin Gottesman, Irv Schoenfeld was consciously dissatisfied with his wife and was on the lookout for opportunities to get his narcissistic needs met by one of any number of women who seemed willing and capable of servicing those needs for a time.

These two cases illustrate differing paths to the single woman–married man syndrome. In the first, the man is oblivious to the ways in which his latent narcissistic needs are not being satisfied by what otherwise appears to be a happy marriage. Only when these needs are met by a new woman does the man awaken to find himself in a relationship, wondering how such a thing had ever happened. The self-deception the man engages in results in the sequestration of a hidden side of his personality. The narcissistic gratification that derived from the contextually liberated emergence of this hidden side of himself was a powerful experience that took Edwin Gottesman by surprise. And once he had experienced this other side, he came to associate it with the venue in which it had arisen, further heightening his need for the relationship. In the second path, the man is in touch with chronic dissatisfaction due to the lack of narcissistic gratification he experiences in his marriage, so he isn't surprised when he seeks to get these needs met in any one of a series of extramarital affairs.

Now that we have examined the single woman–married man syndrome from the perspectives of the woman and man involved, we turn our attention to a consideration of the impact these two individuals' actions have on the third, silent partner in the relationship, namely, the wife.

4

From the Wife's Perspective: Who Is to Blame?

Compare her face with some that I shall show,
And I will make thee think thy swan a crow.
William Shakespeare, *Romeo and Juliet*, I, ii, 92

No book about single women and married men could be complete without giving due consideration to the plight of the wife. How does she come to terms emotionally with her husband's infidelity? What choice does she have about the matter? Did she, in any way, contribute to her husband having strayed by virtue of the type of wife she had been? Let us begin by addressing the question of culpability.

What role, if any, does a wife play in causing her husband to look to another woman for whatever he feels is missing in his marriage? Depending on whose perspective one adopts, the husband's, the wife's, the other woman's, or an uninvolved observer's, one is likely to encounter radically different opinions.

Attitudes run the gamut. The wife may be portrayed as having failed to attend to her husband's most basic emotional needs for a soul mate, that she is someone who could never understand him. Others may protest that the wife has committed no greater sin than having grown less appealing as a result of self-neglect born out of her dedication to selflessly tend to the needs of her family. Still others may insist that no love can withstand the erosive effect created by the conflicts and familiarities that arise from living life together over time. Finally the uninvolved observer may consider the wife naive and/or blind to the well-known antics of her unfaithful spouse.

The most self-destructive attitude that a wife can adopt upon discovering that her husband is having an affair is to take undue responsibility for the situation. Many women have been raised to accept the lion's share of responsibility for the success of their marriage, which makes them vulnerable to feeling inadequate when confronted with the existence of a female competitor. The wife may lament having failed to keep physically in shape. She might feel that she has not performed adequately as a sexual partner, that she has been too prone to nag, that she has somehow failed to be attentive in ways that this new woman has been. She might feel as if she has not shown enough interest in her husband's ventures, or that she has not recognized times when his ego needing stroking. She may even accept as valid claims that she has been unable to provide him with a relationship that would permit him the full expression of every aspect of his personality. Such concerns may be fueled by popular books, such as Marabel Morgan's (1973) *The Total Woman*, which argue that it is the woman's responsibility to hold on to her man and make sure she treats him in ways that will ensure that he does not stray.

One interesting story that speaks to the issue of holding wives responsible for their husband's affairs is told by Rosa, whose husband used to complain that she had let herself go:

> Tony thinks he is God's gift to women. He goes off with other women soon after we were married. I go to the

confessor at church. He says you must be patient, he
will settle down, go have children. A man wants children. So I have my son. Tony is still out every night. I
go back to the confessor. He says treat him better when
he comes home and he'll want to stay home. I make his
favorite foods. I don't ask him to change the diapers, I
don't pretend I'm asleep. He still doesn't stay home. I
get pregnant again so I see even less of him. It is some
sort of miracle I [then] get pregnant with my daughter.
I go back to the confessor who says maybe Tony is just
like that. I say couldn't you have told me that before I
have three children? [Cato 1996, p. 197]

There are two chief problems with a wife's accepting all the
blame for the husband's affair. First, it cannot possibly reflect
reality insofar as it makes her responsible for the actions of another person over whom she has no control. The idea that the
wife drove her husband into the arms of another woman, that
she somehow made him do such a thing, is ludicrous. Furthermore, a husband's extramarital affair often has little, if anything,
to do with how adequate or inadequate the wife is as a lover,
confidante, companion, or soul mate.

FIGHTING OVER MEN

No more divisive condition threatens the solidarity of feminist women than does the single woman–married man situation.
Fighting over a man makes empathizing with the other woman's
position a near impossibility, thus threatening the solidarity
feminists have been struggling to achieve for the last several decades. Wives of men who have taken up with single women typically harbor intense animosity toward the other woman in their
husband's life. The single woman is considered a ruthless home
wrecker, completely devoid of morals, and sinister. In turn, the
single woman often sees the wife as an albatross around the man's

neck. He is noble for putting up with her, for tolerating her abuse, for silently enduring a relationship that offers him nothing other than a chance to be with his kids. Such thinking helps the single woman feel less guilty about having stolen the heart of another woman's man.

Heavy competition for male attention, particularly for a commitment to marry, is stimulated by a confluence of sociological conditions. Richardson (1985) has compiled a list of these conditions, which illustrates the great disadvantage women are at when it comes to competing with other women for a spouse. Richardson found that 40 percent of women are single, due primarily to a relative shortage of men. Divorced women, ages 25 to 44, are half as likely to remarry as are divorced men in that same age group. And, as women get older, the situation only worsens. Between the ages of 45 and 64, one divorced woman remarries for every four divorced men who remarry. These statistics are daunting. In 1980, 90 percent of highly desirable men, as measured by their socioeconomic status, were married, whereas women who were more financially successful or better educated actually found it harder to find a man to marry than women who were less well off economically or educationally. Richardson sums the situation up this way: Because men are scarce, "they can demand more in a relationship and be more cavalier and callous. Women are devalued because there is an 'excess' of them: 'There's always another (newer, younger, fresher) apple in the barrel'" (Richardson 1985, p. 4).

If the statistics are not discouraging enough, Richardson points out that women are socialized to believe that their worth as a woman depends on their ability to land a man.

> From childhood on, parents, peers, and the media reinforce definitions of femininity and womanliness, worth and desirability, that are intricately linked to being in a heterosexual relationship. Having the love of a man is probably the single most compelling demand placed upon a woman by herself and her society. It is

the female equivalent of the male injunction to achieve financial success. Contemporary single women are, consequently, placed in an untenable position: there are not enough "available" men; yet, unless they "have" a man they are not "normal" women. [pp. 4–5]

It is no wonder that many women work as hard as they do to hold on to their marriages, and to improve them to whatever extent they can. Gottman and Levenson (1988) discovered an important difference between how husbands and wives who are unhappily married handle marital conflict. Men tend to withdraw from conflict, whereas women tend to face it head on. In marriages that are troubled, women are typically better advocates for the marriage than are men, insofar as the women tend to work harder at ironing out the couple's differences, whereas men tend to avoid confronting their marital problems. This probably accounts, in part, for why so many divorced men complain that their ex-wives were nags, while their ex-wives complain that the men never wanted to talk things over (Locke 1951, Terman et al. 1938).

The interests of the single woman involved with a married man, and those of that man's wife, are clearly at odds. This situation leads to a less than sympathetic view of the other woman in the man's life, be she wife or mistress. Single women relish thinking of themselves as providing the man with the things his wife seems too uninterested or unequipped to give. The wife may be viewed by the single woman as sick, pathetic, dependent, or needy. The married man does nothing to dispel such ideas. Quite the contrary. He encourages such thinking by portraying himself as unhappily married. After all, were this not the case, his intentions with the single woman would be suspect, and she would have no reason to continue the affair, having lost all hope of its becoming more than what it already is.

Of course there is truth in the man's laments. Typically, his complaints are not manufactured just for the sake of convincing his mistress to continue seeing him when she expresses doubt about his commitment. Certainly, some men are Machiavellians who think nothing of making up whatever story suits their purpose, but this book is not about relationships with this type of man. The truth is that in certain ways the man's marriage does pale by comparison to the romance he has found with his mistress. But what marriage would not? The wife is clearly at a disadvantage for no other reason than that the husband has grown used to her. Falling in love is exciting, refreshing, rejuvenating. But it is a transient state that creates the illusion that it will last forever. How is a wife to compete with so powerful an experience as that?

WHO IS RESPONSIBLE FOR THE MAN'S EXTRAMARITAL AFFAIR?

Some of the best illustrations of the ways wives struggle with their husband's infidelities can be found in short stories written by women over the last 150 years (see Koppelman's 1984 anthology of such stories). These stories illustrate the various ways that wives emotionally cope with the knowledge of their husbands' affairs, offering ideas about the potential responses available to women who are left reeling after their lives have been turned upside down by circumstances beyond their control. These stories additionally address the question of what contributed to the man's having looked elsewhere for the love, comfort, closeness, or sexual satisfaction that he ought to have been able to get from the woman who is supposed to have been his one and only.

Koppelman writes that her collected stories "portray women in roles other than the traditional pitiable, ridiculous, or detestable betrayed wife consumed with jealousy and the devious, desperate, or dumb other woman ruthlessly pursuing another woman's man" (p. xviii). These stories are genuinely sympathetic to the wife's plight. Many of them also excuse the actions of the other woman, picturing her as someone who found herself mixed up with a man who is taking advantage of her. Since someone has to be responsible for this sad state of affairs, that honor goes to the man for having reduced the woman to functions that Koppelman catalogues as "sexual, reproductive, commercial, domestic" (p. xxviii).

Viewing both the wife and the other woman as victims of a male mentality that thinks nothing of reducing women to mere functions helps heal the rifts created when two women vie for the attentions of the same man. This is accomplished, however, at the expense of any understanding of the man's position. He is reduced to a two-dimensional caricature, stereotyped as nothing more than a self-centered, insensitive scoundrel out to satisfy his own needs without regard for what he has done to these women. Such stereotypes cast the man's pursuit of single women "as only one more flawed facet in a badly flawed character" (p. xxii), as Koppelman puts it.

Viewing men as villains serves to repay the insult endured by women of feeling reduced to functions or objects by men. The problem with characterizing men in this way is that it lumps together all men who pursue extramarital affairs, as if there is no difference between philanderers, who regard affairs as sport, and men whose seemingly sincere, if misguided, gropings for rejuvenation lead them astray. While it is true that some men fit Koppelman's portrayal, many others do not. The situation often proves more complex than many imagine.

Certainly, women cannot be blamed for the collective rage they feel over having been mistreated by men who have "done them wrong" (Koppelman 1984, p. xviii). Men seem to have it all, and yet want more. The married man who is having an affair gets two women, while the women end up with half a man. While all of this is true, it does the cause of feminism no good for women to paint all male adulterers with the same brush. By viewing all men who cheat on their wives in the same way, they are treating men two-dimensionally, which is what feminists complain men do to women. By taking the low road, and adopting the mind set of men who see women two-dimensionally, women who lambaste men in this fashion pass up an opportunity to be the "bigger man" by resisting the temptation to retaliate in kind.

The other problem with thinking of extramarital affairs as strictly the man's fault is that such thinking leaves the single woman without motivation. She is seen as a mere victim: vulnerable, naive, and gullible. She means no harm, so she does not deserve the wife's or society's condemnation. Failing to hold the single woman accountable for her actions is, in my mind, just another form of reductionism—this time, one that reduces women while simultaneously trying to protect them.

"NO NEWS," A TALE BY ELIZABETH STUART PHELPS

The first and oldest tale in Koppelman's (1984) collection of short stories differs from many of the others in her anthology in that it examines, in an even-handed way, the various factors that contributed to an extramarital affair. In Elizabeth Stuart Phelps's story "No News" (1868), we are introduced to Harrie Sharpe, a physician's wife who is a hardworking, self-sacrificing mother who suddenly ceases to appeal to her husband once he lays eyes on Pauline Dallas, an old friend of Harrie's who comes for an extended visit.

Early in the marriage between Harrie and her husband, things had seemed idyllic. But all of that changed with the arrival of their firstborn. The narrator notes: "It is surprising what vague ideas young people in general, and young men in particular, have of the rubs and jars of domestic life" (p. 19). Dr. Myron Sharpe was unprepared for, and impatient with, the changes imposed on his relationship with his wife by the arrival of a baby. Over time, he seemed not to have noticed the extent to which he and his wife seemed to be going their separate ways.

Harrie seemed to be turning more and more to her children for comfort. As the narrator of the story notes, "Women whose dream of marriage has faded a little have a way of transferring their passionate devotion and content from husband to child . . . [but] whatever a woman's children may be to her, her husband should be always something beyond and more; forever crowned for her as first, dearest, best, on a throne that neither son nor daughter can usurp" (p. 23).

The day her friend Pauline Dallas shows up, Harrie is stiff, aching, and exhausted from the chores of making clothes for her children. Harrie meets Pauline wearing an ill-fitting, unflattering calico dress that she herself had made to save money. By contrast, Pauline arrives gloved and perfumed, wearing a smart, fashionable, becoming outfit. Dr. Sharpe cannot help but notice how sprightly Pauline is in conversation, and her worldly knowledge seems to put Harrie to shame. As Dr. Sharpe turns in for the night, "it struck him, for the first time in his life, that Harrie had a snubbed nose. It annoyed him, because she was his wife, and he loved her, and liked to feel that she was as well looking as other women" (p. 25).

The narrator notes that another woman would have sized Harrie up as looking old-fashioned and dowdy. By comparison, Miss Dallas has a pleasant air, "like a soft brown picture with crimson lights let in" (p. 26), an air that Dr. Sharpe noted his wife lacked. For her part, Harrie appreciated what Pauline had, and wondered why fate had not seen fit to bestow such niceties on her.

The author cannot find it in her to blame Pauline for capturing the attentions of Dr. Sharpe. She is portrayed as someone who was not bad-hearted, only a bit misguided—someone who "did not know exactly what she was about" (p. 28). Harrie could not compete with Pauline. When Harrie shows up for breakfast "dreary and draggled" (p. 30), after a difficult night tending to the children, Miss Dallas "has a particular color and coolness and sparkle . . . like that of opening flowers" (p. 30).

One evening Dr. Sharpe and Miss Dallas are discussing Tennessee's admittance to the Union. Harrie chimes in: "Tennessee! Why, how long has Tennessee been in? I didn't know anything about it" (p. 27). Miss Dallas smiles kindly, but Dr. Sharpe seems annoyed and impatient, and chastises his wife: "Harrie, you really *ought* to read the papers. . . . It's no wonder you don't know anything" (p. 27). In her self-defense, Harrie snaps back: "How should I know anything, tied to children all day? Why didn't you tell me something about Tennessee? You never talk politics with *me*" (p. 27). This interchange left Harrie feeling low, painfully aware of her deficiencies.

Dr. Sharpe's sin is that he is so taken by Miss Dallas that he seems unaware of the impact his feelings are having on his wife. He grows impatient whenever Harrie tries to emulate Pauline, seeming not to understand these attempts as Harrie's way of trying to win back his affections. Harrie grows more despairing, picturing her children growing up "under the shadow of a wrecked and loveless home" (p. 31). She prays to God to let her die, and becomes physically ill with a shivering fever. Dr. Sharpe fails to notice his wife's condition. The narrator notes that had Harrie been a patient Dr. Sharpe would surely have sent her to bed.

Miss Dallas's announcement that she will soon be leaving the Sharpes has the doctor visibly shaken. He and Pauline decide to go for a final boat ride, during which he admits to Pauline his situation: "An honest man, who loves his wife devotedly, but who cannot find in her that sympathy which his higher nature requires, that comprehension of his intellectual needs. . . . Such a man need not be debarred, by the shallow conventionalities of an unappreciative world, from a friendship which will rest, strengthen, and ennoble his weary soul?" (pp. 33–34). To which Pauline answers: "Certainly not. . . . There are marriages for this world; true and honorable marriages, but for this world. But there is a marriage for eternity,—a marriage of souls" (p. 34).

Deeply absorbed in conversation, neither the doctor nor Pauline notices that the weather is changing, and they become caught in a storm. They are, however, eventually able to make it safely to shore. When the two return home there is no sign of Harrie. The parlor window has been left open, and the rain is pouring in. Dr. Sharpe is clearly annoyed at Harrie's carelessness. The housekeeper explains that Harrie has mysteriously disappeared, which sets the doctor thinking about Harrie's great uncle who had died in an asylum. Suddenly, he envisions the future of his children growing up with an insane mother.

"Shall I go and help you find her?" asks Miss Dallas, "or shall I stay and look after hot flannels and—things? What shall I do?" (p. 35).

"I don't care what you do!" says the doctor savagely. At that moment, Dr. Sharpe experiences a "cold loathing" for Pauline. "He hated the sound of her soft voice; he hated the rustle of her garments, as she leaned against the door with her handkerchief to her eyes" (p. 35).

A search of the area reveals that Harrie's boat is gone from its usual mooring. Dr. Sharpe, accompanied by a trustworthy seaman named George Hansom, takes to the sea and hears cries, but the fog makes it impossible to tell from which direction the cries are coming. Ultimately, they happen upon Harrie's abandoned boat adrift in the water with a bit of a red scarf caught in its stern. After a time, the cries cease. Hansom concludes there is no hope of finding Harrie alive and tells the doctor so. The idea that his wife is gone shoots through Dr. Sharpe, who falls onto the sand "like a woman, and lay like the dead" (p. 37). Hansom suggests that Dr. Sharpe go home, while Hansom and the other rescuers who had joined them continue to search for the remains.

The doctor returns home and is lying on the office floor. Pauline and an older woman friend of Harrie's are sitting in the parlor "when the door swung in and Harrie—or the ghost of her—staggered into the chilly room and fell down in a scarlet heap" (p. 38). Pauline leaps back, and lets out a piercing scream.

Over the next several weeks Harrie hangs on to life, while the doctor and her old friend try desperately to nurse her back to health. She is able to offer an account of what she had been through, how she had taken to the sea in her boat in an effort to rescue her husband from the storm "with some dim, delirious idea of finding Myron [her husband] on the ebbing waves" (p. 38). Her boat became stranded in the matted grass, which left her no choice but to abandon it and try to make her way home through the mud and the ooze, which slowed down her efforts considerably.

Harrie ultimately recovers and regains her strength. Miss Dallas, who had taken care of the children while Harrie was so sick, bids farewell to her hosts. And Dr. Sharpe finds it in himself to approach Harrie and offer her his deepest apologies for how he had acted, along with a proclamation of his love for her. Harrie cries, as does her husband, and, as the narrator notes, does so just as hard as Harrie.

An Analysis

A superficial reading of "No News" leads to the conclusion that it is an I-worked-my-fingers-to-the-bone-and-this-is-the-thanks-I-get type of tale. Koppelman falls into the trap of viewing Phelps's story from this perspective. She sees Harrie as "liv[ing] the life her husband believes a wife should live" (p. 14) and, as a result, is turned into a servant, thus ceasing to be her husband's social equal. Koppelman sees Dr. Sharpe as the sole culprit of the story, seemingly assigning no responsibility for the deterioration of their relationship to Harrie.

Koppelman believes that stories like "No News" are cautionary tales alerting all women that "there is no type of woman who is immune to betrayal and there is nothing that a woman can do or avoid doing to protect herself and the marriage to which she is only one of the partners" (p. xxv). In her rush to blame Dr. Sharpe for the state of the marriage, Koppelman overlooks one of the central points the author is trying to make, namely, the ease with which some women retreat from marriage, even if reactively, to the comforts of motherhood. Harrie is her husband's partner not only in marriage, but in the marriage's near dissolution. "No News" is a cautionary tale, but not the sort that Koppelman thinks. The story cautions couples about the need to remain vigilant to the prospect of slowly growing apart.

Phelps never makes clear whether Harrie's withdrawal into her role as mother was in reaction to conflicts she was having with her husband, but that is a reasonable assumption. If this was the case, it is pointless to argue about who hurt whom first, or who was first to withdraw. In the final analysis, it is usually impossible to differentiate action from reaction in situations such as these. All that ultimately matters is that each party acknowledges how he or she has contributed to the current state of affairs.

Phelps has gone to great lengths to portray the complexities of married life. Her story illustrates what can go wrong between a husband and wife when the wife's life bogs down with the everyday duties of raising a family, managing a house, and tending to her husband's needs. The beauty of Phelps's story is that it resists the urge to make one of the partners the villain. At first glance, Harrie seems to be doing the best she can do, given her circumstances. She is a dedicated, hard-working mother. But upon closer examination we see how Harrie's actions, or reactions, whichever the case may be, must have contributed to the deterioration of the marriage. Harrie ceased to maintain an interest in the outside world. She ceased to keep up with current events, figuring that reading was a luxury she could ill afford. She did this knowing all the while how important such matters were to her husband. Harrie also spent far too much time tending to the children, resulting in her emotionally abandoning her husband, a point the author goes to great lengths to underscore.

Phelps sets the stage for Miss Dallas's arrival by describing how accustomed Dr. Sharpe had become to living alone ever since his wife had begun to spend inordinate amounts of time tending to the children. Though one might consider Harrie's dedication to her children admirable, if not called for, given the demands her three young children made on her, the author suggests that Harrie's maternal dedication may well have gone beyond the call of duty, most likely causing the doctor to feel rejected and resentful. Yet she might well have retreated into the tasks of motherhood in reaction to her husband's withdrawal.

Such conditions are fertile ground for a husband's imagination to be ignited by a woman who seems to provide for him what his wife cannot or will not provide. Miss Dallas's actions are portrayed as innocent, if misdirected. The author makes it clear that readers should not blame her for how alluring she was to Dr. Sharpe. For his part, Dr. Sharpe also cannot be held responsible for having been enticed by so fascinating a woman as Miss Dallas. Throughout the story, Dr. Sharpe reminds himself, over and over again, of how he loves his wife, as if trying to bring himself to his senses and break the spell Miss Dallas unintentionally has over him. But though he is not having a sexual affair with her, he might as well be, given how he is carrying on. Dr. Sharpe's greatest infidelity seems to be his insensitivity to the effect his actions are having on his wife. She is clearly distraught by his being charmed by Miss Dallas. Dr. Sharpe turns neglectful when he fails to recognize how physically sick his wife has become.

Dr. Sharpe never seems to notice the imperfection of his wife's nose until he becomes smitten with Miss Dallas. Prior to that time, the author explains, "Myron Sharpe had always considered his wife a handsome woman. That nobody else thought her so had made no difference to him" (p. 24). So often husbands who find little fault with their wives and consider themselves happily married end up becoming dissatisfied with their wives when the passion of being in love with another woman makes their wives seem to pale by comparison.

In her story, Phelps has captured some of the preconditions that can cause a marriage to become vulnerable to a man's looking elsewhere for female companionship. Myron and Harrie Sharpe had grown apart from one another and no longer shared much in common. Furthermore, Dr. Sharpe had felt rejected by his wife's utter devotion to the children. Quite often, extramarital affairs are triggered by the arrival of children. Whether Dr. Sharpe could be said to have had an affair with Ms. Dallas is a matter that will be covered in Chapter 6. The single woman–married man syndrome—being, as it is, the product of two individuals' needs—can never be said to have developed out of the needs of just one of the partners in the couple.

A WIFE MEETS WITH HER HUSBAND'S MISTRESS: "THE DIFFERENCE," A TALE BY ELLEN GLASGOW

In 1923, at the age of 49, Ellen Glasgow, who later was to win a Pulitzer Prize for literature, wrote a short story, "The Difference," that was published in *Harper's* magazine. This story captures the thinking of a wife who has just learned that her husband has been unfaithful. Though it is fiction, it realistically portrays what many wives feel about their husbands' affairs. Glasgow obviously knows of what she writes. Her own mother had a nervous breakdown upon learning, shortly after giving birth to her tenth child, that her husband was having an affair with another woman. The author lived in the shadow of her mother's illness, an illness that ended in the mother's death. Glasgow also knew about affairs from having personally participated in one, between the ages of 26 and 33, as a single woman involved with a married man.

"The Difference" is a story about a 44-year-old woman named Margaret Fleming who, as the story opens, is agonizing over how to respond to a letter she has just received informing her that her husband is having an affair with Rose Morrison, the letter's author. Margaret had been completely unsuspecting and was devastated by the news. Glasgow describes Margaret's thoughts about her marriage to George: "The thought flashed into her mind that she knew him in reality no better than if she had lived with a stranger for twenty years. Yet, until a few hours ago, she would have said, had any one asked, that their marriage was as perfect as any mating between a man and a woman could be in this imperfect world" (p. 170).

Margaret figures that she must face Rose Morrison. So, on a dark, rainy, fall afternoon, she boards a streetcar and rides to confront her husband's mistress, who is living in a cheap suburban villa that her husband had purchased several years before as an investment. As the scene opens, Margaret has been let in by the mistress's maid, who has told Margaret that her employer is not home. Margaret insists on waiting. She enters the living room and immediately discerns that the woman she has come to see is, indeed, at home. Hearing a sound, Margaret turns and confronts Rose Morrison. What follows is an abridged version of Glasgow's tale told in the author's words:

> "So you came?" said Rose Morrison, while she gazed at her with the clear and competent eyes of youth. Her voice, though it was low and clear, had no softness; it rang like a bell. Yes, she had youth, she had her flamboyant loveliness; but stronger than youth and loveliness, it seemed to Margaret, surveying her over the reserves and discriminations of the centuries, was the security of one who had never doubted her own judgement. Her power lay where power usually lies, in an infallible self-esteem.
>
> "I came to talk it over with you," began Margaret quietly; and though she tried to make her voice insolent, the deep instinct of good manners was greater than her effort. "You tell me that my husband loves you."
>
> The glow, the flame, in Rose Morrison's face make Margaret think again of leaves burning. There was no embarrassment, there was no evasion even, in the girl's look. Candid and unashamed, she appeared to glory in this infatuation, which Margaret regarded as worse than sinful, since it was vulgar.
>
> "Oh, I am so glad that you did," Rose Morrison's sincerity was disarming. "I hated to hurt you. You can never know what it cost me to write that letter; but I felt that I owed it to you to tell you the truth. I believe that we always owe people the truth."
>
> "And did George feel this way also?"
>
> "George?" The flame mounted until it enveloped her. "Oh, he doesn't know. I tried to spare him. He would rather do anything than hurt you, and I thought

it would be so much better if we could talk it over and find a solution just between ourselves. I knew if you cared for George, you would feel as I do about sparing him."

About sparing him! As if she had done anything for the last twenty years, Margaret reflected, except think out new and different ways of sparing George!

"I don't know," she answered, as she sat down in obedience to the other's persuasive gesture. "I shall have to think a minute. You see this has been—well, rather—sudden."

"I know, I know." The girl looked as if she did. "May I give you a cup of tea? You must be chilled."

"No, thank you. I am quite comfortable."

"Not even a cigarette? Oh, I wonder what you Victorian women did for a solace when you weren't allowed even a cigarette!"

You Victorian women! In spite of her tragic mood, a smile hovered on Margaret's lips. So that was how this girl classified her. Yet Rose Morrison had fallen in love with a Victorian man.

"Then I may?" said the younger woman with her fullthroated laugh. From her bright red hair, which was brushed straight back from her forehead, to her splendid figure, where her hips swung free like a boy's, she was a picture of barbaric beauty. There was a glittering hardness about her, as if she had been washed in some indestructible glaze; but it was the glaze of youth, not of experience. She reminded Margaret of a gilded statue she had seen once in a museum; and the girl's eyes, like the eyes of the statue, were gleaming, remote and impassive—eyes that had never looked on reality. The dress she wore was made of some strange "art cloth," dyed in brilliant hues, fashioned like a kimono, and girdled at the hips with what Margaret mistook for a queer piece of rope. Nothing, not even her crude and confident youth, revealed Rose Morrison to her visitor so completely as this end of rope.

"You are an artist?" she asked, for she was sure of her ground. Only an artist, she decided, could be at once so arrogant with destiny and so ignorant of life.

"How did you know? Has George spoken of me?"

Margaret shook her head. "Oh, I knew without any one's telling me."

"I have a studio in Greenwich Village, but George and I met last summer at Ogunquit. I go there every summer to paint."

"I didn't know." How easily, how possessively, this other woman spoke her husband's name.

"It began at once." To Margaret, with her inherited delicacy and reticence, there was something repellent in this barbaric simplicity of emotion.

"But you must have known that he was married," she observed coldly.

"Yes, I knew, but I could see, of course, that you did not understand him."

"And you think that you do?" If it were not tragic, how amusing it would be to think of her simple George as a problem!

"Oh, I realize that it appears very sudden to you; but in the emotions time counts for so little. Just living with a person for twenty years doesn't enable one to understand him, do you think?"

"I suppose not. But do you really imagine," she asked in what struck her as a singularly impersonal tone for so intimate a question, "that George is complex?"

The flame, which was revealed now as the illumination of some secret happiness, flooded Rose Morrison's features. As she leaned forward, with clasped hands, Margaret noticed that the girl was careless about those feminine details by which George declared so often that he judged a woman. Her hair was carelessly arranged; her fingernails needed attention; and beneath the kimonolike garment, a frayed place showed at the back of her stocking. Even her red morocco slippers were run down at the heels; and it seemed to Margaret that this physical negligence had extended to the girl's habit of thought.

"He is so big, so strong and silent, that it would take an artist to understand him," answered Rose Morrison passionately. Was this really, Margaret wondered, the way George appeared to the romantic vision?

"Yes, he is not a great talker," she admitted. "Perhaps if he talked more, you might find him less difficult." Then before the other could reply, she inquired sharply, "Did George tell you that he was misunderstood?"

"How you misjudge him!" The girl had flown to his defense; and though Margaret had been, as she would have said "a devoted wife," she felt that all this vehemence was wasted. After all, George, with his easy, prosaic temperament, was only made uncomfortable by vehemence. "He never speaks of you except in the most beautiful way," Rose Morrison was insisting. "He realizes perfectly what you have been to him, and he would rather suffer in silence all his life than make you unhappy."

"Then what is all this about?" Though she felt that it was unfair, Margaret could not help putting the question.

Actually there were tears in Rose Morrison's eyes. "I could not bear to see his life ruined," she answered. "I hated to write to you; but how else could I make you realize that you were standing in the way of his happiness? If it were just myself, I could have borne it in silence. I would never have hurt you just for my own sake; but, the subterfuge, the dishonesty, is spoiling his life. He does not say so, but, oh, I see it every day because I love him!" As she bent over, the firelight caught her hair, and it blazed out triumphantly like the red lilies in Margaret's library.

"What is it you want me to do?" asked Margaret in her dispassionate voice.

"I felt that we owed you the truth," responded the girl, "and I hoped that you would take what I wrote you in the right spirit."

"You are sure that my husband loves you?"

"Shall I show you his letters?" The girl smiled as she answered, and her full red lips reminded Margaret suddenly of raw flesh. Was raw flesh, after all, what men wanted?

"No!" The single word was spoken indignantly.

"I thought perhaps they would make you see what it means," explained Rose Morrison simply. "Oh, I wish I could do this without causing you pain!"

"Pain doesn't matter. I can stand pain."

"Well, I'm glad you aren't resentful. After all, why should we be enemies? George's happiness means more than anything else to us both."

"And you are sure you know best what is for George's happiness?"

"I know that subterfuge and lies and dishonesty cannot bring happiness." Rose Morrison flung out her arms with a superb gesture. "Oh, I realize that it is a big thing, a great thing, I am asking of you. But in your place, if I stood in his way, I should so gladly sacrifice myself for his sake. I should give him his freedom. I should acknowledge his right to happiness, to self-development."

A bitter laugh broke from Margaret's lips. What a jumble of sounds these catchwords of the new freedom made! What was this self-development which could develop only through the sacrifice of others? How would these immature theories survive the compromises and concessions and adjustments which made marriage permanent?

"I cannot feel that our marriage has interfered with his development," she rejoined presently.

"You may be right," Rose Morrison conceded the point. "But to-day he needs new inspiration, new opportunities. He needs the companionship of a modern mind."

"Yes, he has kept young at my cost," thought the older woman. "I have helped by a thousand little sacrifices, by a thousand little cares and worries, to preserve this unnatural youth which is destroying me. I have taken over the burden of details in order that he might be free for the larger interests of life. If he is young to-day, it is at the cost of my youth."

For the second time that day, as she sat there in silence, with her eyes on the blooming face of Rose Morrison, a wave of peace, the peace of one who has been shipwrecked and then swept far off into some serene haven, enveloped her. Something to hold by, that at least she had found. The law of sacrifice, the ideal of self-surrender, which she had learned in the past. For twenty years she had given freely, abundantly, of her best; and to-day she could still prove to him that she was not beggared. She could still give the supreme gift of her happiness. "How he must love you!" she exclaimed. "How he must love you to have hurt me so much for your sake! Nothing but a great love could make him so cruel."

"He does love me," answered Rose Morrison, and her voice was like the song of a bird.

"He must." Margaret's eyes were burning, but no tears came. Her lips felt cracked with the effort she made to keep them from trembling. "I think if he had done this thing with any other motive than a great love,

I should hate him until I died." Then she rose and held out her hand, "I shall not stand in your way," she added.

Joy flashed into the girl's eyes. "You are very noble," she answered. "I am sorry if I have hurt you. I am sorry, too, that I called you old-fashioned."

Margaret laughed. "Oh, I am old-fashioned. I am so old-fashioned that I should have died rather than ruin the happiness of another woman."

The joy faded from Rose Morrison's face. "It was not I," she answered. "It was life. We cannot stand in the way of life."

"Life to-day, God yesterday, what does it matter? It is a generation that has grasped everything except personal responsibility." Oh, if one could only keep the humor! A thought struck her, and she asked abruptly, "When your turn comes, if it ever does, will you give way as I do?"

"That will be understood. We shall not hold each other back."

"But you are young. You will tire first. Then he must give way?" Why in twenty years George would be sixty-five and Rose Morrison still a young woman!

Calm, resolute, uncompromising, Rose Morrison held open the door. "Whatever happens, he would never wish to hold me back."

Then Margaret passed out, the door closed behind her, and she stood breathing deep draughts of the chill, invigorating air. Well, that was over. [pp. 178–183]

Discussion

Glasgow's tale captures many of the features one typically encounters in the single woman–married man syndrome. For instance, married men are typically incapable of resolving the question of which woman they would ultimately prefer being with—

their wife or their lover. As is often the case with such single women, Rose misunderstands George's seeming inability to leave Margaret as his not having the heart to do that to his wife. Idealization causes the single woman to see her married lover as a nice guy rather than recognizing him for who he is: either an ambivalent indecisive man who wishes to be seen as selflessly sacrificing his needs for the sake of others, or—worse yet—a selfish man stringing the other woman along.

Rose feels that she understands George better than does his wife of twenty years, maybe even better than does George himself. Furthermore, she is completely certain about what she presumes to be in George's best interest. She does not even realize the presumptuous nature of her reasoning. Rose is uncritical about her devotion to George as well as unquestioning of the love she is sure he feels for her. In these ways, she is illustrating additional features of the single woman–married man syndrome.

"My wife doesn't understand me" is a common complaint husbands make to their mistresses. Glasgow is unclear about whether George had ever said such a thing to Rose. Nevertheless, Rose is left with this impression. When she claims to understand George better than Margaret does, this is tantamount to her telling Margaret: "There are sides of your husband about which you are unaware, sides that you are incapable of bringing out in him." If Rose is anything like other single women who have become involved with married men, then she most likely credits herself for having been the catalyst for the emergence of this other facet of George, thus validating her sense of womanliness for having achieved such a feat.

The mistress in the single woman–married man syndrome likes to see her role as central to the married man's transforming rejuvenation. But it could just as well be that her role is incidental. She might serve as a nonspecific catalyst who just happened upon the scene at the time the man was ready to be transformed. The narcissistic gratification of thinking oneself so powerfully attractive as to be capable of initiating such a transformation is too great to pass up, especially for women who, as yet, have not let themselves become involved enough with a man to have wed.

Married men are notorious for seeking out affairs with women who are not necessarily better than their wives, just different from their wives. Rose and Margaret are opposites. Rose is modern, whereas Margaret is old fashioned. Rose is brash, whereas Margaret is reticent. Rose is raw, whereas Margaret is refined. Rose is inattentive to her grooming, whereas Margaret is meticulous. Rose is willing to go after what she wants (all the while portraying such pursuits as selflessly motivated by what is in George's best interest), while Margaret stands ready to sacrifice her own needs for those of her husband, as she has always done. And, in the end, Rose insists she will do whatever is required to promote her self-development, even if that means leaving George at some time in the future. Margaret, on the other hand, is self-sacrificing to a fault, having given no thought whatsoever to the notion of self-development.

Glasgow's tale does not end with Margaret's departure from Rose's home. We now pick up the story as Margaret returns home, sopping wet from having made her way in the rain. She goes upstairs to her room and prepares herself for a confrontation with George. In the following passage that ends her story, Ellen Glasgow captures the interaction between husband and wife that is every unfaithful man's worst nightmare:

> She took off her wet clothes and slipped into her prettiest tea gown, a trailing thing of blue satin and chiffon. While she ran the comb through her damp hair and touched her pale lips with colour, she reflected that even renunciation was easier when one looked desirable. "But it is like painting the cheeks of the dead," she thought, as she turned away from the mirror and walked with a dragging step to the library. Never, she realized suddenly, had she loved George so much as in this hour when she had discovered him only to lose him.

As she entered, George hurried to meet her with an anxious air. "I didn't hear you come in, Margaret. I have been very uneasy. Has anything happened?"

By artificial light he looked younger even than he had seemed in the afternoon; and this boyishness of aspect struck her as strangely pathetic. It was all a part, she told herself, of that fulfillment which had come too late, of that perilous second blooming, not of youth, but of Indian Summer. The longing to spare him, to save him from the suffering she had endured, pervaded her heart.

"Yes, something has happened," she answered gently. "I have been to see Rose Morrison."

As she spoke the name, she turned away from him, and walking with unsteady steps across the room, stood looking down into the fire. The knowledge of all that she must see when she turned, of the humiliation, the anguish, the remorse in his eyes, oppressed her heart with a passion of shame and pity. How could she turn and look on his wounded soul which she had stripped bare?

"Rose Morrison?" he repeated in an expressionless voice. "What do you know of Rose Morrison?"

At his question she turned quickly, and faced not anguish, not humiliation, but emptiness. There was nothing in his look except the blankness of complete surprise. For an instant the shock made her dizzy; and in the midst of the dizziness there flashed through her mind the memory of an evening in her childhood, when she had run bravely into a dark room where they told her an ogre was hiding, and had found that it was empty.

"She wrote to me." Her legs gave way as she replied, and, sinking into the nearest chair, she sat gazing up at him with an immobile face.

A frown gathered his eyebrows, and a purplish flush (he flushed so easily of late) mounted slowly to the smooth line of his hair. She watched the quiver that ran through his under lip (strange that she had not noticed how it had thickened) while his teeth pressed it sharply. Everything about him was acutely vivid to her, as if she were looking at him closely for the first time. She saw the furrow between his eyebrows, the bloodshot stain in one eyeball, the folds of flesh beneath his jutting chin, the crease in his black tie, the place where his shirt gave a little because it had grown too tight—all these insignificant details would exist indelibly in her brain.

"She wrote to you?" His voice sounded strained and husky, and he coughed abruptly as if he were trying to hide his embarrassment. "What the devil? But you don't know her."

"I saw her this afternoon. She told me everything."

"Everything?" Never had she imagined that he could appear so helpless, so lacking in the support of any conventional theory. A hysterical laugh broke from her, a laugh as utterly beyond her control as a spasm, and at the sound he flushed as if she had struck him. While she sat there she realized that she had no part or place in the scene before her. Never could she speak the words that she longed to utter. Never could she make him understand the real self behind the marionette at which he was looking. She longed with all her heart to say: "There were possibilities in me that you never suspected. I also am capable of a great love. In my heart I also am a creature of romance, of adventure. If you had only known it, you might have found in marriage all that you have sought elsewhere . . . " This was what she longed to cry out, but instead she said merely,

"She told me of your love. She asked me to give you up."

"She asked you to give me up?" His mouth fell open as he finished, and while he stared at her he forgot to shut it. It occurred to her that he had lost the power of inventing a phrase, that he could only echo the ones she had spoken. How like a foolish boy he looked as he stood there, in front of the sinking fire, trying to hide behind the hollow echo!

"She said that I stood in your way." The phrase sounded so grotesque as she uttered it that she found herself laughing again. She had not wished to speak these ugly things. Her heart filled with noble words, with beautiful sentiments, but she could not make her lips pronounce them in spite of all the efforts she made. And she recalled suddenly the princess in the fairy tale who when she opened her mouth, found that toads and lizards escaped from it instead of pearls and rubies.

At first he did not reply, and it seemed to her that only mechanical force could jerk his jaw back into place and close the eyelids over his vacant blue eyes. When at last he made a sound it was only the empty echo again, "stood in my way!"

"She is desperately in earnest." Justice wrung this admission from her. "She feels that this subterfuge is unfair to us all. Your happiness, she thinks, is what we should consider first, and she is convinced that I should be sacrificed to your future. She was perfectly frank. She suppressed nothing."

For the first time George Fleming uttered an original sound. "O Lord!" he exclaimed devoutly.

"I told her that I did not wish to stand in your way," resumed Margaret, as if the exclamation had not interrupted the flow of her thoughts. "I told her I would give you up."

Suddenly, without warning, he exploded. "What, in the name of heaven, has it got to do with you?" he demanded.

"To do with me?" It was her turn to echo, "But isn't

that girl—" she corrected herself painfully—"isn't she living in your house at this minute?"

He cast about helplessly for an argument. When at last he discovered one, he advanced it with a sheepish air, as if he recognized its weakness. "Well, nobody else would take it, would they?"

"She says that you love her."

He shifted his ground nervously. "I can't help what she says, can I?"

"She offered to show me your letters."

"Compliments, nothing more."

"But you must love her, or you couldn't—you wouldn't—" A burning flush scorched Margaret's body.

"I never said that I . . . " Even with her he had always treated the word love as if it were a dangerous explosive, and he avoided touching it now, "that I cared for her in this way."

"Then you do in another way?"

He glanced about like a trapped animal. "I am not a fool, am I? Why, I am old enough to be her father! Besides, I am not the only one anyway. She was living with a man when I met her, and he wasn't the first. She isn't bad, you know. It's a kind of philosophy with her. She calls it self . . . "

"I know." Margaret cut the phrase short. "I have heard what she calls it." So it was all wasted; Nothing that she could do could lift the situation above the level of the commonplace, the merely vulgar. She was defrauded not only of happiness, but even the opportunity to be generous. Her sacrifice was as futile as that girl's passion. "But she is in love with you now," she said.

"I suppose she is." His tone had grown stubborn. "But how long would it last? In six months she would be leaving me for somebody else. Of course, I won't see her again," he added, with the manner of one who is conceding a reasonable point. Then, after a pause in which she made no response, his stubbornness changed into resentment. "Anybody would think that you are angry because I am not in love with her!" he exclaimed. "Anybody would think—but I don't understand women!"

"Then you will not—you do not mean to leave me?" she asked; and her manner was impersonal, she was aware, as if Winters [their butler] had just give her notice.

"Leave you?" He glanced appreciatively round the room. "Where on earth could I go?"

For an instant Margaret looked at him in silence. Then she insisted coldly, "To her, perhaps. She thinks that you are in love with her."

"Well, I suppose I've been a fool," he confessed, after a struggle, "but you are making too much of it."

Yes, she was making too much of it; she realized this more poignantly than he would ever be able to do. She felt like an actress who has endowed a comic part with the gesture of high tragedy. It was not, she saw clearly now, that she had misunderstood George, but that she had overplayed life.

"We met last summer at Ogunquit." She became aware presently that he was still making excuses and explanations about nothing. "You couldn't go about much, you know, and we went swimming and played golf together. I liked her, and I could see that she liked me. When we came away I thought we'd break it off, but somehow we didn't. I saw her several times in New York. Then she came here unexpectedly, and I offered her that old villa nobody would rent. You don't understand such things, Margaret. It hadn't any more to do with you than—than—" He hesitated, fished in the stagnant waters of his mind, and flung out abruptly, "than golf has. It was just a sort of—well, sort of—recreation."

Recreation! The memory of Rose Morrison's extravagant passion smote her sharply. How glorified the incident had appeared in the girl's imagination, how cheap and tawdry it was in reality. A continual compromise with the second best, an inevitable surrender to the average, was this the history of all romantic emotion? For an instant, such is the perversity of fate, it seemed to the wife that she and this strange girl were united by some secret bond which George could not share—by the bond of woman's immemorial disillusionment.

"I wouldn't have had you hurt for worlds, Margaret," said George, bending over her. The old gentle voice, the old possessive and complacent look in his sleepy blue eyes, recalled her wandering senses. "If I could only make you see that there wasn't anything in it."

She gazed up at him wearily. The excitement of discovery, the exaltation, the anguish, had ebbed away, leaving only gray emptiness. She had lost more than love, more than happiness, for she had lost her belief in life.

"If there had been anything in it, I might be able to understand," she replied.

He surveyed her with gloomy severity. "Hang it all! You act as if you wanted me to be in love with her." Then his face cleared as if by magic. "You're tired out, Margaret and you're nervous. There's Winters now. You must try to eat a good dinner."

Anxious, caressing, impatient to have the discussion end and dinner begin, he stooped and lifted her in his arms. For an instant she lay there without moving, and in that instant her gaze passed from his face to the red lilies and the uncurtained window beyond.

Outside the leaves were falling. [pp. 185–189]

Limiting Roles and Latent Potential

Margaret copes with her pain by envisioning herself making the supreme sacrifice of not standing in the way of her husband's happiness. By so doing, she continues to play out her role as the self-sacrificing wife, thus providing her life with meaning and purpose. But George's diminishment of the affair, by lumping it together with other forms of "recreation," robs Margaret of a face-saving, self-saving opportunity to be generous.

Margaret's willingness to step aside, though consistent with her personality, is atypical of how most wives react upon hearing about their husbands' affairs. Margaret seems wedded to the practice of self-negation, which she feels is a manifestation of her love for George. It is this final act of love, this method of coping with the pain of the affair, that sifts like sand through her fingers, leaving her disillusioned in a way that is beyond George's ability to fathom. Margaret is just "making too much of it," George exclaims. In George's mind the affair has nothing to do with Margaret, a position that leaves Margaret dumbfounded. The author writes: "When a man and a woman talk of love they speak two different languages. They can never understand each other because women love with their imagination and men with their senses. To [women] love is a thing in itself, a kind of abstract power like religion; to [men] it is simply the way he feels" (p. 174).

Trapped within Margaret lay latent possibilities. There is more to her than George could ever imagine, but she is incapable of ever letting this "more" be known. Even when she longed to cry out that she, too, was capable of great love, that she, too, was a creature of romance, her voice failed her. Had George known about this other side of her, he may not have had to stray from home. The tragedy of this story is not so much about George's meaningless affair; it is about the couple's inability to explore the latent potential locked up within each of them.

Glasgow goes no further in exploring what has caused Margaret to limit herself to the confines of the role of self-sacrificing wife. Margaret seems to have spared George the task of growing up, of having to deal with the fact that he is married to a woman who, like himself, also has needs worthy of consideration. It was she who had (in so many ways) proven indispensable to his attainment of success. She was there to tend to his every need, yet she had failed to demand anything more than to be permitted to live out the role of mothering figure.

It could certainly be argued that it was not only Margaret's fault that significant aspects of her being went completely unnoticed by George. It seems reasonable to assume that he bears some responsibility for having been blind to these hidden aspects of his wife's personality. She had offered a limited view of who she is as a person and he had taken advantage of her failure to indicate what more she needed from him.

The next chapter explores the ways in which role rigidity on the part of either husband or wife can severely limit the marriage's potential. Both wives in the two short stories presented in this chapter lived out the role of selfless wife and/or mother. This may partly be a function of the fact that these stories were written in different eras, in different social climates (1868 and 1923). One would expect the women's movement has opened women's eyes to greater opportunities for deeper personal satisfaction within marriage. But, as we are about to see, role rigidity remains as much a problem in our day as it did generations ago.

II

MARITAL DYNAMICS AND EXTRAMARITAL AFFAIRS

5

Marital Discord:
The Seeds
of Discontent

If men could be contented to be what they are,
there were no fear in marriage.
  William Shakespeare, *All's Well That Ends Well*, I, iii, 51

Short stories, like those presented in the previous chapter, illustrate some of the marital dynamics that may lead a husband to pursue other women. This chapter explores the role that marital discord plays in increasing a husband's inclination to be unfaithful. It begins with a review of a study that examines the marriages of a group of unfaithful men as seen through the eyes of their wives and lovers. By studying all types of marriages and extramarital affairs, not just those that are characteristic of the single woman–married man syndrome, we can provide a context that helps further distinguish this particular syndrome from all other types of marital situations and extramarital affairs.

A STUDY BY LEIGH CATO

In 1996, free-lance writer Leigh Cato wrote a book based on interviews she had conducted with twenty-seven wives and the "other woman" in their husbands' lives. Though her work has its limitations, given the fact that she had no formal training in the methods of scientific research, it is still worth considering since her open-ended interviews are verbatim accounts recorded in these women's own words. It is important to note, however, that in a large majority of the cases that Cato studied (20 of 27), the husbands ultimately left their wives, oftentimes in order to be with the "other woman" with whom they had been having an affair. This differs from what one typically encounters in the single woman–married man syndrome as it has been defined in Chapter 1 of this book. Usually men whose affairs conform to the defined syndrome remain with their wives. If the marriage does end, these men tend to become involved with women other than those with whom they had the extramarital affair.

Only three of the twenty-seven extramarital affairs Cato studied satisfy the criteria of the single woman–married man syndrome. While there is currently no way to know how prevalent this syndrome actually is, I suspect that it occurs more frequently than Cato's work suggests. I believe Cato's sampling is unrepresentative of the universe of extramarital affairs, not only with regard to the frequency of "cases" that correspond to this syndrome, but with regard to how often men who are having affairs leave their wives for the "other woman." Cases in which unfaithful husbands remain married to their wives may be underrepresented in Cato's study because many wives who remain married to husbands who have strayed may not wish to speak about what they believe to be their husbands' solitary indiscretion, wishing to put that painful chapter of their lives behind them.

With all its limitations, Cato's book remains worthwhile insofar as it teaches us about the nature of marriages that lead to extramarital affairs. At least 17 of Cato's 27 wives married when they were quite young, between the ages of 16 and 22. This number may actually be higher, since Cato fails to mention how old some of her subjects were when they wed. Only one of the twenty-seven women is identified as having married in her mid-thirties. Many of the ex-wives wondered if they might have been too young and inexperienced to wed.

Most of the marriages Cato describes had ceased to satisfy either partner. The husband exercised his option by ending a marriage that his wife seemed unprepared to leave. These unhappy wives wished to remain married primarily because they felt insecure being on their own, either socially or financially. The only emotional benefit these marriages seemed to offer these wives was provided by the function of the marriage's structure—its ability to validate their existence or help them feel a part of something—rather than by the quality of relatedness. Once these women were free of marriages that had outlived their usefulness, many of them discovered what they were missing.

Susie, a woman who did not suffer much financial hardship on account of her divorce, nevertheless panicked after her husband left, thinking she had to go right back out and find another man. Subsequently, she has come to prize her freedom, her ability to "eat chocolate in bed and read trashy novels without criticism" (Cato 1996, p. 41). Eve, a woman who came to feel that her husband's interest in her extended only to what she could provide for him materially, ultimately came to realize that there had never been any emotional connection between them: "I think I am mourning the time I have wasted in an emotionally dead marriage more than the loss of Charles" (p. 41). Another woman, Kate, who thought she wanted her husband back, discovered, when that became an option, that she "didn't want to go back to being the understanding, helpful, caring wife" (p. 191). In the time they had been apart, Kate came to realize how hard she had worked providing for her husband's creature comforts, all at the expense of her own needs. Finally, there is Rena, who had not known it at the time he left her, but slowly came to realize that remaining married to her tyrannical husband would have been "emotional suicide" (p. 214) insofar as she had been unable to develop a sense of herself independent of her ex-husband's view of her. One might argue that all of these women have rationalized their single status, but I am not so sure that this completely explains what these women report feeling.

In each of these cases, the man inadvertently did his wife a favor when he left her for another woman. However, none of these women knew it at the time. In some of Cato's cases, it is the woman who kicks the man out when he becomes involved with another woman. These women work up the courage to say goodbye and good riddance, and are empowered by doing so.

Losing the "Function" of Marriage

Rather than feeling relieved retrospectively that a loveless marriage is over, some women remain bitter about being left for another woman. One woman, a professor named Etta, commented, "I feel my life has been devalued. Everything I had—we had—believed in, all of a sudden is worth nothing" (Cato 1996, p. 88). Another women said, "I hate the idea of being alone, not part of a couple. I feel discarded and I don't think I deserve it. I did nothing wrong. I was a good wife and a good mother" (p. 108). A third women observed, "Yes, I was hurt when he ran away, mostly because it doesn't feel nice to be left. Everyone looks at you and says, 'Hey, what's wrong with her?'" (p. 184). Such statements make it unclear what it was that these women missed most: the structuring and validating function of the marriage—its ability to make them feel worthwhile on account of their being part of something—or the continuing opportunity to feel emotionally close to, and to share their lives with, a particular person who was their husband.

Once a husband leaves his wife, the wife often wonders what is wrong with her, what it was about her that "made" the man leave, or what she might have done differently: "I was terribly upset when he walked out—I couldn't figure out what I had done wrong" (p. 15). "I keep asking myself, what did I do wrong?"

(p. 89). "He just packed up his clothes and left. I sat on our bed watching him carefully fold each shirt. It was masochistic. I often wonder if I had fought more and harder, would he have stayed? I guess I'll never know" (p. 109). "I kept thinking . . . what does this woman have that I don't?" (p. 107).

Husbands may also value marriage primarily for its structuring and validating functions. In a number of Cato's cases, the husband seemed to value his wife primarily for how she keeps things in his life running, how she makes sure everything happens. At other times, the wife is valued only so long as she behaves in ways that stroke the husband's ego. With regard to a politician named Richard, his first wife noted that everything was fine until she decided she had a right to offer her own opinions. She observes, "All of a sudden . . . I was no longer the sweet young thing who adored him and hung on his every word" (p. 214). As one wife tells it, "He saw me as someone who did the physical things like bearing the children, cooking for the dinner parties, being witty and charming with his clients and making sure the domestic chores didn't interfere with his life. . . . But there was never, in retrospect, any real emotional connection with myself or my children" (pp. 178–179).

Another such case, from the 1930s, is that of a gynecologist who was married first to Elsa, the mother of his three children. Elsa was a European woman who had, by her reckoning, let her husband down by having failed to live up to his expectation that she would be a "righteous, moral and upstanding wife who despised sex" (i.e., whore/madonna complex) (p. 202). Early in their marriage he had a number of flings, making sure that Elsa would learn about each and every one of his affairs. Elsa and her husband got to the point where they hardly ever spoke. Feeling it unwomanly in that era to express anger, Elsa became depressed. Her husband would be gone for weeks at a time. She "finally snapped" (p. 204) when her husband brought home a young woman whom he had obviously impregnated, in order that she might be properly cared for until she delivered. Elsa threw the two of them out and filed for divorce—unusual at that time. The doctor went on to marry the woman he had impregnated. And, by this second wife's account, he treated her in precisely the same selfish, egotistical way as he had treated Elsa. Throughout that marriage, he never took his wife or daughter on a trip. He was hypercritical of his wife's housekeeping abilities and could turn verbally abusive. And he never ceased having affairs.

Then there is the case of Kate, the woman mentioned earlier, who passed on the option to have her husband back because she had come to realize, in his absence, just how demanding he was. When her husband took up with a woman several decades his junior, that woman came to regret ever having gotten involved with him once she realized that he expected to be waited on "hand and foot. . . . What he wants is a cross between a nymphette and a nurse-maid. I don't fit the bill for either. . . . The relationship is in tatters and neither one of us seems to know how to end it. . . . About six months ago it really came to a head. I said I wanted to leave; he threatened suicide. It was all my fault, according to him. I lured him away from his wife, I wrecked his career. He had given up everything that was important in his life for me" (pp. 192–193). Such cases illustrate just how tyrannical some men can be in the pursuit of getting and maintaining what they feel they need.

Living in Oblivion

One of the remarkable findings in Cato's study is how often the wife is taken completely by surprise when her husband announces his intention to leave. They are stunned and dumbfounded, never having suspected anything was wrong. The fact that so many of the wives had not a clue that their marriages were in trouble might be one reason why they were. How many women blind themselves to the grim reality of their marriage? And what role do their husbands play in ensuring that the wife knows nothing about how they (the husbands) really feel?

Some wives report having realized that they had been naive ("obviously my marriage wasn't what I thought it was" [p. 88], or

"I didn't know anything about [the fact that my husband was unhappily married] until the day he left" [p. 37] or "What has always baffled me is when people say, 'Why didn't you know, everyone else did'?" [p. 3]). Others admit to not having been able to bear the fact that their husbands had left them emotionally years before. The wife's denial is sometimes supported, and may even, at times, be a function of the husband's behavior. A husband who fails to confront his wife with whatever dissatisfactions he has about the marriage, and, instead, acts as if nothing whatsoever is wrong, will leave his wife bewildered when he finally figures it is time to go. One confused wife, Susie, who "would have put any amount of money on the fact" (p. 38) that her husband had always been faithful to her and whose husband had just given her a diamond eternity ring to celebrate their tenth anniversary, was stunned when she found a note from him on her pillow explaining that he no longer loved her and had decided to leave.

Some wives were surprised that their husbands were having affairs, or were leaving them for other women, because they had misread their husbands, considering them incapable of such behavior. One such wife, an overbearing woman who was disparaging of her husband Kevin's character, figured that he did not have the "balls" to pull off such a feat. She quipped: "A bit passive, our Kevin. . . . He was never much of a go-getter. Sort of a plodder. . . . We didn't fight a lot. I just used to get frustrated at how slow he was—a procrastinator of the first order" (p. 29). Another woman, who was married to the consummate "nice guy," saw her husband as the perfect husband and father. She thought of him as "no ladies' man," as someone who was not interested in "that sort of stuff," (p. 108) and, accordingly, not someone who was likely to stray. So it came as a shock to her when her husband told her that he could no longer stay in the marriage, and that he had found someone else. Had his wife completely misread who her husband was? If so, what role might that have played in the demise of the marriage. And what did the husband contribute to his wife's inability to read him for who he was? The woman for whom he left his wife acknowledged that he is a man unaccustomed to talking about his feelings. So it is reasonable to assume that his difficulties in being open with his first wife about his feelings contributed to her having misread him. A third wife, who had been left by her husband, said of him prior to his leaving, "I've got this guy, I really like him, he's a bit dull but I really love him. Boy, is he ever safe. He won't go anywhere" (p. 38).

The Limiting Roles of Marriage

Sometimes a man and his wife fall into a pattern of interacting that leads each to believe that his or her way of relating to the other is strictly a function of who they are as individuals. They do not appreciate that each may evoke specific types of reactions, and ways of being, that are unique to their particular relationship and may not be a feature of any past or future relationships. Mistaking one's mate for how he or she is within the marriage is one of the biggest mistakes a wife or husband can make because it sells the mate short. Just because husbands or wives operate in a characteristic way vis-à-vis their mate does not necessarily predict how they would be with a different partner.

It is not always the case that a man inevitably carries his personality with him and is therefore doomed to repeat the same relationship the next marriage around. Sometimes a man finds it hard to bring out other aspects of his personality in the presence of his wife because the marital relationship proves so limiting that it feels impossible for him to change within the context of such a confining mold.

Cato's book provides a few examples of cases in which the man develops a substantially better relationship with the woman for whom he left his wife, chiefly because he emerged as a different person in that relationship in comparison to who he had been in his marriage. In the case of Kevin, described above, his wife was so disparaging of his character that he felt a desperate need to escape the marriage in order to protect his self-esteem from further attack. Given how his wife regarded him, it is not surprising that the woman Kevin ultimately ran to was someone who saw him as anything but a wimp. Instead, she saw him as someone who "didn't take shit" from others, and "stood his ground" (p. 31) if the need arose. Evidence suggests that Kevin was, in fact, acting a great deal more assertively in his new relationship than he had in the marriage, in which he may well have acted in ways that were provoking, or even deserving of, his wife's criticisms. Once the die was cast, and the marital interactive style had become established, Kevin saw no way of correcting the situation other than escaping it altogether.

In the case of Ray, the consummate nice guy whose ex-wife, Helena, hated the idea of no longer being a part of a couple, a different Ray emerged when he left Helena for Pat. In retrospect, Helena observes: "Pat changed everything. Ray became a different person. He dressed differently, he cut his hair differently, he even walked and talked differently. I kept thinking, what is this woman doing to him? What does she have that I don't?" (p. 107). Though Helena concedes that she and Ray had probably married for the wrong reasons, and acknowledges that they had drifted apart, she still wonders how the relationship might have turned out if only she had done things differently. Her continued attempts to fix the marriage were evidently experienced by her husband as nagging—which brings us to the next topic, how husbands and wives deal with their differences.

MARITAL COMMUNICATION PATTERNS

All marriages—even good ones—have their share of conflict. These differences have been studied by researchers (Fitzpatrick 1984, Gottman 1994) who have classified three distinct types of marriages based on how, and whether, the couple actively engages in the task of conflict resolution. Gottman (1994) boldly asserts that "marriages come in three discrete adaptations, and there are no in-between adaptations that are stable over time"

(p. 185). Fitzpatrick (1984) has dubbed these three types of marriages as independents, traditionals, and separates. Independents tend to become quite volatile when confronting their differences and may quarrel incessantly; traditionals tend to minimize their differences in the name of harmony; and separates tend to avoid addressing conflict altogether.

Individuals in independent marriages insist on pursuing their own interests and relations independent of their spouse. Such partners are determined to exercise their right to express their individuality at every turn, believing that doing so strengthens the marriage. They like to demonstrate that they have remained true to themselves, having sacrificed nothing of themselves to the marriage. Neither partner in such a marriage is interested in submerging an aspect of his or her personality for the sake of the other. Nor is either partner willing to submit to the other's needs or wishes, at least not without a fight. Each partner makes his or her position or desire known to the other in a clear and direct fashion. They do not mince words. They tend to interrupt one another for the right to have their point of view or agenda considered and adopted by the other. They are effective at lobbying their partner to give in to their wishes, which naturally makes for lively debate. Such partners typically lock horns in their attempts to persuade the other of the value, superiority, or practicality of their position. Both partners attempt to gain dominance, though neither loses respect for the other in the process. Though such partners live somewhat independent lives, spending time apart in the pursuit of interests that are not shared, they nevertheless maintain an intensely emotional connection.

Traditional marriages are characterized by the partners' tendencies to downplay their differences in the service of maintaining peaceful cohabitation (harmony). Such spouses view the full expression of their separable individualities (their personal differences) as less important than the couple's ability to maintain a sense of "we-ness." Conflicts are more likely to end in the partners stepping back, observing themselves, and concluding, "What

are two people who are in love with each other as much as we
are doing arguing over so trivial a matter as this?" Such spouses
will argue only about the most important issues they confront
as a couple, but most other conflicts, those that are considered
minor, tend to be swept under the carpet. Unlike independent
marriages, which tend to be emotionally tumultuous, traditional
marriages are characterized by mutual civility between the partners, who are able to understand where their spouses are coming from. Most psychotherapists would judge such couples as
functioning optimally.

Marriages between individuals who live relatively separate
existences (separates) are characterized by emotional distance
(withdrawal) and a tendency to avoid conflict whenever possible.
Such couples exhibit a low level of companionship and sharing.
Studies suggest that, in general, husbands are much more likely
than wives to respond to conflict by emotionally withdrawing
(clamming up or walking out) (Komarovsky 1962, Rubin 1976),
whereas wives tend to hang in and continue trying to confront and
work through the couple's differences (Burke et al. 1976, Gottman
and Krokoff 1989, Huston and Ashmore 1986, Wills et al. 1974).
Husbands who "shut down" in an effort to avoid becoming emotionally overwhelmed by the negative affect that is often generated
during confrontations also tend to avoid the expression of positive affects, thus leading to a deadening of the emotional dimension of the marriage. Fitzpatrick (1984) observed that husbands
of this type end up speaking to their wives less often and for shorter
periods of time than husbands in traditional or independent marriages; while early in marriage the husband may have been able to
freely share his feelings, over the course of time he ceases to self-
disclose to his wife. But this behavior is context-dependent rather
than an invariant feature of the husband's personality. Men who
cease to be open with their wives, who selectively tune their wives
out, are nevertheless able to be open with, and attuned to, other
women (Fitzpatrick 1984, Gottman and Porterfield 1981). While
researchers have yet to correlate personality types with marriage

types, it may well turn out to be the case that couples who engage in separate-type marriages do so primarily because one or both of the partners exhibit exquisite narcissistic sensitivities.

One critical dimension of marriage is the degree to which the partners tend to experience themselves as connected with rather then separate from one another (Raush et al. 1974). While independent-type marriages permit the partners much autonomy and individuality, the couple nevertheless remains emotionally connected. Partners in traditional-type marriages experience connectedness via their sense of "we-ness," while partners in separate-type marriages lack a sense of connectedness and, accordingly, are alienated from one another.

While each of these three types of marriages can be stable over time, those characterized by withdrawal warrant further study since chronic withdrawal threatens the ongoing stability of the marriage and may contribute to a husband's pursuing extramarital affairs. Chronic withdrawal typically creates a sense of loneliness. It may also generate intense negativity, out of the sheer frustration and narcissistic injury that develop when one partner leaves another by withdrawing. If negativity is the only way one can reach a withdrawn spouse, it may accordingly become reinforced. On the other hand, withdrawal can be the effect, rather than the original cause, of the couple's difficulties in successfully resolving their differences. If one partner lashes out at the other for not being sensitive enough to realize when the first partner was needing his or her mate to capitulate, or if one partner feels as if he or she is being emotionally strong-armed into giving in by the other, emotional withdrawal may have the dual function of self-protection and passive-aggressive protest.

Affect Intolerance and Emotional Withdrawal

The degree of physiologic arousal experienced by each partner when interacting with his or her spouse has proven to be a fruitful area of investigation for researchers interested in studying the role that physiologic arousal plays in husbands' tendencies to emotionally withdraw from their wives (for a discussion see Gottman 1994). The physiologic linkage between marital partners is studied by hooking up the subjects to instruments that monitor heart rate, pulse transmission, skin conductance, and general somatic activity. Once the partners have been hooked up to these monitors, they are permitted to interact in a naturalistic way. It is important to note that physiologic arousal is not synonymous with displayed affect since emotional withdrawal, which is unaccompanied by emotional displays, nevertheless produces significant physiologic arousal in the partner who is shut out, or "stonewalled" (see below), in the process (Gottman 1994).

These physiologic studies have contributed to an understanding of the unique problem men have maintaining exclusive intimate attachments over time. Withdrawing from relationships is a decidedly male thing (Gottman 1994, Locke 1951, Terman et al. 1938). This is especially true when it comes to a particular form of withdrawal known as stonewalling. Men are nearly six times more likely to stonewall their spouses than are women. Stonewalling is characterized by the failure of the listener to produce the usual cues that inform a speaker that the listener is following what the speaker is saying, that the speaker's intended meaning is getting across and is being understood. Typical cues that signal to a speaker that the listener is interested in, and attending to, what he or she is saying include head nods, brief vocalizations, facial movements, and small moves of the head and neck. Stonewalling is often interpreted by the speaker as "detachment, disapproval, smugness, hostility, negative judgment, disinterest [sic], and coldness" (Gottman 1994, p. 141).

What contributes to the tendency of husbands to withdraw from, or to stonewall their wives? Gottman and Levenson (1985) discovered that "compared with females, males have a constitutionally heightened vulnerability to sustained levels of physiologic hyperarousal and males experience such states as being highly aversive" (cited in Gottman 1994, p. 261). Gottman (1994) has suggested that this finding accounts for the behavior of husbands who emotionally withdraw when they feel they are under fire. Men's unique difficulty handling intense emotion is not just limited to marriage. For instance, when negative affect enters into a man's relationship with his college roommates, he is much less able to preserve that relationship when compared to women, who are just as skittish about the emergence of negative affects but who seem better equipped to emotionally handle such occurrences (Ginsberg and Gottman 1986).

Men evidently recover more slowly from autonomic nervous system arousal than do women. This might also account for the tendency of men to approach conflict in an overly rational way when compared with women, who are much more prone to permit their feelings to enter into the equation (Kelley et al. 1978, Rubin 1976). Remaining hyperrational is men's way of keeping themselves from becoming emotionally flooded in the process of conflict resolution. Gottman (1994) notes, "The research evidence suggests that, regardless of the level of marital satisfaction, men do not seem to function as well as women . . . in the context of high negative affect" (p. 242).

A husband's tendency to withdraw from his wife leads him to tune her out, thus making it hard for him to understand more subtle forms of communication, ones in which the ambiguity of the message leaves it up to the listener to fill in the blanks. Gottman and Porterfield (1981) studied the effect that withdrawal had on a spouse's ability to read the subtext of ambiguous messages (e.g., the wife says, "I'm cold, aren't you?" which is read correctly by the husband to mean "I would like to snuggle"). The study showed that whereas wives in stable and unstable marriages were just as able to ascertain their husband's underlying message, husbands in dissatisfied marriages demonstrated a "decoding deficit" that left them unable to understand what their wives were saying. It is critical to note, however, that these same husbands had no difficulty whatsoever decoding ambiguous messages sent by someone else's wife. Clearly, when husbands withdraw or stonewall their wives, they exhibit a form of selective inattention that might be considered just another form of passive-aggressive behavior. This is not a character trait, but a situationally determined style of ignoring one's wife.

A Clinical Vignette

Mr. I., a divorced college professor in his mid-fifties, had been carrying on a long-term, long-distance relationship with another college professor who lived several states away. He was a recovering alcoholic who had been sober for over ten years. He came from an English family that tended to be conflict avoiding; all the family's interactions were "proper." His girlfriend, on the other hand, was Italian. She was raised in a household characterized by great emotional turmoil; both words and plates would fly.

Mr. I. sought treatment to see if he could alter his characteristic style of avoiding conflict, something about which his girlfriend, Ms. W., complained bitterly. Ms. W. had grown frustrated and impatient with Mr. I.'s tendency to become hyperrational whenever she expressed upset over his having done something that she deemed insensitive. Mr. I.'s tendency to retreat into hyperrationality left Ms. W. feeling abandoned, chiefly because it placed him on a plane different from the one on which she was operating. Mr. I. favored a measured and rational analysis of whatever situation the couple was discussing, which left Ms. W. feeling that she and the patient were out of sync.

Mr. I. admitted that he felt disoriented whenever he tried to stay on an emotional plane with his girlfriend. Remaining grounded in his emotional reactions caused him to feel like he was losing his intellectual footing. It was as if he became swept up in a whirlwind, utterly disabled by the experience. Under such circumstances, he could neither think nor reason. He would struggle desperately to regain his balance, and would cling to a recitation of the facts about how he and his girlfriend had gotten into their present dilemma. By so doing, he hoped to make clear the correctness of his perceptions, thus putting the conflict to rest.

Reverting to a hyperrational stance caused Mr. I. to overlook the fact that any given person's experience is a highly subjective matter that relies heavily on personal interpretation. The intersubjectivity of experience renders meaningless simple matters such as who is technically right or wrong about, for example, the temporal sequence of events that led to a conflict. He was unable to keep in mind that an understanding of how another person comes to see things often takes precedence over a cool assessment of the objective truth, particularly when one is trying to understand where another is coming from. His girlfriend's typical stance was "don't confuse me with the facts"; his own was "let me remind you of what actually happened." Such confrontations tended to be crazy-making for the girlfriend, who felt that her very perceptions were thrown into question. Mr. I.'s mission was to correct his girlfriend's "misconceptions," feeling that doing so could clarify the actual state of affairs (as he saw them).

Mr. I. admitted that he always experienced conflict as negative, as something that he needed to avoid at all cost. Intense affects were something he could not tolerate because they interfered with his cognitive abilities. In particular, he felt completely unable to tolerate his girlfriend's anger when it was directed toward him. He could not hear what she had to say. He always found himself becoming defensive. He wanted to squelch conflict by solving the problem prematurely, before his girlfriend even had an opportunity to explain what she was so upset about. His girlfriend experienced him as trying to shut her up.

Ultimately, in the course of therapy, the patient developed an ability to understand how his tendency to bring conflict to a premature close was actually causing further conflict. In spite of this understanding, he still found it hard to withstand his girlfriend's emotional barrages for any more than brief periods of time before he would either become defensive or revert to his characteristic hyperrational stance. This case well illustrates Gottman's (1994) contention that "negative affect during marital interaction and the concomitant physiological arousal may interfere with higher order cognitive functions such as problem solving, planning, and creative thinking" (p. 246).

Addressing and Working Through a Couple's Differences

There are three phases by which couples confront and work through their differences: (1) the agenda-building phase; (2) the arguing or disagreement phase; and (3) the resolution phase, during which a compromise is negotiated (Gottman 1979). During the agenda-building phase, the partners air their differences, thus establishing grounds for further discussion. One of them elucidates the conflict by clarifying the issues and asking that they be addressed. During the arguing phase, the partners attempt to persuade one another by arguing their "case." Typically this phase tends to be the most emotionally charged. Heated discussions threaten to erupt into full-scale war as each party fights hard in support of his or her position. More stable couples tend to utilize built-in devices (repair mechanisms) that de-escalate conflict before it gets out of hand, before the fighting turns nasty (Gottman 1979). Repair mechanisms include "feeling probes," which involve one partner's sensitively speculating about what the other might be feeling at the time, and the use of meta-cognitive observations, by which one person sensitively addresses something about how the two partners are currently relating to one another as they attempt to work through their differences. The modifier *sensitively* has been added to underscore that feeling probes and metacognitive observations may be used as weapons that further push a couple apart, rather than as conciliatory efforts to enhance emotional closeness. Finally, in the negotiating phase, the partners work their way toward some sort of resolution of their differences.

Independents tend to maintain a high pitch of emotionality during all three of these phases. Both partners tend to continue to disagree and to criticize one another's position, well into the negotiating phase when the conflict ought to be approaching resolution. Neither partner ever truly gives in, though both somehow feel satisfied that each had been afforded an opportunity to speak and be heard by the other in the process. This style of conflict engagement saves both partners from feeling as if they had been forced to capitulate. The behavior of partners in a traditional-type marriage differs from the behavior observed in independent-type marriages in that emotionality (disagreement plus criticism) in the former only runs high during the arguing or disagreeing phase of the conflict. Such spouses ultimately compromise for the sake of the cherished sense of "we-ness" that is valued over the individual rights of either party.

Marriages characterized by separation and withdrawal tend to exhibit very little emotionality from the beginning to the end of the three phases of the conflict-engaging cycle. Such couples are, in fact, conflict avoiding. Husbands who feel emotionally flooded in the process of attempting to hash things out work to avoid conflict whatever the cost. Furthermore, the partners in separate-type marriages tend to be out of sync with one another in that the wives attempt to persuade more in the first third of the cycle (agenda-building phase), whereas their avoiding husbands attempt to exert influence in the last third of the cycle (negotiating phase).

All three types of marriage discussed above may prove stable or intact over time insofar as they do not end in divorce (Gottman 1994). How partners conduct themselves during the arguing or disagreement phase is an important factor that contributes to marital stability and longevity. Couples who disagree, even those who quarrel violently, need not end up feeling dissatisfied with marriage so long as the partners never lose respect for one another. Gottman (1994) writes, "Neither conflict avoidance or high levels of negative conflict are, by themselves, dysfunctional in terms of the marriage. . . . What is dysfunctional is the response to one's partner with criticism, disgust, contempt, defensiveness, and stonewalling" (p. 184). Fitzpatrick (1988) sums it up as follows:

In all marriages, there is a change from issue attack to personal attack when a conflict occurs. All couples use personal nonsupport statements as linguistic attempts to assert dominance in conflict. *What differs among couples is how a spouse responds to a personal attack*, not the occurrence of the attack in the first place. These results parallel those of Gottman (1979), who finds that in happy marriages, one spouse de-escalates conflict by not responding in kind to the negative communication acts of his or her partner. [p. 133]

In other words, it is not just a matter of not fighting dirty that determines a marriage's stability or instability. It is the ability to cool things down when things start to get out of hand, the ability, when one partner crosses the line, to avoid further deterioration into the realm of interpersonal ugliness.

In summary, the key to marital satisfaction and stability is a couple's ability to approach, confront, and work through their differences without losing respect for one another and without throwing their hands up, resigning themselves to the futility of ever reaching agreement. If a couple spends an inordinate amount of time and energy coping with attitudes of criticism, disgust, contempt, and defensiveness, or has come to believe their differences are irreconcilable, withdrawal is likely, thus setting the stage for extramarital affairs that are free of such painful and frustrating interactions.

THE REWARDS AND RISKS OF DIFFERENT TYPES OF MARRIAGES

Independent Marriages

Independent marriages are intensely passionate relationships. The partners are permitted a full range of emotional expression. They fight a lot and laugh a lot. They have big fights and big reconciliations. Compared with other couples, they tend to be very interested in what the other has to say, not just when they are arguing, but when they are having everyday conversations. Hence, they are quite intimate with one another. Yet with all it has going for it, such marriages have the potential for a great deal of turmoil and upset. Because both partners are permitted to be themselves, they don't harbor resentment over feeling that they have to hide an aspect of their personality for the good of the relationship. Such couples insist on confronting every conflict, even the most minor ones. But while there are advantages to being committed to the elucidation of each and every difference, this degree of rigor may lead the partners to be open with one another to a fault. Sometimes being honest leads to revelations that are hurtful and hard to recover from, leading to the very real prospect of violence.

I would speculate that independent type marriages would rarely, if ever, lead to the single woman–married man syndrome. The passion expressed in the marriage, the freedom to be oneself, and the lack of a sense of having to capitulate for the sake of the relationship ought to immunize a husband against such an outcome. This is not to say that husbands in such marriages never have extramarital affairs. But if they do, I suspect they would be more purely sexual in nature, rather than a reaction to dissatisfactions with the marriage.

Traditional Marriages

By contrast, couples in traditional (conflict-minimizing) marriages run the risk of the relationship becoming a passionless arrangement, less romantic and less satisfying than it otherwise might be were the couple not so determined to sacrifice individual gratification for the sake of harmony and peaceful cohabitation. Such a couple emphasizes sharing and friendship. Such marriages are likely to be judged as good or satisfying marriages by the husbands. Gottman (1994) concludes that such marriages are at risk for experiencing a loss of romance and a loss of the spouses' sense of themselves as individuals. As the partners' differences become de-emphasized, the risk increases of the partners' overlooking real conflicts that are much in need of addressing. Gottman speculates that such marriages are particularly vulnerable at major life transitions, such as having a child.

Except for times when the traditional couple is forced to confront issues that it cannot possibly ignore, the partners tend to downplay their individual differences, which are considered unimportant in the larger scheme of things. In place of a pursuit of their separate goals, they emphasize their communal goals or opinions. At first glance this latter approach has the appearance of being quite mature. In fact, such an approach has a lot going for it. But when one considers how seldom such couples reach resolution about their differences, and how often their differences end up being swept under the carpet, one develops doubts about whether this approach is all it's cracked up to be. The problem such couples have is that once both partners have stated their positions, they often feel as if there is nothing left to say! Neither partner tries very hard to convince the other to accept a position. So they settle for a standoff. Compromise is never reached. There is no give and take and no true problem solving. The best such a couple can hope for is to be philosophical about their differences.

I suggest that this type of marriage can lead to the single woman–married man syndrome. Husbands who feel they are locked into a limiting and rigid relationship that does not permit free expression of all aspects of their personality are at risk for looking for opportunities to be freed of the need to sacrifice themselves for the good of the marital relationship. Yet these men love their wives and cannot fault the overall marriage, apart from the fact that it limits them in ways they may never have realized until a certain somebody enters their lives, awakening them to what it was they were missing. While such husbands may harbor some degree of resentment toward the marriage for having limited them in this way, they are not likely to blame the wife for this state of affairs. They accept responsibility for having made the marriage what it is, so their extramarital affairs are not as covertly hostile as the ones that develop in the context of marriages marred by excessive amounts of criticism, disgust, contempt, and defensiveness, as is seen in conflict-avoiding marriages, particularly those that have disintegrated into unstable relationships due to the constant presence of hostility.

Separate-Type Marriages

Conflict-avoiding relationships (separate-type relationships) also tend to be less passionate marriages, similar to what one encounters in traditional-type marriages. If such couples succeed at avoiding negativity altogether, regret may become the emotion that defines the relationship. Under such conditions, intimacy ceases to be a feature of the relationship altogether. What is left in its place is intense loneliness. This is particularly true when the husband has become withdrawn. Gottman (1994) raises the question of whether such couples "lack the social skills necessary to resolve conflicts that are unavoidable" (p. 191). He also notes that such relationships are at risk for evolving into hostile ones when the couple encounters a problem that cannot be ignored.

I would speculate that the conflict-avoiding type of marriage is also likely to result in the husband having extramarital affairs. It is interesting to note that in about one-third of this type of marriage, the husband complained that he wanted sex more often than the wife did. Given this, the affairs that such husbands pursue may stem partly from a wish for better, or more frequent, sex. If the relationship disintegrates into one marred by excessive amounts of criticism, disgust, contempt, and defensiveness, it may shift from a passionless affair into a loathsome connection. At this point, an extramarital affair may also represent an act of hostility.

TYPICAL GENDER DIFFERENCES

Men may enter marriage thinking of women as submissive, given how many women appear when they are out in public. Gottman (1994) quotes Aries (1976) as noting that "the social behavior of women in stranger groups is tentative, polite, and subordinate" (p. 283). It is easy to see how men might expect, based on women's public tentativeness and deference, that they would be likewise tentative and deferential within marriage. However, this conclusion overlooks the fact that women, in Gottman's (1994) words, "have been socialized to be experts at close personal relationships. . . . [They] are more emotionally expressive than men and far more competent with close social relationships than men" (p. 283). Many men may find themselves surprised when they marry and discover the woman they married can be outspoken in support of the couple's talking out their differences rather than avoiding them, as many men want to do (Locke 1951).

Gottman (1994), drawing on the work of Burke and colleagues (1976), Huston and Ashmore (1986), and Wills and colleagues (1974), concluded that wives play a special, and essential, role as "manager of marital disagreements" (p. 135) insofar as they are more prone than their husbands to ask that the couple's problems be addressed. In exchange for this tendency to engage in conflict, wives tend to be viewed by their husbands as complaining, criticizing, and escalating emotion (Terman et al. 1938). Wives' interactions with their husbands have been consistently described as more confronting, demanding, coercive, and highly emotional (both positive and negative emotions) than the husband's behavior vis-à-vis their wives (e.g., Gottman 1979, Raush et al. 1974, Schaap 1982). Men, on the other hand, have been described as conflict avoiding, withdrawing, placating, logical, and avoidant of emotions (Kelley et al. 1978, Raush et al. 1974). Gottman sums it up: "Wives could be described behaviorally as conflict engaging and husbands as conflict reducing (and, in the face of high conflict, as withdrawing)" (pp. 241–242).

Gottman (1994) underscores the importance of the wife's function: "It is important for the longitudinal satisfaction of couples that wives confront disagreements and not be overly compliant" (p. 238). Though women tend to be blamed, in the short run, for stirring up the pot, the turmoil created by their doing so tends to have positive effects on the marriage over the long haul.

POWER AND DOMINATION

To a greater or lesser extent, power and control are ever-present factors in every marriage. In many marriages the battle rages over who will wear the pants in the family. If the husband defers, he retains power; if he capitulates, he loses it. Deferring can be done from the position of strength as the recognized best alternative, given the circumstances. To capitulate is a different matter. It implies submission and defeat and retains no such claim to dignity. The difference between the two is primary attitudinal. If a partner feels forced to yield ground by the other, he or she is likely to feel defeated in the process. Backing down as a strategy for conflict resolution may be seen as something about which one had no choice—as if a gun were placed to one's head.

Does a man's withdrawal from conflict lead him to feel he has capitulated? And does a man's withdrawing under such circumstances lead him to feel as if he has been dominated by his wife? If a wife is seen by others as "wearing the pants" in the family, the man may feel that he is viewed as if having been castrated, "whipped." Such an outcome is most likely to occur in marriages of the separate type. The wife may become the parental figure in the process, feeling she needs to take the reigns, given the power vacuum left by the weak husband. The husband's inability to stand up for himself may further reinforce this dynamic. The man may withdraw and find another woman who supports an entirely different version of who he is, as illustrated in Cato's case of Kevin (presented earlier in this chapter), whose new girlfriend helped support an image of him very different from his wife's appraisal of him as a wimp.

Domineering behavior is a particular type of controlling behavior (see Gottman 1994 for a discussion of this topic). The goal of domineering is to stifle the partner's attempts to argue his or her case. The domineering partner acts much like a bully, discounting the validity of the other's position, hogging the floor so that the other has no chance of making his or her point. There is no such thing as agreeing to disagree since the domineering person regards the other person's view as null and void. Disputes are never permitted to be won on the sheer weight of the argument. The domineering partner makes sure of having an unfair advantage by doing whatever possible to prevent a fair hearing of the other's position. One may dominate the conversation by not even permitting the other to speak. Typical domineering maneuvers include intimidating, glowering, lecturing, patronizing, persuading, invalidating, threatening, or some combination of these tactics. Certain body postures and gazes support one's efforts to dominate: "A domineering gaze is usually steady and intense with a fixed quality, as if the eyes alone will convince of the speaker's authority" (Gottman 1994, p. 301).

A Clinical Vignette

The following vignette illustrates a marriage in which the husband felt that his domineering wife left him no power to either get what he wanted from the marriage or set things right between them. Accordingly, he had succumbed to sneaking about behind his wife's back to avoid her wrath. Such passive-aggressive maneuvers are quite typical in the single woman–married man syndrome, and at times are precipitated by a basic power imbalance in the relationship that leaves the man feeling castrated. This case illustrates a conflict-avoiding marriage in which the husband and wife had lapsed into living relatively separate existences.

Mr. M. is a 40-year-old married architect who sought treatment for the anxiety and confusion he was experiencing over the state of his love relations. Though the patient had known his wife, Mary, for thirteen years and been married to her for eight years, it was only recently that he had become aware of just how unhappy he was with their relationship. For years he had been motivated to accommodate to Mary's every wish, since his moods were completely determined by hers: When she was happy, he would be happy; when she was sad, he would be sad. It seemed to Mr. M. that Mary took advantage of his wish to please her. She was self-centered, never seeming to give any consideration to what he wanted from the marriage. When Mr. M. did speak up in defense of his wishes and needs, Mary responded judgmentally about his wishes and became jealous about the time he wanted to spend with his buddies.

Mary was a highly competent woman who tended to take charge to such a degree that she was considered controlling in her interactions with others. Mr. M. had grown tired of his wife's stubborn and domineering personality and the two partners had grown distant. When they did interact, they tended to snipe at one another. Mr. M. experienced his wife as a nag. She would "get in my face" by speaking to him in a critical tone as she questioned him about his decisions and whereabouts. Within this context he became increasingly secretive about his activities, figuring that if Mary were oblivious to what he was up to she would have no cause to give him grief.

Though earlier in the relationship the patient had begun talking with his wife about this pattern of relating, he doubted how motivated or capable she was of changing, figuring she was too inflexible to be able to set the relationship right. Mr. M. wanted to please his wife and would bend over backwards to avoid conflict. She, I suspect, was completely unaware of his extreme self-denial in order to avoid her wrath. These factors complicated the couple's efforts to recognize and work through their differences.

Mr. M. had never given much thought to how happy or unhappy he was in the marriage until he became involved with Terri, a single woman he had met through work. At that point his eyes were opened to the fact that life with Mary could not hold a candle to what he was experiencing with Terri. The personal attacks Mr. M. had endured, and returned, in his marriage had worn him down to the point that the marriage no longer contributed to his sense of well-being. Mr. M. felt deadened in his relationship with his wife and was revitalized by his interactions with Terri. While his wife "made" him feel criticized, put down, and treated like a child, Terri made him feel alive and desired, like a self-respecting adult.

Mr. M. felt grateful that he had learned how much better life could be. He saw life with Mary as slavery under the rule of Pharaoh and thought of life with his new girlfriend as the promised land of milk and honey. But, in the meantime, he had been wandering in the desert for what seemed like an interminable time.

The patient's greatest dilemma was his inability to decide how to proceed. He found himself completely unable to tell his wife that he no longer wished to remain married to her. Part of what made it so hard for him to leave her for his girlfriend was the fact that he felt like an absolute cad for even thinking of doing such a thing. After all, his wife was not a bad person, far from it, even if she did things that "made" him feel smothered and "made" him feel as if he had to sneak about to avoid her scolding him, like a mother would a son, were she to learn what he was up to. Mr. M. felt ashamed of his inability to confront his wife with the truth: "Why can't I just tell her what I'm up to, what I want to do and suffer whatever reaction she would have in response?"

Mr. M.'s inability to actively confront his wife led him to wish for divine intervention to help resolve his dilemma. He had always thought of himself as a nice guy and he especially wished to be able to avoid feeling like a "worm" for making a decision that would be hurtful to either of the two women in his life. Rather than extricating himself from a marriage in which he felt like a slave to his wife's every wish, he had just added another person, his girlfriend, to the roster of those whose feelings mattered, and whom he had to do everything in his power to please.

Mr. M. was unhappy and sensed his wife was too. But for him to take the aggressive step of initiating the separation, to be the one to file for divorce, was more than he could stand. Staying with Mary was his way out of feeling that he was a miserable husband. Yet he was not really there with her. He knew this, and turned to me to help him find some magical, guilt-free way out of what seemed to him an impossible situation.

The patient experienced his wife as being much like his mother, a woman whose strong personality ensured that no one in the family dared cross her. The patient's father tended to give his mother a wide berth, and the patient, taking his cue from father, learned early to be overly accommodating to women. Mr. M. subsequently carried this accommodating style over to his marriage with Mary. Only recently had he come to realize how he had grown resentful of the inequities in the marriage.

Mr. and Mrs. M.'s style of relating had deteriorated into frequent sniping, rather than direct confrontation of their problems. Neither partner was able to raise the level of discourse to a higher plane. When he felt attacked, Mr. M. resorted to counterattacks, rather than making the metacognitive observation about the way in which the two of them had, yet again, been relating to one another. No truce was ever called, so the two continued to take pot shots at one another, thus perpetuating a vicious downward spiral. Defensive reaction begot defensive counterreaction. Neither would forgo the satisfaction of getting back at the other, and neither seemed equipped to seize the opportunity to gain distance from the situation by demanding that they both look at what they were doing to each other and to their marriage.

Were Mr. M. to leave his wife for Terri, what are the odds that things would ultimately be any better with her? What Mr. M. liked about Terri is that she agreed with him about so many important issues in life, unlike his wife. But if Terri did not start out having the same controlling personality as Mary, would Mr. M. interact with her in ways unconsciously designed to bring that side out in her? Or might Mr. M., this time around, turn out to be the one who got to play the domineering figure that his wife got to play in the first marriage? Any one of these alternatives was possible. There was no telling, this early in their relationship, in which direction things were headed. However, the factor that would determine whether this relationship proved viable might not depend so much on which of the above interactional configurations the couple adopted. It might instead depend more on whether this new couple's approach to problem solving replicated the marriage's conflict-avoiding pattern (with hostile resentment and intermittent sniping, punctuating an otherwise cold and distant relationship), or, instead, adopted a healthier pattern of conflict resolution, such as that seen in traditional-type couples. To date, Mr. M. remains in limbo between the two women in his life.

This case brings us to the point of needing more information about why men, in general, have extramarital affairs. The next chapter reviews the scientific data currently available that addresses this question. Not all of what is to be discussed has a direct bearing on the single woman–married man syndrome. But no book about extramarital affairs, even ones that are a subset of all such affairs, would be complete without a discussion of the larger phenomenon.

6

Extramarital Affairs: Recreation, Rejuvenation, Triumph

Full many a lady
I have ey'd with best regard, and many a time
Th' harmony of their tongues hath into bondage
Brought my too diligent ear; for several virtues
Have I lik'd several women.

William Shakespeare, *The Tempest*, III, I, 43

Restating the defining traits of the single woman–married man syndrome: this syndrome represents a type of extramarital affair that differs from other extramarital affairs in the following ways: (1) the woman is single, has typically never been married, and is usually unencumbered by the demands of children; (2) this is the man's first extramarital affair, or, if the man has had others, this affair will differ from all of them in that he will become deeply emotionally involved with, and attached to, the woman; (3) the man feels incapable of deciding which alternative he would ultimately prefer: staying with his wife or committing to the other woman; (4) the affair runs an emotionally tumultuous, on-again-off-again course; (5) the affair almost never ends in marriage—if the man divorces, his next wife is rarely the one with whom he had been having the affair; (6) the affair is not primarily about sex, but rather is chiefly about emotional attachment and the satisfaction of emotional needs that had, for whatever reason, gone unmet in the marriage.

The term *extramarital affair* may mean any number of things to different people. Most would agree that an affair refers to an extramarital relationship that takes place over the course of time. It makes no sense to call a one-night stand an affair. Most would further agree that an extramarital relationship includes a sexual dimension. A platonic relationship between a married man and a single woman would not usually be thought of as an affair, no matter how close the two individuals had become, if that relationship was completely devoid of sexual attraction. Grounds for disagreement about what constitutes an affair relate to questions about whether all instances of extramarital sex constitute extramarital affairs, and whether the extramarital relationship must be kept secret.

SEXUALITY

Glass and Wright (1992) take issue with a tradition, reflected in the literature on extramarital affairs, of adopting the male bias by emphasizing sexual intercourse as the criterion that defines extramarital behavior. They draw a distinction between extramarital sex (EMS) and extramarital emotional involvement (EMI) and, by doing so, differentiate types of extramarital relationships based on whether they include emotional intimacy.

These two categories—extramarital sexual behavior and extramarital emotional involvement—entail some blurring at the boundaries. Yet the distinction is an important one to make, since, at the extremes, these two types of relationships have little in common other than the fact that both involve going outside the marriage for some form of satisfaction.

Shirley Glass (Glass and Marano 1998), a leading researcher in the area of extramarital affairs, proposes that a relationship must satisfy three criteria to be considered a full-fledged affair: the partners must be emotionally intimate, there must be sexual chemistry, and the wife must be kept in the dark about the affair's existence for as long as possible.

Differentiating extramarital sex from extramarital emotional involvement entails very real consequences. Many men, but fewer women, would be disinclined to think of a "just for sex" arrangement with a member of the opposite sex as an affair, so long as the relationship does not also include either emotional intimacy or attachment. For the men in Morton Hunt's (1969) survey, "infidelity means caring for another woman, seeing a lot of her, and spending part of the family income on her" (p. 9). Repeated visits to the same prostitute, or trysts with "nonprofessionals" that are wholly sexual, involving no emotional intimacy whatsoever, are not considered affairs by many men. Some men have casual, meaningless sexual encounters with a woman. Between such encounters, the man has no contact with the woman, and she occupies no space in his mind. Such partners are sometimes referred to in the vernacular as "fuck buddies." Though most men would not be inclined to dignify such encounters by calling them affairs, women tend to think otherwise. Because women are much less likely than men to have affairs that do not involve emotional intimacy (Thompson 1983), they tend to be distrusting of their husband's contentions that their "strictly sexual" extramarital activities truly lack a dimension of intimacy and emotional attachment. Glass and Wright (1992) note, "When women discover their husband's sexual involvement with another woman, they automatically assume that their husbands have fallen out of love with them and in love with the extra-marital sexual partner because that would be [the wife's] own justification for [such] involvement" (p. 383). Such thinking, Glass notes, places an undue burden on women by leading them to hold themselves responsible for their husband's having strayed (Glass and Marano 1998).

Let us consider the example of a husband who meets a woman friend for coffee on a routine basis. Their conversations are intimate insofar as the man shares his personal feelings on different issues with his friend. Now, suppose these two happen to share a mutual sexual attraction. Even though their rendezvous takes place at a coffee house rather than a motel, and goes no further than infusing the couple's interactions with sexuality, the relationship is verging on becoming, or, in Glass's thinking, has already become, an extramarital affair, so long as the other two conditions of secrecy and intimacy are met. Though many would take issue with such reasoning, Glass believes that one need not consummate a sexually charged relationship for that relationship to be an extramarital affair. The couple may have never even held hands, yet each knows there is a force that is drawing them together. This brings us to a consideration of whether there is ample justification for Glass's position.

In spite of the clear dangers of continuing to meet under such circumstances, the couple cannot resist the force that draws them together. But while they give in to the temptation to meet, they resist taking things further, and this mutual task of resisting sexual temptation serves to further bind the couple together. The situation is an unstable one since sexual attraction and fantasy keep alive the possibility that someday something might happen. Whether or not the couple goes on to live out the relationship's sexual potential, the two are clearly playing with fire. If this is not an extramarital affair, it is awfully close to being one! In fact, in Hollander's (1976) study, fully 25 percent of the single women she studied who had had affairs with married men failed to sexually consummate, or had barely sexually consummated, their relationships via sexual intercourse even though the relationship had gone on for significant periods of time.

Now, let us consider a different scenario. A man and woman act out their attraction for one another by openly flirting whenever they meet. Such flirting can be relatively harmless depending on the circumstances, and, in the absence of secrecy or emotional intimacy, such behavior cannot be confused with an extramarital affair.

SECRECY

Though not all would agree, there are good reasons to include secrecy as one of the defining features of an extramarital affair. However, knowledge of the affair need not be kept a complete secret. It is only the wife who must be kept in the dark about her husband's extramarital sexual encounters, for were she to discover that his interests lie elsewhere, the entire dynamic of the affair and the marriage would change. Extramarital sexual relations that are conducted with the wife's knowledge and consent have been described as "open marriages" rather than as affairs.

Needing to keep an affair secret is necessitated, in part, by the reaction the husband anticipates his wife would have were she to learn about it. Wishing to avoid the wife's hurt and rage, and an awareness that the wife's knowledge of the affair would make her hypervigilantly suspicious of her husband's behavior, thus making a continued pursuit of the affair nearly impossible, are the pragmatic reasons for keeping knowledge of the affair from her. Hunt (1974) writes that this "very great emphasis on secrecy [is] based on the clear recognition that such extra-marital acts will be *perceived* by the spouse as disloyalty, partial abandonment, and a repudiation of marital love" (p. 270, emphasis added). But these reasons alone cannot completely account for the need to keep an affair secret. There are additional benefits.

In the single woman–married man syndrome, secrecy is as much a goal of the affair as it is a necessary procedure to maintain calm on the home front. Secrecy is compelling for three reasons. First, needing to keep an affair secret lends danger to the enterprise. An affair is made all the more thrilling by virtue of its forbiddenness, a forbiddenness that requires that the affair be kept from the wife's sight. Second, men sometimes unconsciously pursue affairs to find someone with whom they can try out a different persona than the one they employ in the marriage. If a husband's role vis-à-vis his wife has become static, stale, and stultifying, he may feel the need to look elsewhere for rejuvenation. An affair gives a man the chance to experiment with another way of being, and secrecy helps the man compartmentalize ways of being. When affairs represent the manifestation of a split between different facets of the man's personality, secrecy is the ingredient that facilitates the actualization of such a split. Third, in marriages where the wife is experienced by her husband as so domineering or controlling that she begins to feel like a fun-squelching parent, secrecy becomes an important way of hiding the passive-aggressive acting out of the husband's rebellious or revengeful impulses toward his wife. By having an affair, the man can thumb his nose behind the wife's back without her being any the wiser.

Most marriages tolerate the existence of a certain degree of personal privacy, so long as what is kept private is of no great consequence to the marriage. However, were a husband to fail to mention so significant a ritual as his daily meetings with a member of the opposite sex, a meeting that has as its sole purpose the furtherance of a close personal bond, such an omission is likely to be considered a deception and a betrayal by the wife. Being emotionally intimate with someone other than one's wife, even if the relationship is devoid of sexual tension, is a potential threat to the marriage, especially when it results in the husband's confiding in another woman about significant matters that he has failed to share with his wife, doubly so if the main topic is the man's dissatisfaction with his marriage.

Under such circumstances, the man might defend his decision to keep these meetings to himself lest his wife misinterpret the meetings, which, in turn, would cause her to blow up. But no matter how the man attempts to justify his actions, it is still an omission that ultimately erodes whatever intimacy and trust he has established with his wife. Even if these meetings are truly platonic, a man who avoids a confrontation with his wife by reasoning what she doesn't know can't hurt her may have, by so doing, limited the closeness he might otherwise have with his wife.

INTIMACY

Mr. R., a man in his mid-fifties, comes for psychiatric consultation at the behest of his wife. She has become quite concerned and upset about the amount of time he has been spending in front of his computer monitor in search of Web sites that offer an opportunity to engage in virtual cybersex. As far as the wife is concerned, her husband's activities constitute infidelity and are tantamount to his having an affair. Mr. R. disagrees. He thinks that what he is doing is no different from a husband who masturbates looking at girlie magazines.

For hours each week, Mr. R. seeks out Web sites that visually connect a number of participants, each of whom has a camera attached to his or her computer. The participants communicate with each other and engage in sexual acts with themselves or with a partner aimed at satisfying their own sexual needs (primarily exhibitionism), and arousing and satisfying the sexual needs of the others (primarily voyeurism). Mr. R. spends so much time at his computer that he is left emotionally and sexually sapped by these marathons. As a result, he is no longer able to engage his wife to the degree he once had. The fact that the sex Mr. R. has been having involves actual people, not just pinups, and the fact that he dedicates so much time and energy to this hobby make it something more than just idle bathroom masturbation. But does it constitute an affair, as Mrs. R. claims?

Is the essence of an affair the fact that one goes outside the marriage in search of satisfactions that one ought to find in the marriage? Or is the essence of an affair the fact that energy that ought to be invested in the marriage is invested elsewhere? The toll that Mr. R.'s extramarital sexual activities have taken on his marriage is, in Mrs. R.'s opinion, comparable to her husband carrying on with another woman. As a result, she has become exasperated, and the marriage appears to be in jeopardy. But just because extramarital sexual activity has the same detrimental effect on a marriage as would an extramarital affair does not make the two synonymous.

Certainly, Mr. R's. activities cannot have satisfied his needs for intimacy. Whatever attachment he feels to his pursuit of sexual satisfaction via the Internet, this attachment represents an addiction rather than a genuine human connection. In fact, Mr. R.'s sexual activities seem fetishistic, since he is not relating to a whole object, but only to the visual images (part objects) of people. No matter how lifelike these sexual acts may be, they remain *virtual* experiences in every sense of the word, even though they create a powerful illusion that may blur the distinction between reality and fantasy in many people's minds.

This is not to say that men cannot conduct extramarital affairs via the Internet that go on to become extramarital emotional involvements. Being in the physical presence of another is no longer required for one to have an affair. Every day, men and women are logging on and conducting secret, emotionally intimate, and sexually charged affairs with people they have come to know via the Internet. They may not even know what the other person looks like, though commonly pictures do get exchanged. The couple may engage in sexual interplay via the keyboard and screen. They may go on to talk by phone, may meet, and may even wed.

WHAT IS KNOWN ABOUT EXTRAMARITAL AFFAIRS

The term *extramarital affair* covers a wide variety of relations: heterosexual pairings, such as married men with married women, single men with married women, and single women with married men; and homosexual pairings, such as married men with other married men, married men with single men, married women with other married women, and married women with single women. Affairs between single women and married men constitute a subtype of extramarital affair; the single woman–married man syndrome is a subset of the subtype.

Incidence

Thompson (1983) reviewed twelve surveys that focus on extramarital sex, beginning with the seminal work of Kinsey and colleagues (1948, 1953), and concluded that between 20 and 50 percent of men will have at least one extramarital affair during the course of their lifetime. More recent surveys of the literature, conducted by Laumann and colleagues (1994) and Wiederman (1997), found that about one-fourth of married men had engaged in extramarital affairs. At any given point in time, between 2 and 4 percent of men are pursuing extramarital affairs (Billy and colleagues 1993, Smith 1991).

Many of these studies suffer from methodologic problems that make it hard to accurately estimate the number of married men who have affairs. To begin with, determining the lifetime incidence of extramarital affairs is difficult if one is primarily studying men who are in the prime of their sexual lives. When Kinsey and colleagues (1948, 1953) lumped men by age into incremental five-year age groups, they found that about a third of married men in each of five age groups had, at some point, been involved in an extramarital affair. In an effort to estimate the cumulative lifetime occurrence of such affairs, Kinsey and colleagues (1953) extrapolated their data and came up with a projection that about half of all married men had intercourse with women other than their wives at some time during their marriage.

Other methodologic problems include how interviews are conducted. For instance, in the Laumann and colleagues (1994) study, about one-fifth of the respondents were interviewed with either a child, spouse, or other person in the room, making it less likely that those respondents would be as candid as those afforded greater privacy. Trust also limits what one is willing to disclose to a stranger about one's private life. In a study of patients engaged in intensive psychotherapy, Greene and colleagues (1974) found that while only 30 percent of patients early in the course of treatment admitted to having been unfaithful to their wives, another 30 percent revealed secret extramarital affairs later in the course of treatment, presumably as a result of their having established greater trust in the therapist.

Why Do Men Have Affairs?

Conventional wisdom suggests that a man's tendency to look outside marriage for sexual satisfaction is a direct function of his dissatisfaction with his wife as a sexual partner. This conclusion is much more likely to be reached by women than by men (Kinsey et al. 1953, Petersen 1983). One of the surprising findings that emerges when one reviews the extramarital literature is that some men who claim to be quite happy with their wives and their marriages on all counts nevertheless pursue opportunities to have sex with women other than their wives. In Whitehurst's (1969) study, 79 percent of men who had pursued extramarital affairs, yet considered their marriages "total" or "vital," attributed their extramarital behavior to the strength of their sexual drive. They admit to being "sexually curious" even though they report sex with their wives as relatively satisfactory. This point is emphasized by Glass (Glass and Marano 1998), who has concluded, after conducting years of research in the area, that "there are many men who do love their partners, who enjoy good sex at home, who nevertheless never turn down an opportunity for extramarital sex. In fact, 56 percent of the men I sampled who had extramarital intercourse said that their marriages were happy" (p. 36). When an extramarital affair is represented as being about the man's dissatisfaction with marriage, there are three main factors that account for this dissatisfaction: sexual boredom; role stagnation; and persistent, though often unexpressed, anger and resentment.

These three reasons may not represent isolated, unrelated factors. Stagnant roles may lead either to a failure to be able to openly address one's resentments or to sexual boredom. Resentments that arise outside of one's sexual relations may impact negatively on the partners' ability to enjoy sex with one another. A primary difficulty in getting one's sexual needs met may lead a husband to harbor long-term resentments.

Sexual Boredom

Over the course of time, sexual relations between a husband and wife inevitably become less exciting. Humphrey (1982) states, "Perhaps one of the greatest enemies of sexual monogamy is monotony. No matter how innovative and sensitive marital partners are, doing the same thing (even if it is sexual intercourse) with the same person in the same settings and often in the same way can become dull" (pp. 586–587).

Nothing can compete with the refreshing newness and stimulating unpredictability offered by sexual encounters with a person other than one's spouse. Stoller (1979) confirms that novelty is an important ingredient in sexual excitement. He writes of how unpredictability introduces the illusion of risk, and, conversely, unvarying predictability begets boredom. Once the mystery is gone, and a degree of disillusionment has set in, sex is never the same. Sometimes sex becomes a chore on account of its becoming mechanical, predictable, boring, and stagnant.

Since one can assume that few marriages are spared the fate of diminished sexual intensity, one would think that this factor alone could not explain why some men look outside their marriage for added sexual satisfaction while other men do not. Could the intensity of a man's sexual urge be enough to explain why some men settle for lesser amounts of sexual excitement while others feel a need to go looking for more? While many men contend that this is precisely the case, one must not confuse the conscious reasons men offer to explain their extracurricular activities with actual causes of extramarital behavior (Humphrey 1982). Pittman (1989) notes that when people were asked to give reasons for why they had affairs "the initial answer was likely to be shallow and naive" (p. 127). Greene and colleagues (1974) echo this point of view: "Infidelity is the kind of behavior which demands a reason, whether it is an accurate one or not. Hence, the conscious reasons for infidelity are often rationalizations meant to defend against the revelation of deep conflictual material. We expect rationalizations and excuses because infidelity is often an acting-out defense against remembering and verbalizing intrapsychic material from the past" (p. 91). Kernberg (1980) observes, "If the couple's presenting complaint is sexual indifference, it is helpful to remember that boredom is the most immediate manifestation of lack of contact with deeper emotional and sexual needs" (p. 107). Maykovich (1976) and Whitehurst (1969) suggest that an additional factor is needed, that of personal alienation (a sense of isolation and powerlessness), in order for marital or coital dissatisfaction to lead a man to have an extramarital affair.

Role Stagnation

Apart from sexual stagnation, the marital couple may fall into routine, stereotypic ways of interacting with one another. Some couples find it hard, if not impossible, to break free of such confining roles and, as a result, come to consider marriage a prison. What is it that makes it hard for couples to break out of such pathologic role fixations that lead to boredom and indifference in marital relationships? Kernberg's (1991) answer lies in the couple's denial of some of the more intense affects generated in the relationship, affects that underscore the ambivalent aspects of the marital relationship: "What destroys passionate attachment and may appear to be a sense of imprisonment and 'sexual boredom' is actually the activation of aggression, which threatens the delicate equilibrium between sadomasochism and love in a couple's sexual and emotional relationship" (p. 50). By defending against the emergence of aggression, the couple suffers "a loss in the capacity for real depth and intimacy in the couple's relationship as the price exacted for the protection that is provided against aggression" (Kernberg 1980, p. 102).

Adherence to rigid rules or an inability to confront issues head-on inhibits the couple from introducing novel behaviors into the relationship. Such relations appear brittle on account of the unconscious belief that the relationship would not survive any alteration in the way the partners relate to one another. Under such conditions, husbands may grow increasingly resentful, thus priming themselves for an extramarital encounter. One-third of the studies that were reviewed by Glass and Wright (1992) suggested that boredom was an often-stated reason for extramarital affairs.

Glass (Glass and Marano 1998) states,

Affairs are often a chance for people to try out new behaviors, to dress in a different costume, to stretch and grow and assume a different role. In a long term relationship, we often get frozen in our roles. When young couples begin at one level of success and go on to many achievements, the new person [the one with whom one is having an affair] sees them as they've become, while the old person sees them as they were. [In affairs] people seem to take on a different persona, and one of the things they liked best about being in that relationship was the person they had become. The man who wasn't sensitive or expressive is now in a relationship where he is expressing his feelings and is supportive. [p. 42]

Pittman (1989) writes that affairs are often not about a man's having found someone who is better than his wife. Instead, they are often a man's way of finding someone who is somewhat different from his wife. "More often people are not seeking an alternative to their marriage, but a supplement to it. They just want a friend for whatever they aren't getting at home" (p. 43). Pittman concludes that affairs "were thus three times more likely to be the pursuit of a buddy than the pursuit of a better orgasm" (p. 122). Rather than being about sexual boredom, often affairs serve as a vehicle for a man to bring out a hidden aspect of himself that he seems unable or unwilling to bring out in his marriage.

Persistent, Unexpressed Resentments

A man sometimes emotionally flees marriage via an extramarital affair because he has grown angry with his spouse and has begun to harbor resentments toward her. If the husband is unable to deal directly with such anger and resentment, it may get expressed in the passive-aggressive act of turning to another woman. Half of the studies reviewed by Glass and Wright (1992) identified revenge, rebellion, and hostility as significant reasons given for why married men have affairs. The ability to face the depth of ambivalence one feels toward one's mate is a function of that individual's ability to experience mature love.

TYPES OF EXTRAMARITAL AFFAIRS

One of the problems in reviewing the literature on extramarital relations is that the studies typically lump together all forms of extramarital relations (Glass and Wright 1992). There are clear differences between types of affairs. One difference is how soon after marriage the first affair begins. Pittman (1989) says that men who were unfaithful early in the course of their marriage ended up having multiple extramarital relationships. The only thing capable of altering this pattern was the intervention of "dire and unusual circumstances." By comparison, about a third of men in Pittman's study began affairs about a decade after they were married. These men, Pittman notes, "treated their marriages with respect and tenacity, and they then did the same with their affairs, usually the first and only sex partner they had had outside the marriage" (p. 124). J. Ross (1996) echoes Pittman's findings when he describes cases in which men had married early and had developed, over the course of time, a sense that they needed to seek what they felt they had missed out on by virtue of their having married young.

Another basis on which affairs can be differentiated is whether or not the man has any regard for who the woman is as a person. Romantic affairs are those that are emotionally involving above and beyond the physical attraction the couple shares. Many men and women reserve the term *affair* for those extramarital sexual relationships that involve "depth of feeling" (Hunt 1969, p. 9). By contrast, extramarital sexual encounters conducted by men who have no interest in, or patience for, who the woman is as a person, or for what she wants from the relationship, are referred to as "philanderings."

An extramarital emotional involvement, as is seen in the single woman–married man syndrome, is a romantic affair that stands in contrast to philandering. Romantic affairs take place over the course of time. They are motivated by the man's need for rejuvenation and for the liberating experience of transcendency. Such affairs can be almost spiritual in their dimensions, and can have a dramatic effect on the participants' senses of self. The affair is less about sex than about the emotional excitement that is generated. The man's focus may be on selflessly pleasing the woman, something no self-respecting philanderer would ever be caught doing. The man caught up in a romantic affair is emotionally involved with the person he takes his beloved to be. By contrast, philandering results in brief sexual encounters. It is fear based and is all about power and control, safety and triumph. The philanderer is sexually, rather than spiritually, obsessed. He is only interested in pleasing himself, and he makes no pretense about trying to figure out who the woman beneath the skin might be.

Naturally, as is the case whenever so clear a distinction is drawn, the line between romantic affairs and philanderings becomes blurred under certain circumstances. Sometimes, in the course of his philanderings, a man becomes more emotionally involved than he had ever anticipated becoming. Rather than remaining comfortably uninvolved, he finds himself caring more for a particular woman than he had for any other woman. At this juncture, the philanderer finds himself in over his head. The very thing he had spent his energy trying to avoid has come to pass. This is one route by which a man may land in a romantic extramarital affair. The other route is taken by men who have been faithful to their wives over the course of years, and then find themselves uncharacteristically involved with another woman. The philanderer-turned-romantic was illustrated in Chapter 3 by the case of Irv Schoenfeld; the happily married man who strays was illustrated in the same chapter by the case of Edwin Gottesman.

Romantic Affairs

Nothing is more deadly to a romantic than marriage. When the thrill has gone and the man awakens to the cold reality that is his wife, he may begin to wonder: "Is that all there is?" Such romantics start to feel that something is terribly amiss. Disillusionment, the inevitable hard pill each married person must swallow, does not go down easily for romantics. The problem, as Pittman (1989) puts it, is that "romance seduces people into expecting too much" (p. 189).

Men may become dissatisfied with their marriages for reasons that have little to do with the unsatisfactoriness of their wives as mates. For certain individuals, chiefly those suffering from narcissistic-spectrum pathologies, mature love cannot hold a candle to romantic love—the ecstatic excitement that often results from romantically charged extramarital affairs. This is particularly true of men in the single woman–married man syndrome.

There is a place for romance in every individual's life. In fact, it is romance that typically catapults a marriage into orbit. Pittman (1989) argues that couples who can enjoy intense romance while it burns hottest, and yet can accept, as inevitable though regrettable, the years that follow where romance is but a memory, are likeliest to consider themselves happy or content with marriage. For Pittman, true love is what is left "after the romance is cool ash and memory" (p. 189). In Kernberg's (1974b) terms, such patients cannot only fall in love, they can go on to achieve "mature love." Pittman (1989) figures that it is the romantic beginnings that lend the marriage its sense of specialness. "A marriage that began as a great love has a momentum and a magic that less inspired matches lack. Romance doesn't have to be revived to bring back the sense of specialness; the romance can merely be recalled" (p. 188).

Pittman (1989) elaborates:

> Mild romantics can drift along peacefully in a pleasant marriage, missing the romance and not knowing quite how to go about getting any. Their marriage is placid and workable, with no crazy excitement but all the comfortable love and unquestioned commitment of longstanding marriage. Such romantics may have no real complaints, but may have a vague sense of something missing. They may be reasonably happy, but vulnerable. [p. 193]

Romantics such as these are at risk for having extramarital affairs, since many of their narcissistic needs go unsatisfied in the context of a long-term marriage. A study by Buss and Shackelford (1997) shows the existence of a positive correlation between narcissistic personality traits and the inclination to have extramarital affairs. Husbands who suffer from narcissistic vulnerability are much more likely to end up feeling hurt or rejected by their spouses and, as a result, are more likely to look to another woman to help replenish their damaged "ego" (Humphrey 1982).

Love relations based primarily on the satisfaction of narcissistic needs prove to be unusually intense, thus convincing the lovers that what they are experiencing is, in fact, true love. Such relationships may prove so intense as to lead the lovers to idealize the relationship and to imagine that what they share is unparalleled in the history of mankind. This was precisely what Edwin Gottesman, presented in Chapter 3, described experiencing.

Lovers engaged in such a relationship figure that what they are experiencing must be true love. What other name would one give to such an intense emotion as this? Isn't this the very thing of which poets speak? To this, cynics may ask, Isn't that how the addict loves his addiction?

If an affair acts to bolster one's sense of oneself, the individual is likely to completely fall apart at the prospect of losing such a self-sustaining relationship. In the course of mourning the loss of the relationship, the lovelorn often complain of how they have lost a piece of themselves in the process. And, given the self-object functions (Kohut 1971) that the other had served, the complaint is not that far from the truth. For individuals who bring such narcissistic needs to relationships, being in a relationship is not an option, it is an absolute emotional necessity. Accordingly, they hold onto the relationship for dear life.

Philandering

Philanderers have brief sexual encounters that are all about sex and have nothing to do with intimacy or romance. Some regard philandering as a testament to the strength of the man's sexual drive, a drive that cannot tolerate the constraints of monogamy and can only be satisfied through encounters with multiple sexual partners. Such reasoning overlooks a host of other factors, beyond the pleasure principle, that co-determine such behavior. Philandering is no more about sexual drive and impulsivity than is rape. Both are primarily about exerting power and control over women. To think otherwise ignores the multi-determined nature of such complex behaviors and the narcissistic pathology that underlies the philandering adaptation to object relations.

Philanderers fear emotional involvement with women because they believe it exposes them to the risk of being teased ("made" to want greater emotional involvement only to be rejected in the end) and the risk of becoming utterly submissive in the process. Such fears lead men to employ counterphobic defenses in their dealings with women. By repeatedly exposing themselves to the feared prospect of emotional entanglement, such men reassure themselves that there is nothing to fear. Each time the philanderer escapes a sexual encounter unscathed, every time he demonstrates himself capable of becoming sexually involved without becoming emotionally involved, he experiences exhilaration in place of dread. Stealing cheese from the mousetrap without getting caught becomes sport for these men. Such men remind one of the child's joke about the man who, approaching a pile of what appears to be dog excrement, attempts to confirm his suspicions: first he scoops up some on his finger and takes a closer look. "Yeah, it looks like dog shit!" Then, he smells it. "Yeah, it sure smells like dog shit!" Then, he sticks some in his mouth. "Yeah, it tastes like dog shit. . . . Phew, I'm glad I didn't step in it." Philanderers do everything but step in what they consider "shit"—the shackles of an emotional relationship that so mars the beauty of the sexual act.

Philanderers may go beyond merely dreading women. They may hate women and may treat them in hostile and cruel ways. Kernberg (1974a) notes, "One finds envy and hatred [toward women] in many male patients" (p. 494). Out of fear or hatred of women, men may depersonalize them by failing to recognize the difference between one woman and another apart from the woman's looks. They accordingly see women as interchangeable. They take note of the ways in which the women's bodies differ but have no regard for who they are as human beings.

Let us look at the case of a classic philanderer, whom we shall refer to as Mr. P., who is presented in Pittman's (1989) book *Private Lies: Infidelity and the Betrayal of Intimacy*. During the course of his 20-year marriage, Mr. P. had, on average, one extramarital encounter per week. He claimed that his wife was "too stupid" to have ever suspected. Mr. P. was a self-made man who had become wealthy enough to do "anything his heart desires," which mostly involved, in his words, "chasing pussy." This illustrates Kernberg's point that philanderers are notorious for being fetishistically focused on the body's surface (breasts, buttocks, vaginas, etc.) rather than on the woman as a whole person. For the philanderer, women *are* breasts, women *are* buttocks, and so on.

Ever since making the mistake of liking one of the women he had pursued early in his "career," Mr. P. had made it a rule to never see the same woman more than twice. His preferred sexual encounter was the "quickie." Pittman (1989) quotes one of Mr. P.'s jokes that sums up his attitude about relationships with women. Q: "What is a romantic?" A: "A romantic is a man who suffers from the delusion that one woman is different from another."

Over the course of time, Mr. P. came to realize that getting a women to the point of demonstrating her willingness to have sex with him was actually more important to him than the ultimate sexual act. This realization makes clear the nature of Mr. P.'s motivation: to derive narcissistic gratification from having been proven sexually desirable rather than the libidinal discharge of pent-up sexual tensions. Conquest came in the form of seducing a woman into caring more about him than he did about her. Having disarmed a woman in this way disabled her from being in a position to narcissistically injure him. He had been Delilah and she Samson in this gender-reversing drama. Such reversals form the very nature of triumph (Stoller 1979).

Philandering is all about one's power over another. The philanderer works hard to avoid any relationship that looks permanent or controlling. In his marriage, he exerts undue control over his mate. "A philanderer's marriage is guerrilla warfare. His wife is the enemy to be escaped or subdued. He will bully, charm her, disorient her, whatever it takes to keep her from understanding him and getting him under her control" (Pittman 1989, p. 179).

Pittman (1989) suggests that what drives philandering behavior is the philanderer's fear of women. Philandering is an attempt to exert sexual domination over women in order to "keep women and their dangerous sexuality under male control. [Philanderers believe that] the greatest loss of status would be to come under the control of a woman. Escape from female control is an affirmation of masculinity. Such men recoil from the idea that a man would give a woman enough control over him to determine such personal matters as whom he has sex with. Philanderers can't believe in monogamy" (p. 157).

By making it appear as if it is the woman who is left wanting, the woman who is forced, by virtue of her emotional needs, to submit to the man's whims, he can reassure himself that he is in no danger. Kernberg (1974a) states that promiscuous patients experience a desperate need to escape involvement that runs counter to their desperate search for love. Once the woman has been conquered, once she has been made to give up what she has been withholding, the mysterious and enviable "it" that she alone possesses, the man loses interest and moves on. Her danger as a woman, capable of frustrating the man's needs and arousing his envy, has been defused. The man need no longer fear her. In summary, by devaluing female sexuality, by denying his need for a particular woman's love, and by relating to women as part objects, the narcissistic male finds himself incapable of maintaining a deep emotional and sexual involvement with women.

SUMMARY

Many presume that if a man is having an affair it is because he is sexually starved as the result of a discrepancy between his sexual appetite and that of his wife. This was comically captured in Woody Allen's movie *Annie Hall*. The image on the movie screen is vertically split: Woody Allen is lying on his analyst's couch and his girlfriend, played by Diane Keaton, is lying on her analyst's couch. Their respective analysts ask each how often the two are having sex. He answers, "Never"; she answers, "Always." The two analysts then ask each to clarify precisely how often that is, to which we hear a simultaneous answer: "Three times a week."

Men go outside of their marriage for sexual gratification for many reasons other than wanting sex more often than do their wives: the men have grown too accustomed to having sex with their wives and are sexually bored, or they were young and inexperienced when they married and regret having forgone the opportunity to experience other women.

Men are also driven to have affairs for nonsexual reasons. Romantic-type affairs fill a man's need to find another woman with whom he can be another way than the way he has been with his wife. Affairs also serve as an "ego boost." Some men feel unconsciously constrained by the marriage from experiencing and expressing some aspects of themselves. Some men cannot be passionately sexual with the mother of their children, toward whom they feel deep and tender affection. Some men fear it is not safe to have too many of their needs met by just one woman, be they sexual needs, the need for self-expression, or the need for intimacy and attachment. Romantic-type affairs also provide narcissistic gratification; the man is so desired by the woman that she is willing to continue to pursue him despite the chronic frustration she may suffer as a result, as is seen in the single woman–married man syndrome. Such an experience is likely to make an aging married man, like Chapter 3's Edwin Gottesman, feel young again. Most extramarital affairs of the single woman–married man syndrome are romantic affairs pursued for these reasons.

Finally, there are the extramarital sexual encounters of philanderers that are commonly referred to as affairs but that would not satisfy the strict definition presented at the beginning of this chapter. Such men contend that their behavior is nothing more than their way of satisfying a robust manly sexual urge. But a deeper consideration of such behavior reveals just how scared and counterphobic such men are. Having multiple affairs with dozens of different women helps men reassure themselves that they are not vulnerable to women, and therefore need not fear that they would ever be seduced by, or have to submit to, the charms of a woman.

The next chapter addresses men's dread of women and men's fear of submission to a woman rather than allowing themselves to surrender in her presence and along with her.

III

PERSPECTIVES ON GENDER, TREATMENT, AND LOVE

7

The Emerging Man as Manifested in Heterosexual Relationships

Love may transform me to an oyster.
William Shakespeare, *Much Ado About Nothing*, II, iii, 24

Having presented a number of illustrative examples of the single woman–married man syndrome, and having established its relationship to extramarital affairs in general, we now turn our attention to the psychological dynamics and intersubjective conditions that contribute to the development of this syndrome. This chapter considers the psychodynamics of the married man, and Chapter 8 discusses the psychodynamics of the single woman.

This chapter discusses several issues: why husbands blame their wives' shrew-like behavior for driving them into the arms of other women; the role a husband's passive-aggressive, pseudosubmissive behavior plays (1) in incurring his wife's shrew-like wrath and (2) in keeping certain of his selfish needs and wishes under wraps, thus protecting his image as a "nice guy"; the ways in which men unconsciously hide aspects of themselves, which then primes them to have extramarital affairs that provide a venue for the full expression of this latent side of their personalities; the role that a man's indecisiveness, born of ambivalence, plays in keeping his motives, thoughts, and feelings hidden from himself and others; and the developmental basis of men's unique vulnerabilities to women, which leads them to dread women.

BLAMING THE WIFE

The simplest explanations offered to account for a man's tendency to look outside the marriage are also the most misleading. The wife is blamed for being inadequate as a mate. She does not "put out" sexually, is unstable, or is an emotionally withholding shrew who stifles her husband's ability to "be all that he can be" by placing subtle restraints on the expression of his personality. Often, the man would have us believe that his wife's failings completely account for, and justify, his having strayed. Who can blame the guy for wanting a bit more of what every husband ought to have by virtue of being married?

While many extramarital sexual encounters may be the result of a man's not feeling satisfied with his sexual life at home, this is not, by definition, a typical contributing factor to the genesis of the single woman–married man syndrome. Therefore we will dispense with discussing this factor and proceed to discuss the latter two factors.

The "Saint" Who Stays with His Emotionally Unstable Wife

Playing the part of the long-suffering husband who is staying with his wife for her sake, not his, is one condition likely to prime a man to have an affair. Take, for example, the case of Simon and Ella described by Cato (1996). Ella, who had always thought that she would make the "perfect wife" (p. 96), married Simon, a collegiate football player, who envisioned himself as "the family patriarch, providing for the family and playing football with his sons" (p. 96). But things did not turn out as the couple had planned. Ella ended up giving birth to two daughters, both of whom proved disappointments for Simon. The elder was born deaf, and Simon would have little to do with her, treating her as if she were "damaged goods" (p. 96). Ella felt he held her responsible for their daughter's imperfections. Simon hoped their second child would be a son, but instead Ella gave birth to a "gangly and skinny" (p. 97) tomboy.

Whether Ella felt guilty for not having been the perfect wife because she had failed to provide her husband with perfect children or was made to feel guilty by her husband's blaming attitude toward her is, in the final analysis, academic. Most likely, both factors contributed to the eventual outcome. Even if Simon had played no role in causing her guilt, his inability to help lift that burden off Ella's shoulders made him an accomplice in her self-blaming attitude.

In the end, the disappointment and guilt this couple suffered caused Simon to withdraw from Ella, who, in response, became seriously depressed, resulting in her being referred for group therapy. It was not until the other patients in the group pieced together the facts she had shared with them, and confronted her with their strong suspicion that her husband was having an affair, that Ella was able to consider such a possibility.

When Ella confronted her husband's boss with her suspicion that Simon was having an affair with someone at work, the boss looked at her as if she were "some sort of lunatic" (p. 100). When Ella confronted him with what she perceived his attitude to be, the boss admitted that Simon had told everyone that his wife was emotionally disturbed and that he only stayed with her out of fear that, were he to leave, she would commit suicide. Simon was evidently considered a saint for having endured her as he had. The boss then went on to confirm her worst fears about her husband's extramarital activity.

If Simon had, in fact, considered his wife seriously emotionally disturbed for having become depressed for "no good reason"

(p. 100), he may well have conveyed this belief to Ella, thus furthering Ella's tendency to question whether she was a reasonably rational person. In turn, this may have contributed to her being unable to piece together the facts until she was helped to do so by the members in her group therapy.

The Blaming of the Shrew

Sometimes men consider extramarital affairs as a way to escape the hold of an overly aggressive, controlling, domineering wife, who not only "forces" the man to submit to her ways but affords him little space within which to elaborate the full range of his personality. This was precisely how Mr. M., the 40-year-old architect discussed in Chapter 5, saw his situation. He felt he had become a slave to his wife's needs. His happiness hinged on making her happy. But, by Mr. M.'s estimation, she took advantage of his wish to please by remaining dissatisfied and critical of him. For a time, his wife's chronic displeasure stimulated Mr. M. to try even harder. But he became increasingly aware of how his wife's sour attitude robbed him of an opportunity to experience himself as a successful husband. Eventually, he grew tired of forever trying to please her, and the two began to snipe at one another. Being married to his wife ultimately contributed to Mr. M.'s feeling worse about himself as a person. So it was not altogether surprising that he began an affair with Terri, the woman who helped him restore his positive sense of goodness and with whom he finally felt free to be himself.

It is easy to blame Mr. M.'s wife if one accepts his account of the marital relationship. But any seasoned therapist is likely to wonder about a host of different issues to which Mr. M. may have been blind, issues that would point to his own culpability in the ultimate deterioration of the marriage. Even though Mr. M. portrayed himself as selflessly wanting nothing more than for his wife to be happy, it appears as if he was oblivious to how unsatisfying it could potentially be for a wife to be married to so seemingly selfless a man. Furthermore, while Mr. M. thought he knew what it took to please his wife, it is questionable whether his hunches were on the mark. Furthermore, Mr. M. shares the responsibility for not having dared to express more of himself in the marriage. Yes, he may have risked incurring his wife's wrath by doing so, but he had shown cowardice by taking his wares elsewhere.

Mr. M. ultimately came to see his wife as characterologically incapable of being happy. In his opinion, it would be no different if she were married to another man. By thinking of her in this way, he could deny the intersubjective aspects of their relationship, how his way of interacting with her brought out certain facets of her personality that may not have been elicited by a different man.

Another case that lends itself to such one-dimensional thinking is the case of Irv Schoenfeld (Ross 1996), presented in Chapter 3). It was Ross's initial impression that Irv's affairs were in reaction to his wife's "compulsion to deprive him of any narcissistic satisfaction" (p. 118). In other words, it was another case of a reasonable man and his shrew wife. Ross notes that this interpretation hinges on a perception of the wife as "a phallic, controlling, castrating mother from whom the patient must escape for his own good" (p. 128). This, of course, is just what some husbands believe and would have others believe. But after having worked with this patient psychoanalytically over the course of several years, Ross came up with a different understanding of the patient's perception of his wife. It was Ross's ultimate understanding that Irv's wife had become the recipient of the projection of the patient's primitive superego functioning onto her, which led him to experience her as if she were a cold, demanding, no-nonsense figure who wanted nothing more than to deprive him of any satisfactions he desired. Ross concludes that "by transforming his wife into a father figure who demands duty and performance and imposes her notions and values on his way of thinking" (p. 127), the husband creates a primitive ego ideal that he tries to live up to, yet has no hope of ever succeeding in doing.

This illustrates a point Kernberg (1977) makes with regard to the development of a mature superego as one of the prerequisites of an adult's ability to experience mature love. As Kernberg sees it, the capacity to love maturely is the result of a developmental process whereby boys evolve from experiencing their father as a "primitive, controlling, sadistic male, who represents the fantasied jealous and restrictive father of the early oedipal period" (p. 91) to identifying with the "'generous' father who no longer operates by means of repressive laws against the sons. The capacity to enjoy the growth of the son without having to submit him to punishing initiation rites reflecting unconscious envy of him signifies that the father has definitely overcome his own oedipal inhibitions. The practical implication of these formulations is that one important source of instability of love relations in adult men derives from incomplete identification with the paternal function" (pp. 91–92).

PROVOKING THE WIFE'S AGGRESSION VIA PSEUDOSUBMISSION

Let us look a little further into the dynamic alluded to above in the case of Mr. M. By his having neglected to advocate for his own needs or wishes, by his having failed to assert his own beliefs, Mr. M. played the role of the selfless husband. While some wives may think that makes him an ideal husband, in the long run this proves not to be the case. Most wives want another complete human being with whom to relate, rather than a passive manservant who leaves them feeling partnerless and lonely for adult companionship. This is true even though a relationship with another sovereign adult inevitably leads to conflict. Any power imbalance between a husband and wife that is the product of a man's failure to stand up for himself, to speak up in support of his needs and in defense of his beliefs, is likely to incur the wife's wrath even though part of her wishes to have the upper hand in the relationship. Sometimes a wife's shrew-like behavior is the product of resentment over being left to fill a power vacuum. Getting to be the one who makes all the decisions is something she half desires and half abhors.

Kernberg (1980) presents a case that speaks to this point. The patient is a man in his early forties who presented with serious marital conflicts and numerous problematic sexual proclivities: compulsive masturbation that lasted hours, thus interfering with the discharge of his professional and marital duties, and a tendency to have extramarital affairs characterized by sadomasochistic features. One of these affairs was with a woman who seemed sexually interested in him yet charged him money for the privilege of her company in bed.

At the beginning of the marriage the patient acted passively and irresponsibly with regard to his professional duties and his social and financial obligations. He was overly dependent on his wife to straighten his life out for him. "He unconsciously forced her into the role of a giving mother dealing with a passive, irresponsible little child" (Kernberg 1980, p. 88). Because the marital relationship had taken on this character, it lacked depth, which the patient tried to make up for by being overly solicitous of his wife.

Their relationship underwent significant change when the husband became professionally successful. Then the wife grew uninterested in her work and in having sex with her husband, and developed a series of minor illnesses. His efforts to satisfy her by selflessly catering to her every sexual need ceased to please her, causing him to feel guilty and frustrated. The husband redoubled his efforts to satisfy her by submitting to her every demand, even when doing so seriously interfered with his professional obligations. "It appeared that her unconscious envy of his success and his guilt over it increased his conscious submissiveness toward her, and he displaced his sadistic sexual need to the woman who decreased his guilt by demanding payment" (Kernberg 1980, p. 89).

Kernberg (1980) summarized the case: "Analytic exploration revealed strong sadistic and masochistic needs related to oedipal and preoedipal sexual and aggressive impulses toward a sadistic, controlling, guilt-inducing mother that had broken through the superficial, socially appropriate, but emotionally inadequate marital relationship of the early years of marriage" (p. 90). Kernberg figured that the couple's sexual relations early in marriage had been constricted by the patient's repression of these sadistic and masochistic impulses. At the point the patient came for treatment,

> a deeper, predominant, dissociated object relation emerged from repression and became expressed in a dissociated or split-off way. His equilibrium became that of a *masochistic pseudosubmission* to his wife, while he acted out his sadistic and masochistic needs in the relationship with the paid woman friend and in his masturbatory fantasies. The more mature functioning of his superego was replaced by the simultaneous expression of guilt and rebellion in a sadomasochistic relation with his wife, who represented his mother. . . . As he became increasingly aware of the temptation to provoke her angry outbursts in order to then submit to her (temporarily), he became concerned about what was happening between them. [p. 90, emphasis added]

Yet another example of such pseudosubmissive behavior is illustrated by the case of Mr. I. presented in Chapter 5. Mr. I. could not tolerate the emotional upheavals triggered by conflict between him and his girlfriend. While this case is not an example of the single woman–married man syndrome in that Mr. I. was a divorcé rather than a married man, it nevertheless well illustrates how a man's way of relating to his girlfriend can serve as a serious impediment both to intimacy and to the prospect of a courtship culminating in marriage.

Mr. I. was eager to satisfy his girlfriend's every whim because he felt that this was the least he could do, given what a louse he had been at the outset of their relationship when he had shown interest in some of his female students. This had proved tormenting for his girlfriend, who would never let him live it down. She told him that she considered him untrustworthy and demanded that he submit to conditions that, at one level, he resented and knew to be excessive. For instance, she requested, and he granted her request, that she be permitted to listen in on all of his voice mail messages, something she claimed she needed to do to reassure herself that no further hanky-panky was going on.

Having to go along with this request rankled Mr. I. However, he denied these feelings out of fear that were he to oppose her, she would "go ballistic," as was her style. Such emotional outbursts frightened him and led him to feel that such conflict must always be avoided for the good of the relationship. His girlfriend felt just the opposite, and took any sign of omission (not letting her in on his feelings) as an act of unfaithfulness.

The patient's guilt over having acted selfishly at the outset of their relationship led him to want to make it up to his girlfriend through acts of supposed selfless submission. The patient deceived himself into consciously believing that he was doing everything he could to comply with her wishes, everything, that is, but be frank about how upset he was at her for having asked him to submit in ways he actually could not stomach. He seemed not to have the courage to think, let alone say: "You've got to be kidding. Do you really expect me to give up that much of myself for the sake of our relationship?" And this failure to assert himself proved, for his girlfriend, to be one of the most bothersome aspects of Mr. I.'s behavior.

In spite of his conscious desire to keep these rebellious feelings from manifesting, intermittently and inevitably they would

emerge in one way or another. The patient's covert rebellious-
ness became readily apparent to his girlfriend, who was always
on the lookout for discrepancies between what he said and what
he did. Whenever she discovered such discrepancies, she would
become enraged, leading the patient to return to his psychotherapy session seeking ways to keep such unfaithful impulses
from emerging. Trying harder to comply with his girlfriend's
wishes only served to keep him out of touch with how angry he
was at being required to submit in this way.

After months of investigation, it emerged that the patient was
afraid that he was losing himself for the sake of saving the relationship. So he unconsciously held on to a small piece of himself
that lay safely sequestered out of his awareness and away from his
girlfriend's sphere of influence. But it become readily apparent to
his girlfriend that there was something he was keeping from her,
and this hidden side interfered with their ability to remain close.
He covertly resisted being controlled, all the while acting as if he
were willingly submitting to his girlfriend's wishes and needs. He
feared that to be controlled by her was to risk being destroyed in
the process. He acted as if he were at her beck and call, yet nothing was further from the truth. He felt that in order not to be at
odds with her, he must comply with her every wish. Yet this proved,
in a larger sense, not to be her wish at all.

COMPARTMENTALIZATION
AND THE HIDDEN SELF

One critical aspect of the single woman–married man syndrome is the way the married man expresses an entirely different aspect of his personality when with the other woman as compared to how he acts when with his wife. It seems reasonable
to assume that such acts of withholding would seriously limit
the degree of intimacy that these men are capable of achieving
in marriage. Monica Lewinsky quotes President Clinton as having revealed to her, at the time he terminated their affair, that

he was adept at letting others see only selective aspects of himself—that no one knew the "true Bill Clinton" (Morton 1999, pp. 113–114). We will never know whether she has accurately quoted him, so this could never, on its own, constitute data regarding this point. But there are plenty of other examples to support the conclusion that married men who pursue extramarital relationships that conform to the single woman–married man syndrome exhibit this tendency to manifest significantly different aspects of their personality when with different women.

Both Mr. M. and Mr. I., who were discussed in Chapter 5, kept hidden aspects of their emotional lives and activities from the women in their lives. Mr. M. had taken to lying to his wife about the time he spent with his buddies golfing or drinking. He felt she disapproved of such activities, both because they robbed her of time she might otherwise have with him and because she considered Mr. M.'s male friends sophomoric. Mr. M. would make up stories as his "cover," but whenever his wife discovered what he had been up to, she would give him "grief" not only for having lied but for having selfishly spent time apart from her, which made her feel unwanted. When he was "found out," Mr. M. acted like a schoolboy who had been caught with his hand in the cookie jar, an attitude that cast their relationship as that of mother and child, which contributed to a further deterioration of the marriage. With Terri, his girlfriend, Mr. M. felt he could be completely honest about who he was and how he felt. But as emotionally fulfilling and open as that relationship seemed to be, Mr. M. was never able to commit to Terri, largely because he remained indecisive and ambivalent, confused as to who he was and what he actually wanted. Not only had he become accustomed to lying to his wife, he also lied to himself. This parallels what President Clinton was alleged to have shared with Monica Lewinsky when, in her words, he admitted to having become "increasingly appalled at himself, at his capacity not only for deceiving others, but also for self-deception" (Morton 1999, pp. 113–114).

Mr. I., who had never been able to form a tight enough bond with his girlfriend for them to wed, also hid a great deal from the woman in his life. However, he did this unconsciously in that he also hid from himself the knowledge that he could not accept the concessions he had made to her "for the good of the relationship." However, a deeper analysis revealed that he was primarily trying to maintain his own emotional equanimity given his intolerance of intense emotionality. He deceived himself into believing that he did not mind making these small sacrifices and that he was doing so for her sake, not his. But his girlfriend was able to see through both of these assertions. She could sense when he was keeping things from her and would confront him about this long before he became aware of how he was feeling. However, she incorrectly assumed that he was fully conscious of these deceptions, which fueled her distrust of him.

Another case illustrates how some men compartmentalize their lives to keep portions out of the woman's sight and reach. Sometimes it appears as if men need a second woman with whom they can express aspects of their personality that have gone unexpressed with their wives.

Mr. L., a married man in his mid-thirties, was universally attractive to women, not just because of his good looks but also because he had a well-developed feminine side that made it easy for him to empathize with the female experience. He was considered a nice guy by men and women alike, not the type one would ever think capable of cheating on his wife. Even he was shocked when he became romantically involved with a teacher at his children's school. He sought treatment in order to come to terms with how he found himself feeling and acting.

Mr. L.'s mother did not tolerate any sign of disloyalty, a trait the patient was well aware of from a very young age. Anyone who crossed his mother was as good as dead to her. This had been the case with the patient's father, who, when the patient and his brother were still quite young, had left his wife for another woman. Even though decades had passed since the father had left, the patient's mother would not tolerate any mention of his name.

The patient learned early on that he had to take care of his fragile mother, who, though loving, was quite needy. This contributed to his unusual ability to be empathic with women. As a child he had unconsciously suppressed significant aspects of his personality so as not to endanger the stability of his bond with his sole remaining parent. And he remained unaware of these hidden dimensions of his personality until they emerged in the context of his relationship with a single woman. These dimensions were inconsistent with the person he knew himself to be in his relationship with his wife.

The patient loved his wife and twin sons, and could not face the prospect of living without them. Yet for a time he found it equally hard to imagine giving up the intimacy he had developed with the other woman, a woman who had never previously permitted another man to get as emotionally close as she had allowed Mr. L. What made it hardest for Mr. L. to let go of his relationship with this other woman was his realization that once he let go of her, there would be no other relationship that could serve as an avenue for the expression of these newly discovered dimensions of his personality.

Mr. L. felt satisfying intimacy with his wife. But she was nothing like the other woman, with whom he had learned another way of being. What saddened the patient was that he could not express this newly discovered aspect of his personality with his wife. Their relationship was about certain ways of relating and not about others, and it seemed unreasonable to expect her to relate to him in a new way after having spent their adult lives together. To have expected this would have been to change all the rules. What they had was actually quite good. It was satisfying, but it was what it was. They had been married too long for him to expect her to contend with his new way of being.

What remained a mystery at the time Mr. L. left therapy was whether he had sold his wife short by assuming she was incapable of coping with this other aspect of his personality. Might she have been like Margaret in Glasgow's (1923) story "The Difference" (see Chapter 4), who says, "There are possibilities in me that you never suspected. . . . If you had known it, you might have found in marriage all that you have sought elsewhere" (p. 186). Is Mr. L.'s belief that his wife could not tolerate a renegotiation of their relationship to include previously hidden dimensions of his personality a way to protect himself from feeling too exposed, vulnerable, and dependent on his wife?

I have spoken of a "hidden self" as if such a thing exists, as if it were akin to a dissociated part of one's personality that has an independent existence just waiting for a chance to be expressed. In fact, the hidden self that emerges in the context of a particular relationship is not something that had preexisted as a sequestered organization. The hidden self is the product of a process set in motion by one's beginning to relate to a facilitating (transforming) other. This newly emergent self is context-dependent, just as all intersubjective processes tend to be. Were no such interaction ever to take place, all that would exist of this hidden self is latent, untapped potential. In fact, one can only speak of a hidden self in retrospect, after a previously latent aspect of the self makes itself known via its context-dependent manifestation. Once this self has been brought to life, it remains somewhat dependent on the context within which it first emerged, which serves as the primary vehicle for the continued expression of that aspect of one's self. For this reason, such contexts tend to be ones upon which people grow quite dependent as they come to relish the expression of these new dimensions of their personality.

INDECISIVENESS, BLESSED CONFUSION, AND AMBIVALENCE

Being out of touch with hidden dimensions of one's personality makes it difficult, if not impossible, for one to decide between alternatives. The inability of a man to decide which of two women he prefers is a predictable characteristic of the single woman–married man syndrome. Men who in all other aspects of their lives are capable of great decisiveness turn to me early in the course of treatment, when I barely know them, to tell them which woman to choose. They feel as if they have no basis upon which to act, no internal compass indicating who it is they would ultimately be happiest with. Feeling completely ambivalent, such men are prone to draw up lists of pros and cons as if such an exercise could help them resolve their dilemma.

It is often through one's choices that one becomes known to others. If one unconsciously wishes to keep certain personality aspects hidden, it behooves that individual to avoid making choices. And, by becoming utterly confused as to what one wants, one is rendered indecisive, thus keeping that individual from revealing himself through his choices.

Blessed Confusion

The following clinical description summarizes what was learned in the initial phase of a married man's analysis about his tendency to become confused about what he wanted, what he felt, and what he thought.

The patient had sought help for his severe depression. But early in the course of his analysis, he began to deal with how confusing it was to lead a life that included emotional involvement with two women—his wife and his lover. For the patient, confusion seemed to be a blessing insofar as he would hide behind it, thus protecting him from having to expose his true self. "If someone starts to ask me why I feel as I do, I begin to lose my mind. I can't always offer a logical explanation to support my position, so I conclude I must be mistaken—the other person must be right. I have a hard time sticking to what I feel is true. Confusion defines me. I can't imagine being without it."

Confusion was typically followed by the patient's acceptance of others' positions as correct. "I consider others' views more objective than my own." The patient would allow himself to be molded by others' needs, demands, or expectations of him. "I'd be lost if it weren't for others who help determine me by their expectations of me." He would be angry at others for not letting him be himself and live his own life. Yet, if left to his own devices, he seemed clueless as to who he was and what he wanted.

Confusion also operated defensively, helping the patient deny his own drives and needs. It was always the other who made demands on him, always he who was the poor slave to the other's unreasonable demands. Much of the beginning phase of analysis was focused on helping him see why he felt so inclined to view things in such a way. Thinking along these lines proved to the patient that he was not selfish, as his parents had always said he was. Such thinking also satisfied certain masochistic tendencies, and it kept him unaware of just how needy he was for attention and affirmation from others.

Ambivalence and the Single Man

Indecisiveness is seen in single as well as married men. Psychotherapists frequently encounter single men who just cannot seem to bring themselves to propose marriage to a woman whom they have been dating long enough to know whether she is right for them. Though they claim to love the woman, there is just one thing about her that bothers them, just one little thing that leads them to wonder whether they will later regret having settled for a woman who falls short in this particular area. These men seem incapable of overlooking this particular thing in favor of a consideration of the overall package. So that particular thing becomes a deal breaker that leaves the man feeling as though he ought to back out and see if he can find a woman who could more completely satisfy his expectations. He typically does nothing of the sort, however, and instead remains ambivalently attached to the woman until she tires of his inability to resolve these lingering doubts.

The following clinical example illustrates just such a patient.

Leonard G. was an affable man in his early forties who had become very depressed over the breakup of his eight-year relationship with his girlfriend, Molly T. Leonard and Molly seemed ill-suited, given their differing backgrounds, temperaments, and life goals. He was an intense, highly ambitious, fast-thinking East Coast executive who had dozens of ideas about what he wanted to accomplish in life; she was a laid-back, low-key, self-satisfied West Coast woman who seemed to want nothing more than to "hang out." While the patient felt "grounded" by his girlfriend's "down-to-earth" nature, this trait also led him to have misgivings. He just could not see himself making so unambitious a woman his life partner. Yet he could not bring himself to leave the woman he claimed to be "crazy" about. Molly gave Leonard an ultimatum to which he responded by proposing marriage. But by the next morning his intense ambivalence prevented him from following through on his promise to wed. Molly regretfully broke off their relationship, saying that she could not see Leonard ever resolving his ambivalent feelings about her.

Freud (1909) wrote that doubt leads some men to

paralysis of the will and an incapacity for coming to a decision upon any of those actions for which love ought to provide the motive power. . . . The *doubt* corresponds to the patient's internal perception of his own indecision [that] takes possession of him in the face of every intended action. The doubt is in reality a doubt of his own love—which ought to be the most certain thing in his whole mind; and it becomes diffused over everything else, and is especially apt to become displaced on to what is most insignificant and small. A man who doubts his own love may, or rather *must*, doubt every lesser thing. [p. 241]

As was described by Freud, Leonard G. feared commitment of any sort. He was metaphorically claustrophobic, forever needing to have a way out, an alternate option that protected him from feeling trapped by whichever situation he was currently in. This was true of his line of work, the coast on which he lived, the house he planned to inhabit, the analysis I proposed he begin, and the woman he claimed to love. He feared that once he committed wholeheartedly to a job, a locale, a house, an analysis, or a woman, he would become imprisoned and defined forever after by those choices, damned by the facts of his life. He feared becoming reduced to a mere stereotype that he would be unable to transcend. A year before, after having reached an agreement to purchase a house in the suburbs, the patient was struck by a fear that he was about to become a suburbanite. He found this prospect so disturbing that he backed out of the deal, just as he had pulled out of his engagement to Molly. If she had become his wife, he feared that others might see him as the husband of a woman who lacked ambition and drive, and he could not tolerate being limited by such a view. Hannah, another girl he had begun dating, had the intellect, the drive, and a shared cultural background that Molly lacked. Yet, as one would expect, Hannah had one flaw that ruled her out as a prospect: she was not nearly as good in bed as Molly had been.

MR. NICE GUY'S SELF-DECEIVING SELFLESSNESS

Another feature of the single woman–married man syndrome is the characteristic way married men portray themselves as selflessly satisfying their wives' and lovers' wishes and needs, which they have seemingly permitted to take precedence over their own. This was precisely the case with Mr. M., who asserted that his happiness hinged entirely on whether his wife was happy, and with Mr. I., who contended that he willingly chose to do things that were not in his best interest just because doing so pleased his girlfriend.

Convincing oneself that others' needs come before one's own creates a flattering self-image, one that can be projected in order to seem appealing. By denying one's selfish needs, one can come to think of oneself as a nice guy who wishes nothing more than to selflessly satisfy the wishes and needs of others. Feeling indecisive, confused, and ambivalent about what one wants can help one effectively deny one's less flattering wishes and intentions in the service of appearing selfless.

Self-deception is a concept that has received renewed attention lately. It refers to the creation of a self-image that is at odds with the true characteristics of one's personality. It differs from reaction formation, which refers to the vicissitudes of specific drives and impulses; for example, unconscious hate is defended against by overstated, consciously avowed, love, or vice versa. Self-deception has more to do with the management of one's feelings about who one is as a person, one's self-image. One may like to think of oneself as being kinder, gentler, and more thoughtful than one actually is. Self-deception is a mechanism that assists in creating an image that might prove more pleasing than the truth.

The cases of Mr. M. and Mr. I. demonstrate self-deception in action. Mr. M. portrayed himself as wanting nothing more than to please his wife; her happiness meant all the world to him. But upon further investigation. it turned out that what primarily made Mr. M. happiest was the knowledge that he alone had been the one responsible for his wife's happiness. Accordingly, he was much more interested in the narcissistic gratification he derived from having been the cause of his wife's happiness than he was in her happiness per se. This is much like the man who is pleased about having brought his wife to orgasm rather than taking pleasure, via identification, with the wife's primary experience of pleasure. Furthermore, Mr. M.'s own narcissistic difficulties made it hard for him to be attuned to what would, in fact, be most pleasing to his wife. As for Mr. I., while he liked to portray his intentions as strictly motivated by a desire to do as his girlfriend wished, as therapy proceeded it became clearer that he wished nothing more than to be able to avoid intense emotional conflict. He tried to accomplish this by deceiving himself into believing that he was willing to do what, in fact, he could not stomach. What he could not give his girlfriend was the one thing she desired most— access to his inner thoughts and honesty about his true feelings.

Barkow and colleagues (1992), writing from the perspective of evolutionary psychology, suggest that "if especially altruistic people exist, it may be profitable to try to convince others that one is such a person in order to get them to try to establish relationships with you (Alexander 1987). This strategy is facilitated by the ability to systematically exclude impure motives from consciousness, an ability that requires the subtle use of many defenses" (p. 616). Barkow and colleagues (1992) go on to note that one is more likely to convince others of the purity of one's own intentions if one first sells oneself on the truthfulness of that very idea.

> Self-deception could increase fitness by increasing the ability to pursue selfish motives without detection. The full argument has several stages: Human reproductive success requires human social success, social success requires success in reciprocity relationships, success in reciprocity relationships comes from getting a bit more

than you give, getting a bit more than you give requires
the ability to deceive others, and the ability to deceive
others is enhanced by the ability to deceive yourself.
[p. 606]

Typically, married men who have affairs consistent with the
single woman–married man syndrome think of themselves as nice
guys who are not out to hurt anybody. They find it objectionable
when their girlfriends accuse them of taking advantage of them.
"How ungrateful can a woman be?" such men wonder. This
was the gist of what Monica Lewinsky claimed to be President
Clinton's attitude toward her in the waning days of their relationship. Part of what contributes to the difficulty the man has
bidding adieu to the girlfriend is his awareness that once he ends
the relationship, it is likely that there will be someone walking
the earth who sees him as nothing but a "creep." And this the
man's "ego" will not allow.

This dynamic is illustrated in the following clinical example
about Mr. L., the charming and empathic man, described earlier in this chapter, who discovered a hidden dimension of his
personality once he became involved with a woman other than
his wife.

Mr. L. relished thinking of himself, and having others think
of him, as a nice guy. His girlfriend had never trusted a man
before him. Accordingly, Mr. L. felt he had done her a favor
by showing her what men can be like, that men can be sensitive and caring. Being the only man capable of getting
through to her was a source of deep narcissistic satisfaction
for Mr. L. But in leaving her, he feared he would destroy all
that he had done for her. No longer would she be able to
think that some men are kind, sensitive, and self-sacrificing. If he continued to be caring and warm as he attempted
to extricate himself from the relationship, it would make it
that much harder for his girlfriend to let go. His inclination
was to tell her that he still loved her but just could not be

with her, since this was, in fact, true. Yet he realized that would make it all the harder for her to get over him. Unless he let her be angry with him, it was unlikely that she would be able to get over him and move on. But what he feared most was that she would end up thinking of him as just another selfish bastard who had taken advantage of her. He could not tolerate someone thinking this way about him after all the years he had spent perfecting ways of gracefully avoiding his mother's wrath. He also could not tolerate the guilt of having reinforced her worst impressions of men, thus contributing to her distrust of men. But, to his credit, he was able to bring himself to tolerate risking her thinking unflattering thoughts about him so that she could break free of him.

THE TANGLED WEB OF SELF-DECEPTION

Self-deception is not a foolproof method of ensuring that others will accept one's self-portrayal as altruistically motivated. Mr. I.'s girlfriend saw through his contention that he wholeheartedly wanted to do whatever it would take to reassure her that he was trustworthy. She saw past his seemingly sincere demeanor and was able to discern the selfish motives that lay beneath his seeming concern for her needs.

Let us return to a hypothetical situation we originally discussed in Chapter 1, in which a man is caught in the unflattering position of having his baser motives recognized in spite of his best efforts to hide them. A married man has begun a relationship with a single woman and everything is going along swimmingly until the woman asks the man whether he cares for her as a person above and beyond his enjoyment of her as a sexual partner.* If the man

---

*Though this situation is similar to what Monica Lewinsky claims to have occurred between her and President Clinton, there is no reason to believe that what follows has anything to do with their particular circumstance. I base the following formulation on clinical experience, which applies only to certain cases.

wishes to see himself, and have her see him, as a nice guy, he is not likely to admit to himself, or to her, that he is primarily interested in her as a sex object, even if that is, in fact, the case. Instead, he is likely to take offense at her having thought such a thing, and will, from that point onward, tend to act in ways designed to prove to himself and to her that he *is* the caring man he would like to believe he is. And, if the man's actions conform to this image, he may begin to appear, and may even become, the very thing he is trying to prove himself to be.

Some may take exception to the notion that this hypothetical man has in reality become a caring lover just by acting the part of one. But the situation may turn out to be a great deal more complicated than it appears. By initially deceiving himself into believing that he is only interested in this woman as a sexual partner, the man successfully defends himself from the prospect of growing vulnerably dependent upon the woman. The woman then confronts him with her perception of him as just another selfishly motivated man. The man is now in a difficult position. Will he maintain his defense against true intimacy at the expense of being thought a louse? Or will his primary interest be to protect his narcissism? If so, he may then be willing to admit feelings that may potentially expose him to vulnerable dependency. In this way the man has backed himself into admitting something he had been motivated to deny, having been shamed into having to admit the very thing from which he had been running.

MEN'S UNIQUE VULNERABILITY

By now it should be clear just how important a role men's narcissistic vulnerability plays in their relationships with women. Though men might act as if nothing could be further from the truth, it is patently obvious just how sensitive many men tend to be when it comes to the issue of permitting themselves to become emotionally attached to a woman. Unconsciously limiting the amount they reveal about themselves serves as a defense against the prospect of growing increasingly dependent upon just one woman to satisfy their emotional needs. Hiding significant aspects of themselves becomes a way of making relationships with women safe.

These dynamics can be illustrated by the consideration of another commonly encountered phenomenon that points to men's exquisite sensitivity to the vicissitudes of their lover's investment in, and attention to, them. It has often been said that if one is looking for the husband of a woman who is in the delivery room, he is apt to be found in another woman's bed. This adage captures the fact that men often experience much unconscious conflict about their wives becoming mothers. While many men consciously wish to become fathers, to be the patriarch of the family, they are ambivalent about the prospect of welcoming a third party into their love nest.

The problems that develop as lovers become fathers and mothers is well illustrated in Phelps's (1868) short story "No News" (see Chapter 4). Harrie and her husband grow further and further apart as Harrie dedicates herself to the task of child rearing. Ultimately the two are living relatively separate existences, a fact made painfully clear with the arrival of a sophisticated and urbane friend of Harrie's, with whom Harrie's husband feels he has much in common. Cato, in *The Other Woman*, which has been discussed in Chapter 5, also describes several cases in which the married man's extramarital affair appears to have been in reaction to the anticipated or actual arrival of the couple's newborn.

A husband may feel ignored when his wife turns her attentions to the newborn. He may even feel he has become expendable, having outlived his husbandly function by providing his wife with the babies she had always wanted. One patient states:

> a woman has two separate distinct functions for me— as a sexual object and as a companion and mother to my children. It is hard for these two to interact with each other. If these two aspects get blended together, would I then feel jealous of my kids' demands on my

wife? Like—my kids' needs come before mine. Therefore I have to abandon hope of needing my wife to satisfy my sexual needs so as not to be in competition with
my kids. Is that merely a justification for going outside
the marriage for sex? It sounds like I am having affairs
for the kids' sakes.

This provides yet another in a string of explanations of the
"whore–madonna" complex.

What is it about a wife's becoming a mother that causes men
such trouble? The answer may lie in certain specific features of
the childhood sexual development of males. Kernberg (1977),
drawing on the work of Braunschweig and Fain (1971, 1975),
notes that "for the boy, the pregenital relationship with mother
already involves a special sexual orientation of her toward him,
which stimulates his sexual awareness and the narcissistic investment in his penis. . . . Braunschweig and Fain state that, normally,
mother's periodically turning away from the male child to return
to father . . . frustrates the little boy's narcissism" (pp. 88–89).

A mother's involvement with her son is discontinuous in that
the mother periodically retreats from her son and returns to her
husband as his sexual partner, thus becoming momentarily
unavailable to the son (see Kernberg 1991, 1995, who cites Braunschweig and Fain 1971, 1975 and Andre Green 1986, 1993). Tuch's
(1975) findings lend support to this theory: the level of attentive-
ness mothers pay to their sick children is, at least in part, a function of where the woman is within her menstrual cycle. During
mid-cycle, mothers seemed to be more annoyed by, and less attentive to, their children's illnesses. Presumably, this is because
mothers are less offspring-oriented and more spouse-oriented at
times when they are most likely to be fertile.

Kernberg (1995) notes, "Ideally, a woman can alternate her
two roles and move easily from being a tender, subtly erotic, affectionate mother to her infant and child to being an erotic sexual
partner to her husband" (p. 83). Depending on the child's innate sensitivities to these discontinuities, and the mother's ca-

pacity to carefully handle these discontinuities, the child may grow up to be an adult who is either tolerant or intolerant of similar discontinuities in his intimate sexual relations. If a mother is overly seductive with her son or withdraws too quickly from him as she switches into her sexual role as an adult woman vis-à-vis her husband, she is likely to cause him undue difficulties dealing with frustration and disappointment with women in his later life. He might then become uniquely sensitive to times when his mother (and, subsequently, his wife) turns away from him as she attends to the needs of her husband (and later, to the needs of her children).

If a son becomes overly frustrated by such discontinuities, this may stimulate his aggression, which may in turn contribute either to the intensity of his superego (via projection of his aggressiveness into the father, which then becomes, via identification, enshrined within the superego) or to the hostility experienced toward women in general (Horney 1966, Kernberg 1995). Kernberg (1995) writes, "In men, the predominant pathology of love relations derived from oedipal conflicts takes the form of fear of and insecurity vis-à-vis women and reaction formations against such insecurity in the form of reactive or projected hostility against them" (p. 56).

Why is it that women do not exhibit the same degree of narcissistic vulnerability as do men? This can be accounted for by a striking difference in the developmental histories of men and women. Throughout childhood boys retain an investment in their mothers as the focus of their romantic interest, whereas girls go through the process of relinquishing their romantic involvement with their mothers in order to turn their attention to their fathers. The experience of having had to make such a switch has profound effects on female development. Some writers have used these developmental differences to explain why women have a greater capacity for heterosexual commitment than do adult males (Altman 1977, Braunschweig and Fain 1971, 1975). They reason that men who have remained attached to their mothers may be inclined to search the world for the perfect mother, thus proving to themselves that they never had to give up hope of being able, one day, to be sexually reunited with their primary object. Women, on the other hand, have already renounced their love interest in their primary object of affection, so they are free to commit themselves elsewhere as they see fit.

Kernberg (1991) concludes:

> The capacity for discontinuity is played out by men in their relationships with women: separating from women after sexual gratification reflects an assertion of autonomy (basically, a normal narcissistic reaction to mother's withdrawal), and is typically misinterpreted in the—mostly female—cultural *cliché* that men have less capacity than women for establishing a dependent relationship. In women, this discontinuity is normally activated in the interaction with their infants, including the erotic dimension of that interaction, which leads to the man's frequent sense of being abandoned, once again, in the cultural *cliché*—this time a male one—of the incompatibility of maternal functions and heterosexual eroticism in women. [pp. 51–52]

This latter cliché refers to the whore–madonna complex.

Triangulation

A husband's difficulties handling the discontinuous nature of his wife's swings from her role as mate to mother can produce serious trouble for the marriage. One way men have of emotionally protecting themselves in case of rejection is to have another woman in the wings, to be wanted by two in order to defend against the prospect of being in competition with another for one's wife. Kernberg (1988, 1995) coined the term *triangulation* to describe fantasied triadic situations. *Direct triangulation* is Kernberg's (1995) term to describe "both partners' unconscious fantasy of an excluded third party, an idealized member of the subject's gender—the dreaded rival replicating the oedipal rival" (p. 87). By contrast, reverse triangulation "has a reassuring and revengeful quality, and consists in fantasies of being involved with two persons rather than with one. . . . The fantasy is, of course, the reverse of the original oedipal situation in which the little boy, for example, competed with father for mother. Now, in contrast, a man fantasies a relation with another woman, and the rivalry of two women fighting over him" (Kernberg 1988, p. 72).

The following material, which comes from a session with the patient who was quoted above as feeling that he could not compete with his kids for the affection of his wife, illustrates just how difficult it can be for a man to acknowledge his needs for a woman and how he might defend against the awareness of such needs via a reverse triangulation.

> The patient's wife was aware that he had had an extramarital affair and, in the spirit of reconciliation, was trying to bring herself and her husband closer together. The patient was somewhat leery of her attempts and, in this particular session, reports the following dream: "I had come home early and found Sally [his wife] at home with another guy starting to have sex. Sally was defensive about it, saying, "Well, you did it, so I can, too."
>
> After reporting the dream, the patient added that he had awakened feeling "really pissed off at her. Just when I put my trust more in her, I am exposed to getting hurt like that." I responded by wondering whether he had constructed the dream to serve as a kind of a cautionary tale warning him about the dangers of going along with his wife's wishes that they reconcile, as if he were warning himself about what can happen if he let himself become more emotionally invested in Sally. To this, the patient replied: "The feeling of anger was so intense that when I woke up, I wondered if *that* is the big block to my letting myself feel closer to Sally. If she

were to break that trust, my anger would be uncontrollable. I don't know what I would do at that point. I would have to get over that hurdle of feeling uneasy about committing to someone before I could let myself get close to her. What if the trust was ever breached? I would be totally out of control, feeling angry, taken advantage of, betrayed. I don't know if I could recover from that kind of rejection." I asked, "So is that why Sally had to experience those feelings rather than you?" The patient seemed not to have heard my question and responded, "What?" I repeated myself: "Since you unconsciously felt that you couldn't possibly tolerate the feelings of being betrayed, then Sally had to go through experiencing that." Patient: "Sally has to occupy the faithful spouse territory. In the dream, I tried to react with 'What do I care if she's doing the same thing I had done?' But I was angry at myself for letting her have that power over me. I wanted to kill myself and I wanted to kill her."

Then the patient went on to enumerate some of the other issues over which he had felt angry with his wife: "My underlying anger justifies my having an affair in the first place. Sally can't deliver the degree of security I want. And maybe it's unrealistic to expect that degree of security from anyone. I thought my partner's love would be unconditional —that she would selflessly support me so that all my insecurity would go away. Sally never provided me with that, so I feel cheated and angry about it. I get angry that Sally isn't the perfect wife for me—not giving me what I need. I assumed in marriage I would get someone who would take care of all these problems. But now I see, as an adult, how on your own one can be, on a trapeze without a net with no one to save you. I assumed when you were married your spouse gave you that additional strength to deal with anything. But that's a bunch of crap. In a way, it's ironic my father died. I never thought about what it would be like to be an orphan. You're right. Sally invited me to get closer and I feel 'What sort of sucker do you take me for?' By inviting me to be closer, it invites me to get further away because I found myself wondering what her real agenda was."

Men's Dread of Women

Men's dread of women has been well described by Horney (1966), who provides cultural examples indicative of this dread: Ulysses's admonition to his seamen to tie themselves to the ship's mast lest the allure of the Sirens cause them to jump into the treacherous seas, and Delilah's ability to rob Samson of his strength. To this, we might add reports that the female black widow spider bites the head of her mate off as he dismounts.

Horney (1966) asks whether there is an ontogenic explanation for this dread of women, whether it is "an integral part of the masculine existence and behavior" (p. 88). She then goes on to ask "Is any light shed upon it by the state of lethargy—even the death—after mating which occurs frequently in male animals? Are love and death more closely bound up with one another for the male than for the female, in whom sexual union potentially produces a new life? Does the man feel, side by side with his desire to conquer, a secret longing for extinction in the act of reunion with the woman (mother)?" (p. 88).

Horney argues that man's disparagement of women has its roots in man's need to render women harmless. She references Freud's (1912) article "On the Universal Tendency to Debasement in the Sphere of Love," in which Freud develops a theory to account for the frequently encountered tendency, on the part of some men, to be unable to feel sexually aroused by women who would otherwise prove to be an excellent choice for a mate. "Where they love they do not desire and where they desire they cannot love" (Freud 1912, p. 183). Freud's thesis is that these men cannot feel sexually aroused by women toward whom they feel affection because such women remind them of their mothers, thus triggering the incest taboo. Horney (1966) and Pittman

(1989) suggest an alternate explanation to the one offered by Freud: A man might need to debase women because to do otherwise, to value women, places women in a position to be able to cause serious narcissistic harm to the man's sense of self. Any man who has already suffered such injury at the hands of his mother may find relief, even triumph, in rendering women harmless.

Horney (1966) argues that the male dread of women can be explained as follows:

> The boy . . . feels or instinctively judges that his penis is much too small for his mother's genital and reacts with dread to his own inadequacies, of being rejected and derided. Thus he experiences anxiety which is located in quite a different quarter from the girls: his original dread of women is not castration-anxiety at all, but a reaction to the menace of his self-respect. . . . The boy is hit in a second sensitive spot—his sense of genital inadequacy, which has presumably accompanied his libidinal desires from the beginning. . . . According to my experience the dread of being rejected and derided is a typical ingredient in the analysis of every man. [pp. 91–93]

It is interesting to note that Kernberg (1974a) echoed these sentiments: "One finds envy and hatred in many male patients" (p. 494).

Horney's explanation offers an alternative meaning for the term *castration*, one that is based not on a fear of harm that may come to a boy's body, as is seen in the castration threat that the boy anticipates at the hands of the father, but the harm that may result from a narcissistic injury, this time coming from the boy's mother.

Horney goes on to suggest that the biological condition that makes men narcissistically vulnerable to the prospect of rejection from women is the fact that the sexual act requires him to perform (get an erection and maintain it through ejaculation), which is something not required of the female sexual response.

Ultimately, Horney (1966) suggests that the dread of women might manifest itself in an "overwhelming inner compulsion to prove their manhood again and again to themselves and others. A man of this type in its more extreme form has therefore one interest only: to conquer. His aim is to have 'possessed' many women. . . . [Such men] are very indignant with a woman who takes their intentions too seriously, or . . . cherish a lifelong gratitude to her if she spares them any further proof of their manhood" (p. 95). One might ask whether the behavior of philanderers is merely a defense against their fear that were they to surrender and become emotionally involved with a woman, they would become dangerously vulnerable in the process.

THE SELF-VALIDATING FUNCTION OF EXTRAMARITAL AFFAIRS

Thus far, it may appear as if my main thesis is that married men become involved with single women because doing so offers them a venue for another aspect of their personality that had gone unexpressed within the marital relationship. While I believe this explains why certain men have affairs, I would like to return to the issue of the narcissistic gratification that derives from being sexually wanted by another. It may turn out that certain affairs are about the expression of a different dimension of a man's personality while others are about the revitalizing validation that comes from knowing that another finds him so irresistibly appealing that she is willing to have sexual relations with him. Let us begin by looking a bit more closely at the issue of sexual arousal.

A man's propensity to have extramarital affairs can rarely be explained completely on the basis of his sexual drive. Sexual arousal is driven by fantasy and is vulnerable to disruption by a host of psychological and emotional issues that can lead to premature or retarded ejaculation and impotence. Sometimes sexual responsivity requires certain conditions for an individual to become aroused by another. For instance, some men cannot become sexually "turned on" unless their sexual partner smokes, wears fishnet stockings or stiletto-heeled shoes, or mistreats or humiliates them. Stoller (1979) has suggested that the basis of sexual excitement is the triumph that comes from magically undoing past traumas by re-creating them in the present in ways that make it clear that one is no longer the victim of another since one is now responsible for orchestrating the situation previously endured passively when younger.

The sexual act often includes pleasing the other sexually, though at times it may become exclusively about "getting off" without regard for the other's satisfaction. Shifting the focus from one's own pleasure to that of another is part of what complicates the human sexual response. The fear that he will be experienced as an inadequate lover may become foremost in a man's mind, resulting in his being too much in his head to be able to achieve a state of abandon that a successful sexual act requires. Such fears can become self-fulfilling prophecies. On the other hand, using another in the selfish pursuit of his own satisfaction without regard for what would please the other represents an impersonal act that could be likened to masturbation. Learning how to satisfy another without becoming crippled by self-consciousness in the process is part of what is required in order to be successful sexually.

The self-validating aspect of another's becoming sexually aroused by one's appearance or sexual performance can become, for some, a more important component of the sexual act than sensual pleasure itself. *Cruising* is a term used by gays to describe the practice of rendezvousing with other gays in a particular locale with the express purpose of establishing who desires whom. Though some might emphasize the culminating act of connecting sexually with another, for others this is not the central focus of the act of cruising. The narcissistic satisfaction that derives from being wanted is at least on par with that of sexual gratification.

The same can be said for certain types of heterosexual affairs. While the man in pursuit of an extramarital affair may be focused on the ultimate goal of orgasm, a careful analysis of the situation reveals that a great deal more is often at work. By emphasizing his orgasm, the man downplays his need to be validated by the woman's interest, arousal, and acceptance. Many men think that needing a woman in these ways is unmanly, since it harks back to a time when they needed their mother.

Some men who pursue extramarital affairs do so chiefly because they are in need of narcissistic replenishment. The marriage has ceased to make them feel special as it had earlier. These men are on the lookout for signs of female interest, and when they perceive a likely prospect, they move in to see if the interest is genuine or just a tease. If the woman proves willing to become sexually involved, that removes all doubt about the man's desirability, at least for a time.

For such men, needing to be deemed worthy places undue pressure on their sexual performance. Once the woman has consented to take the relationship to the next level, such men's narcissistic gratification now rides on whether she thinks they are among the best lovers she has ever had. Under such conditions, it becomes hard to enjoy the sensual pleasure of the sexual act since proving oneself becomes everything.

These dynamics are illustrated by the following material taken from a session with a man who struggled with his urge to pursue extramarital affairs. The patient begins the sessions by sharing his feelings of insecurity about his physical attractiveness, his perceived lack of physical endowment, and his discomfort sharing such insecurities with another, particularly with a man.

> *Patient:* It makes me sexually stimulated if I know the woman is enjoying it. I feel sex is about delayed gratification. It's never about *my* pleasure. I feel I owe more to the woman and I feel I've drained my own pleasure out of the equation. It's as if my pleasure isn't the issue.

Therapist: That gives the woman a lot of power.

Patient: But it feels the other way too. The goal is to have the woman want you more than you want her. That factors out the element of rejection.

Therapist: It seems you achieve that by factoring out your own sexual pleasure.

Patient: I am *very dependent* on the woman for validation and reassurance. But I never permit that to become explicit. Getting to the sexual place in a relationship with a woman feels like such an achievement. Ideas and feelings of love come up right at the start. I feel so gratified to be in the position I'm in. Like someone has taken pity on me.

Therapist: It seems to organize the relationship around a particular concept you have of yourself.

Patient: Sharing these feelings with you worries me, because I fear that your knowing how I feel places you in a position where you could exploit me on account of my fears. The idea that I care about how a woman feels sexually might appear less masculine. It seems odd to share my feelings of physical attractiveness with another man. What are you going to do, tell me I'm a good looking guy? But I have to talk about this stuff, because it's tiresome to keep up the façade. It would be nice if these issues didn't become part and parcel of the sexual relationship.

Therapist: You feel you need continued reassurance and that the only way out of feeling insecure about yourself is for more and more women to weigh in on the issue of your attractiveness.

Patient: In an ongoing relationship it's hard to keep asking for that kind of reassurance.

Therapist: It reminds me of *Phantom of the Opera*, or *Beauty and the Beast*, where the men are transformed out of their feelings of inadequacy in the process of being loved by a woman.

Patient: Seeking it out is more important than getting it. Once the woman says "yes" and the relationship becomes physical, the need to perform kicks in, which makes the act not all that much fun. I satisfy the woman by focusing on her physical pleasure and by permitting her to feel dominant. It doesn't occur to me to seek out a situation where the woman is just as concerned about pleasing me as I am about pleasing her. Such a thing seems incomprehensible to me.

To round out the list of potential contributing factors that account for a man's inclination to seek out extramarital affairs, I would add one more. For men who feel emotionally dead, for whom life offers no sense of aliveness, joy, adventure, pleasurable anticipation, or gratifying satisfaction upon the consummation of their drives or the achievement of their goals, an extramarital sexual encounter can act like a drug that provides a much-needed emotional rush. Giving in to an irresistible urge, becoming totally absorbed in the process, can provide necessary relief from the chronic state of detachment.

I suspect that men who have multiple extramarital affairs may be in search of either the narcissistic validation or the emotional rush that comes from being wanted by a series of different women. By comparison, I suspect that men who end up having one extramarital affair (or a very limited number of affairs) are those who feel stifled by marriage and are looking for someone with whom they can experiment being different. Naturally, both factors may contribute to a man's proclivity to have affairs, as may others not described or detailed here.

8

The Other Woman:
The Masochistic
"Solution"

Sigh no more, ladies, sigh no more,
Men were deceivers ever,
One foot in the sea and one on shore,
To one thing constant never.
                    William Shakespeare, *Much Ado About Nothing*, II, iii, 62

When Monica Lewinsky testified before the grand jury, one juror asked her why she kept having affairs with married men: "You're young, you're vibrant. I can't figure out why you keep going after things that aren't free, that aren't obtainable." That question left Ms. Lewinsky feeling, in her words, as if she were "standing naked in front of the whole world" (Morton 1999, p. 252). She responded by offering the following: "There's work I need to do on myself. . . . A single young woman doesn't have an affair with a married man because she is normal." She then added that in order to understand why she had acted as she had, one would need to know her entire life history from birth on. And while she had lived that history, she had to admit that even she did not yet understand what had motivated her actions (*Los Angeles Times* 1998, p. A17).

It would be unfair and inaccurate to describe every woman who has been romantically involved with a married man as abnormal. Laurel Richardson (1985), who has studied the phenomenon of the "other woman" from a sociologic perspective, takes exception to society's tendency to label single women who become involved with married men as "economically parasitical, psychologically sick, and sociologically deviant" (p. 9). She feels such stereotypes go unchallenged in part due to the paucity of empirical research on the subject. Society's tendency to marginalize such women as socially unacceptable, as sociologic lepers, places them in the category of shunned minority. But unlike other categorically marginalized groups who have organized themselves, such as gays and lesbians, single women who have had affairs with married men have yet to speak with a unified voice, or to be studied scientifically, leading to the perpetuation of society's stereotypes of such women as cold-hearted and calculating, self-centered and manipulative, devious and deviant.

Richardson (1979) notes that "other women" rarely fit society's stereotype of the "kept woman," a woman who provides sexual favors to make up for what the man's wife, for whatever reason, cannot or will not provide, and who, in exchange for being sexually "on call," is provided a level of material comfort she could not otherwise afford. Such an arrangement makes a kept woman not much different from a call girl.

Richardson (1979, 1985) also objects to stereotyping the other woman as psychologically sick. She rejects two of the explanations commonly offered to account for the behavior of these women: (1) the woman's expectation and acceptance of yet another unrequited love relationship (masochistic repetition of early childhood trauma), and (2) the woman's expectation and acceptance of her need to settle for limited gratification given her belief that she is not desirable enough to attract anything more than a man's divided attentions (narcissistic undervaluation of her worth). In other words, such explanations rely on the idea that the pursuit of relations with married men is driven either by a single woman's unresolved oedipal fantasies or by low self-esteem that leads her to believe that no man would pick her as his sole love interest. Naturally, these two explanations might well be related in a cause-and-effect fashion.

Richardson (1985) argues that some single women enter relationships with married men because doing so suits a variety of women's needs. For instance, women who are primarily dedicated to pursuing their careers may see marriage as an impediment to professional advancement. To compete with men who, married or not, seem ready and able to commit substantial amounts of time and energy to the job, such women may feel it necessary to be free of encumbrances that might interfere with the achievement of their goals. Such women may look for temporary relationships with married men because such relationships do not require the commitment of time and energy that marriages typically do.

Affairs with married men also provide women with a seeming solution to their fear that marriage poses a serious threat to a woman's ability to maintain an identity separate from that of her husband. There was a time when "a woman became Mrs. Man's First and Last Name and lived out her female destiny through her husband and children" (Richardson 1985, p. 7). Fearing that marriage might mark the beginning of her end, a woman may elect to have an affair with a married man, believing that such a relationship promises the peace of mind that a woman will be able to retain a piece of her mind.

Given women's needs to compete professionally, to maintain a sense of themselves as independent individuals, and to experience emotional intimacy with a particular man, Richardson (1985) predicts that in the future "it is likely that the single woman over 25 who has never had a relationship with a married man will be in the minority" (p. 9). This is particularly true, notes Richardson, because there just are not enough available single heterosexual men to go around, especially for women who are financially successful and better educated. "Generally, when people lack the socially approved means to achieve a culturally desirable goal, they find alternative ways to attain it" (p. 5). For many women, the alternative—dating much younger men, much older men, or gay men—are unappealing. Thus, they date men who are already spoken for.

As a result of open-ended, semi-structured interviews with twenty-six single women who had previously been involved with married men, Richardson (1979) concludes that affairs between single women and married men can be distinguished on the basis of whether or not the single woman was in a position of power vis-à-vis the married man during the course of the relationship. Richardson defines power as "the probability that a person's will will prevail" or as "the individual's recurrent ability to impose his/her will and that the threat of punishment or the withholding of rewards is compelling enough to generate compliance from the less powerful" (p. 401). Conversely, a woman's powerlessness is defined by Richardson as "the subordination of [her] own interests to those of the male, dependence upon and submissiveness to his decisions, temporal passivity, and an incorporation of a socioemotional orientation" (pp. 401–402).

Richardson (1979) suggests that single women who exhibit a dominance style vis-à-vis their married lovers fare better emotionally throughout the course of the relationship than do women who exhibit a hypersubmissive style of relating. Dominant women place their priorities on the pursuit of individual goals, which they feel are incompatible with marriage. They describe their relationships with married man in pragmatic, rather than romantic, terms. Interviews with dominant women tended to be matter-of-fact and intellectual. When such women did exhibit emotionality, it was in response to self-expressed doubts about their abilities to maintain close, intimate ties with men over time, rather than in reaction to the potential or actual loss of a particular man with whom they have been involved.

While the behavior of dominant women is more stereotypically male than female (more active than passive) just the opposite can be said of the behavior of single women who exhibit hypersubmissive styles of relating. For the submissive female, the man's needs typically come before her own. Accordingly, she tends to spend inordinate amounts of time waiting until he becomes available and she is grateful for whatever crumbs are left for her. One such woman, who had seemingly lost all self-respect, told her lover that she was willing to adopt whatever role he deemed fit, that all he needed to do is let her know what she was supposed to be, and she would be it (Richardson 1979). When interviewed after their affair had ended, such women differed from dominant-style women in that they typically became emotional, often expressing both anger and sadness over the affair. Such women are highly romantic, tend to idealize the men with whom they had once been involved, and "continued to surround the relationship with an aura of sacredness" (Richardson 1979, p. 402).

Women who exhibited a dominant style of relating were not nearly as emotionally vulnerable to the vicissitudes of the affair, or to its ending, as were hypersubmissive women. If the man sought a greater commitment from her, dominant-style women tended either to bolt or to permit the relationship to peter out. By contrast, hypersubmissive women tended either to be dumped suddenly or to suffer through an on-again–off-again relationship, which typically tended to drag on for extended periods of time because of the man's ambivalence and indecisiveness about whether he ultimately wanted to remain married or leave his wife for the other woman. Sometimes these men would leave their wives for brief periods of time, only to end up returning to them. This repetitive pattern of comings and goings takes the single woman on an emotional roller-coaster ride, her hopes soaring and plunging each time the man gets closer to, then further from, ultimately committing himself to her.

Rarely do hypersubmissive women take the initiative and break off the affair. When they do, it is either the result of intensive therapy or in response to a major disappointment that suddenly awakens them to the ultimate limits of the relationship.

Richardson (1979) illustrates this point when she quotes one such woman whose father's death led her to a realization: "I was so alone, he [her married lover] had to go to a . . . picnic . . . a *picnic*. Hers. He said he couldn't get out of it. Her picnic versus me. . . . I hated him then. . . . Nothing was ever right after that" (p. 405).

Richardson (1979) summed up her findings:

> If a woman adopts a submissive management style, she can expect to be emotionally vulnerable; and if she adopts a dominance management style, she can expect to be emotionally limited. To the extent a woman incorporates the feminine stereotypes, she will be powerless and subordinated and the probability of emotional labileness and vulnerability will increase. However, to the extent a woman adopts the masculine stereotypes, she will limit the emotional involvements and her depth of intimacy. [p. 413]

Richardson (1979) contends that "individuals do have some freedom to choose to create intimate relationships that are power balanced" (p. 413), though she admits that egalitarian-style affairs between single women and married men are not easy to come by. Richardson believes that balanced relations between single women and married men, when they do occur, offer the greatest chance for women to feel emotionally fulfilled without running the risk of becoming emotionally devastated in the process.

I am skeptical about Richardson's claim that one's unconscious tendencies to relate in a particular fashion can be controlled by sheer willpower. It appears that relatively few, if any, of the women Richardson interviewed were able to establish the type of well-balanced relationship she views as ideal. This, I believe, is because of the inherent power tilt that inevitably characterizes nearly all single woman–married man relationships. Richardson (1985) states:

The single woman loses control over how her time is spent because it is his free time which determines when and for how long they can be together. Wherever one looks in social relationships, the person who determines when and for how long an encounter will last is the powerful person in the relationship. . . . [Given] the near total subordination of the Other Woman's time to the married man's . . . the potential for her feeling confined, powerless, and worthless is exponential. Being unsure whether one will be summoned or dismissed keeps one emotionally and psychologically off balance. Unable to predict what will come next, one feels less and less control over one's life . . . [and over one's] perceived ability to alter one's life. [pp. 108–110]

The single woman's self-esteem typically is enhanced at the beginning of a relationship because of the married man's initial eagerness to become emotionally involved with her. The single woman typically idealizes the man with whom she has become involved. He is clearly a desirable catch, given the fact that another woman has thought enough of him to marry him. The single woman's success in luring the married man away is seen by her as a testament to her own attractiveness, especially given how logistically difficult and potentially dangerous such liaisons can be. The married man shares his intimate thoughts and feelings with the single woman, thus revealing himself to her in ways he had been unable to do with his wife. The married man's lament, "My wife doesn't understand me," is more than just a line. The man genuinely experiences such sentiments as a fair account of his situation. Richardson (1985) writes, "Being his trusted confidante, the single woman feels ennobled, for to be trusted with a secret means you are judged a worthy person, a moral person" (p. 62).

Because their time together is limited, the single woman goes to great lengths to ensure that petty arguments or disagreements do not intrude and spoil what little time they have together. As a result, such relationships may, at first glance, seem superior to other relationships that are marred by apparent conflict. One single woman describes how their relationship "didn't have to deteriorate because of having to be in a day-to-day domestic situation where demands are made on each other that are unpleasant or mundane. It was never mundane. It was encapsulated" (Richardson 1985, p. 59).

Relationships between single women and married men are distinctively different from those between single women and single men in that the former are carried out in secret, whereas the latter are conducted in the open as a social relationship. This fact heightens the woman's sense that her relationship with the married man is special. The single woman and married man spend most of their time in isolation, which tends to heighten the sense of intimacy. Furthermore, conducting a relationship free of social constraints and social definition also contributes to the sense of the relationship's specialness. But this isolation has other, more insidious, effects. If a relationship is not exposed to the eyes of others, it exists in a closed system. Without feedback from others as to how the couple is functioning as a couple, the woman's idealization of the man and their relationship may persist longer than it would were it to be challenged from without. Single women engaged in relationships of the single woman–married man syndrome type become enamored with their special relationship and are therefore slow to realize how limiting, neglectful, and, ultimately, hopeless such affairs usually turn out to be. Lacking feedback from others that may clue the single woman to how such relationships typically play out, she has no opportunity to rethink aspects of the relationship, to open her eyes to its drawbacks.

The secret/isolating aspect of the affair has other effects. Fearing that she might inadvertently slip and reveal her secret relationship when speaking with friends and relatives, the single woman's conversations with others tend to become less revealing and more distant in general. Thus, her support system narrows. Because the single woman clears her schedule to be at the married man's beck and call, she increasingly neglects her woman friends. In many ways, a single woman involved with a married man is at risk of ceasing to be the person she once was and of growing more and more dependent on the married man. Richardson (1985) notes: "If a woman retreats further into social and emotional isolation, the one person who does remain in her life is her married lover: He does, de facto, become her 'whole life.' In some ways, she becomes like a traditional wife, removed from circulation, at home, waiting" (pp. 72–73).

In the end, a relationship that starts out making the single woman feel good about herself often leaves her feeling neglected, humiliated, and used. The regression she has suffered on account of her having grown increasingly dependent on the man leads her to feel as if she has no choice but to continue to pursue the relationship. The man's continued refusal to leave his wife for her becomes painful in that it robs the woman of the one event that might help her recoup her losses. The single woman begins to regret having lost precious time. Yet she feels unable to extricate herself from the relationship. As Richardson (1985) notes, "When people, generally, lose feelings of self-esteem and self-determination, it is difficult for them to *act*. They accept ill-treatment as their due because they believe they deserve it and cannot imagine better alternatives" (p. 123).

PSYCHOPATHOLOGICAL REASONS FOR DATING MARRIED MEN

Richardson's main thesis, based on an expanded sample size of fifty-five women (Richardson 1985), is that many women who end up involved with married men have not selectively pursued such relationships but instead just happen to find themselves with married men largely because of the demographic dearth of available single men. Richardson feels this is particularly true of well-educated, professionally successful women, who are less likely to attract men because many men are uncomfortable maintaining intimate relations with women who are their equals. A corollary to Richardson's theory is that when women do selectively pursue relationships with married men, they do not do so for "neurotic" reasons. Such women may be pursuing careers that they feel are not compatible with dividing their attentions between work and marriage. Or they may have been hurt in their relationships with single men and may therefore feel safer having a relationship with a married man, whose limited attention is not taken personally because it can be attributed to the fact that he is otherwise engaged. Finally, women may pursue married men as a way of ensuring that they are not eclipsed by the man's shadow, as a wife might be. But while Richardson accepts such rationalizations and justifications at face value, I believe such explanations are often defensive in nature.

Richardson does not believe that single women pursue relations with married men because they lack self-esteem, are masochistic, or are attempting to work though unresolved oedipal issues. While she does not deny just how psychologically devastating such relations can turn out to be for women, she contends that this is primarily the result of the women's having become involved in a relationship that is inherently skewed in that interpersonal power in the relationship is decidedly in the man's favor. She further contends that single women do not date married men looking to find themselves in a "one down" position, but, instead, pursue married men in spite of, or because they are completely ignorant about, the power imbalance that is bound to ensue once the relationship is in full swing.

The upshot of Richardson's thesis is that single women involved with married men are slow to catch on to just how unequal such relationships ultimately turn out to be. Once the single woman has gotten emotionally in over her head, and is no longer in a position to easily extricate herself from a relationship she has grown emotionally dependent upon, she incurs a diminution of her self-esteem on account of her continued involvement in a relationship that no self-respecting woman would, or should, remain in. This lowering of self-esteem is, according to Richardson, the result of being in an unequal relationship, rather than the cause for the woman's having pursued such a relationship in the first place.

Richardson's thesis, while interesting, can be faulted on two counts. While naiveté about how such relationships typically play out may explain why some young women tend to experiment with dating married men, once many such women get a taste of what such relationships are like, they break off the relationship and swear they will never again become involved with another married man. The idea that most single women fail to catch on to where their relationship with the married man is headed until it is too late is insulting to the intelligence of the women. The other problem with Richardson's methodology is that it relies heavily on the accounts provided by single women who had affairs. Richardson makes no attempt to look beneath the surface, beyond the explanations these women offer, to account for their behavior. Psychological tests and psychoanalytic interviews aimed at accessing unconscious motivations ought to provide additional information that would prove helpful in better understanding why single women become involved with married men.

THE OTHER WOMAN'S EARLIEST OBJECT RELATIONS

Very little formal psychological research has studied single women who become repeatedly involved with married men. To date, the most comprehensive study on this subject was conducted by Lynne Hollander (1976), whose subjects were self-selected by responding to handbills Hollander posted at various locations in the San Francisco Bay area. Like Richardson's subjects, these women were not a clinical sample selected from a pool of women in psychotherapy or psychoanalysis. Accordingly, neither of these studies could be considered clinical. But unlike Richardson's subjects, many of whom may have pursued only one affair with a married man, Hollander required that her subjects have pursued romantic relationships with more than one married man, thus ensuring that she was studying a tendency rather than an isolated instance. Accordingly, Hollander's study speaks more directly to the single woman–married man syndrome.

All of the subjects in Hollander's study were single women between the ages of 25 and 35 who had never been married, yet who wanted to be in a long-term intimate relationship with a man. The study group was composed of women who had been romantically involved with at least two married men, while the control group was made up of women who had never pursued a romantic involvement with a married man. The ten women who made up Hollander's study group collectively had twenty-seven lengthy and meaningful affairs with married men. This group also had sixteen long-term affairs with unmarried men. But while these women reported having been in love with 74 percent of the married men they dated, they reported having been in love with only about 38 percent of the single men. By comparison, the eleven women who made up the control group reported having been in love in 81 percent of the thirty-two long-term relationships they had collectively pursued.

Hollander (1976) interviewed each of her subjects and administered a battery of psychological tests to ascertain whether women who pursued married men differed psychologically from women who had never sought out such relations. On the basis of her data, Hollander was able to demonstrate that single women who have been repeatedly involved with married men do not exhibit gross psychopathology. But she also was able to demonstrate that, as a group, these women differed significantly from the control group of women who had never dated a married man. The most glaring differences were in the area of the quality of the relationships these women had with each of their parents. While the study group (women involved with married men) reported having closer, more loving relationships with their fathers than with their mothers, the control group (who had never been involved with a married man) reported the exact reverse situation, leading these women to favor their mothers over their fathers ($p < .04$). The control group also reported experiencing their mothers as having been more loving to them than their fathers had been ($p < .025$); 64 percent of the control group women described their fathers as having been emotionally absent or uninvolved in their lives, whereas none of the women in the study group reported a lack of paternal involvement. Eighty percent of the women in the study group were judged by raters as "father oriented," which was defined as a woman's having had a "more unequivocally positive relationship with father; father seen as warmer, more affectionate, more nurturing, more accepting; little ambivalence in the father–daughter relationship. Mothers seen as more critical, nagging, demanding, or angry. When warm and positive feelings expressed toward mother, strong ambivalence also expressed" (p. 98). By comparison, 82 percent of the control group women were seen as "mother oriented," as defined by a reversal of the terms *father* and *mother* in the above definition of father orientation.

One further difference between the ways in which these two groups of women experienced their parents is that the control group experienced their parents as being much less easygoing and more demanding in comparison to how the study group (those involved with married men) described their parents. Control-group mothers and fathers were described by their daughters as having had more rigid behavioral expectations of them and having allowed them much less freedom when compared to the descriptions of parents of study-group women. Hollander speculates that the perceived strictness of their parents was not interpreted by control-group daughters as an expression of the parents' need to control the child; rather, it was seen as an expression of the parents' belief in the need for well-established limits about what constitutes acceptable and unacceptable behavior, which, Hollander concluded, most likely included an acknowledgment of the inherent boundaries between parent and child.

What these findings suggest is that women may pursue relations with married men because they have become fixated on their father on account of his having been overly gratifying of his daughter's wishes for closeness with him. Hollander was surprised by these findings since she had anticipated precisely the opposite. She had originally hypothesized that fathers who had frustrated their daughters' wishes for closeness would leave them hungering for an opportunity to get from a father surrogate (i.e., the married man) what they had failed to get from their fathers. Instead, these fathers formed unusually tight bonds with their daughters that may have proven seductive, thus stimulating the daughters' fantasies that father preferred them over mother. This would be in line with Hollander's finding that suggested that the parents of women who went on to become involved with married men tended to be less limit setting than their control counterparts.

While closeness is generally thought to be a good thing, one can clearly have too much of it. An overgratification of one's wishes to be close to father can produce as much trouble as one's failing to be able to garner father's love. Additional support for the father-fixation hypothesis is the fact that study-group women date married men who are, on average, eight years their senior. Even the unmarried men this group of women date were comparatively older than the unmarried men that the control-group women date.

These findings tend to support the lay opinion that single women date married men because they are "hung up" on their fathers, upon whom they remain unduly attached. Rather than accepting and working through the inevitable and undeniable fact that they will never get to be Daddy's "one and only," these women find a surrogate with whom to reenact the original oedipal triangle.

What is remarkable about Hollander's findings is that they point to a preoedipal dimension to these women's relationships with their fathers. Her study suggests that a girl's oedipal strivings may become heightened as a result of insufficient nurturing by her mothering figure during the preoedipal phase. In fact, the ways in which the study-group women described their fathers—"nurturing," "caring," "soft," and "approachable and accepting"—make the fathers sound stereotypically maternal. Given these findings, it is not particularly surprising to learn that almost 22 percent of the affairs these women had with married men were never, or were barely, consummated.

One might assume that having a loving relationship with one's father would translate into a girl's developing a positive attitude about herself as she grows to be a woman. But this proved not to be the case. The study group tested as being significantly more withdrawn and socially introverted than control-group women. In general, study-group women found it harder to initiate conversations with men, which, in part, may be a reflection of the fact that these women were more conflicted over the direct expression of their aggression when compared with control-group women. They judged themselves to be less physically attractive when compared to the self-assessments of women in the control group. As a result of their lack of self-confidence, study-group women approached interpersonal situations assuming that they would be rejected, ignored, or, in one way or another, not given the warmth, love, care, or approval they were seeking. The women in the study group suffered in these ways in spite of their having experienced a great deal of warmth, love, and caring from their fathers.

Hollander offers two explanations for why women who describe their fathers as accepting and loving end up having less self-esteem and being more socially anxious and inhibited around men: (1) Given the fact that a woman's primary self-worth as a woman is rooted in a positive identification with, and positive reinforcement from, her mother, the father's love and acceptance proves insufficient—it can never make up for what she failed to get from her mother; and (2) closeness with one's father, while comforting on one level, may actually generate feelings of anxiety and guilt in the girl due to conflict over her fantasied oedipal victory. Such feelings of anxiety and guilt may spill over into a woman's interactions with men who are available. Given such circumstances, Hollander reasons, "The 'other woman' may not want to get too close to any man. The relationship with a married man provides her with some gratification, but in its lack of an ultimate reward, it also provides a defense against the anxiety and guilt of being too close to the father figure. She keeps herself from winning the ultimate oedipal victory" (p. 121).

It must be noted that Hollander's control group is, in certain ways, anything but a control group. It is composed of women of marrying age who wanted to find a life mate but had not yet done so. Also, 70 percent of the control group and 82 percent of the study-group women had been in psychotherapy, a figure larger than one would expect of a true control group, which should be a representative sample of the population. Thus, it might seem unreasonable to delineate a group of woman who become repeatedly involved with married men by comparing them to a group of women who may themselves, in fact, have had difficulties landing a man and who felt disturbed enough to seek professional help. These facts may help explain a peculiar feature of Hollander's control group: fully 64 percent of these women reported that their fathers had been emotionally distant and uninvolved in their lives. If this statistic is representative of the population, such a finding would suggest an unrecognized mental health epidemic! While Hollander's study is based on a very small sample size, it remains one of the only attempts to date that has attempted to study this group of women in a systematic way. While we may not be able to reach definitive conclusions based on her study, it does provide statistical evidence suggesting that in certain ways single women who pursue relations with married men share characteristics in common that distinguish them from women disinclined to pursue such relationships.

In the final analysis, Hollander might have ended up studying women who had encountered difficulties navigating through oedipal waters in two different ways. The study group would have come to grief on account of their having had seductive fathers who made it hard for their daughters to ultimately realize that they would never get to have father all to themselves. By contrast, the control might be thought to represent a group of women who had felt overly frustrated during the oedipal phase, leaving them decidedly less inclined to want to have anything to do with a man who might remind them of their father (e.g., married men) and who were failing to find men to marry.

While Hollander's study goes far beyond Richardson's in that it delineates some of the psychological traits of women who are prone to pursue relationships with married men, in the end Hollander had to admit that the measures she had used in her study were not geared toward uncovering the unconscious motives and dynamics that distinguish women who are inclined to become romantically involved with married men from women who are not so inclined. To gain greater insight into the unconscious psychodynamics of single women who become involved with married men, we must now turn our attention to a study by Akhtar.

A CLINICAL STUDY OF THE "OTHER WOMAN"

Salman Akhtar (1985) reported on ten women whom he had either treated in ongoing psychotherapy or psychoanalysis or whom he otherwise had occasion to evaluate. All the women were dating married men and all displayed deep conflicts and intense ambivalent feelings about the men with whom they were involved. While Akhtar's sample size, like Hollander's, is small, its value lies in the fact that he had occasion to examine some of these women psychologically in great depth. Akhtar assigned the ten women into two groups depending on the woman's ability to integrate the two conflicting opinions ("representations") each developed about the man she was seeing. If the woman could simultaneously consider both opinions at the same time, she was said to have better integrated her ambivalent feelings than if she alternated between the two diametrically opposed views. Women who demonstrated an ability to integrate their conflicting images were assigned to group 1, while those who could not were assigned to group 2.

Of the ten women Akhtar (1985) studied, seven were assigned to group 1 and three to group 2. The first group of women were aware of, and were disturbed by, the intensity of their ambivalent feelings about the men with whom they were involved. They described these men as "charming, handsome, sophisticated, and efficient at work" but simultaneously acknowledged that they seemed "weak, childlike, potentially callous, afraid of genuine intimacy, selfish, and unreliable" (p. 219). In other words, these women were not as prone to idealize (and to subsequently devalue) the men in their lives as were the second group of women.

Akhtar notes that the second group of women seemed unable to consciously experience mixed feelings about their lovers. They alternately thought of the man in their life as "loving, witty, empathic, and sexually gratifying" or as "petty, cruel, dishonest, or fundamentally untrustworthy" (p. 220), depending on whether they had most recently been satisfied or disappointed by him. Akhtar notes that these two descriptions

> carried comparable conviction, and alternately each appeared to these patients as valid and truly representative of the "real" nature of the men with whom they were involved. The disregard they showed toward the discrepancy in their two accounts was striking. . . . It became apparent that the two images of their lovers existed independently of each other in their minds. . . . [These women's] knowledge of the real objects was, in general, dim as it was determined by the need-satisfying potential of the external objects rather than by the objects' autonomous existence and inherent qualities. In addition, their selves were not solidly established; hence, these patients were vulnerable to extreme oscillations of their self-esteem. [p. 220]

When Akhtar compared the presenting symptoms and developmental backgrounds of these two groups of women, he found significant differences. While the first group of women presented with relatively few symptoms (mostly dysthymia), the second group exhibited a variety of diffuse symptoms. This second group of women felt confused about their identities, were emotionally labile, and often felt empty; they had fewer friends and tended to have had many frustrating and futile relationships with men when compared with women in the first group; they exhibited ego weakness as evidenced by a lack of impulse control; they drank more, experimented with drugs more, and were less sexually inhibited than women in the first group. Finally, all three women in the second group had attempted suicide at one time or another.

With regard to these women's developmental histories, all the women who had described their childhoods as happy were in the first group. By comparison, all three women in the second group reported having been beaten as children. While this second group of women remembered their mothers as "rejecting, critical, and unempathic" and as being ill at ease with their own femininity, mothers of the first group of women were described by their daughters as "generally affectionate though a little strict" and as being "comfortable with their own femininity" (p. 222).

Diagnostically, the women in the second group tended toward the borderline spectrum (preoedipal issues), whereas women in the first group exhibited intrapsychic conflicts that were of the "structuralized" (oedipal) type. The first group of women had solidly established ego identities and lived stable lives (with the exception of their romantic involvement with the married man), whereas the women in the second group seemed to live more chaotic, conflict-ridden, and fragmented lives.

Attempting to integrate the findings of Richardson and Hollander with those of Akhtar leads us to note important parallels and differences in the women each studied. It appears as if Akhtar's stable group of women (group 1) corresponds to the group Richardson refers to as women who seem to remain strong vis-à-vis the married man, and who seem to never regress to the point of feeling powerless in relationship to him. But Akhtar's second group of woman differs markedly from Hollander's study group (those women who pursued married men). Akhtar's women exhibited gross psychopathology, unlike Hollander's subjects. Furthermore, Akhtar's subjects "complained about having been unfairly treated, inadequately appreciated, and harshly judged by their fathers" (Akhtar 1985, p. 222), whereas the study group in Hollander's research had the exact opposite experience, having decidedly positive relationships with their father relative to the relationships they had with their mother. It is important to note that Akhtar's second group represented a very small sample size (n = 3), which might explain why he failed to encounter a Hollander-type "other woman."

THREE DISTINCT TYPES OF "OTHER WOMEN"

If one combines the findings of these three researchers, it appears as if there are at least three types of "other women." The first group is represented by what Richardson (1985) refers to as the "new other woman." These women enter into relationships with married men for pragmatic reasons, because doing so suits their needs in that such relationships tend not to place undue demands on the woman's otherwise busy schedule. Richardson contends that these women are not driven by unconscious psychological needs but make a clear-cut, dispassionate choice based on a rational assessment of their priorities and needs. Such women are not likely to lapse into feeling powerless vis-à-vis the man they have been seeing. Quite the contrary. Such women are prone to continue to feel in control throughout the course of the relationship. But they pay a heavy price to remain in control; they remain somewhat aloof and emotionally uninvolved, unconsciously figuring that it is better to be safe than sorry. Such a woman would never permit her relationship with a man to deteriorate to the point where she would be at his beck and call. In fact, in some instances, it is the woman who proves to be the stronger of the two in that she is less emotionally invested in the relationship than is the man, making her less likely to feel as if she needs to make sacrifices to hold on to the relationship. If these women can be said to have a psychological issue, it would be intimacy, but Richardson presents no developmental data about these women's childhood relations with their primary caregivers.

The second group of "other women" is made up of those who can be said to exhibit the signs and symptoms of a benign form of the single woman–married man syndrome. This group further divides into two subgroups based on the characteristics of the woman's earliest object relations. The first subgroup is represented by Hollander's study group of women who tended to have had positive relations with their fathers and negative relations with their mothers. The second subgroup is represented by Akhtar's group 1, women who had positive relations with their mothers and more distant relations with their fathers. Both subgroups of women become involved with married men to the extent of feeling somewhat powerless in the relationship. But neither subgroup was prone to regress to the point of developing a more malignant form of the single woman–married man syndrome, which constitutes the final group of "other women." Most likely, this was because each subgroup experienced a positive relationship with at least one parent during their childhood.

The malignant form of the single woman–married man syndrome is represented by Akhtar's group 2. These women function in a borderline fashion; they live fragmented, chaotic lives. They had negative relations with both of their primary caregivers during childhood and are prone to severe regression in the context of relationships with married men. They tend to go to extremes when the relationship shows signs of breaking apart. They are prone to develop "fatal attractions." They may stalk, or otherwise terrorize, the man upon whom they have become dependently attached, and may feel so desperate a need to maintain this relationship that they will stop at nothing to ensure that he never leaves them. Losing their link to the married lover threatens such women with utter psychological dissolution, so they feel justified in doing whatever it takes to hold on to him.

I suspect that these three groups of women responded differently to the developmental challenges presented during the oedipal phase. Nothing can be said regarding the first group of women since Richardson provides no data about their earliest object relations. I suspect that women who experience positive relations with their mothers during childhood (Akhtar's group 1) have an easier time negotiating the challenges of the oedipal period than do women who had difficulty receiving adequate emotional provisions from their mothers when they were young (Hollander's study group). This latter group is doubly challenged by the inevitable frustrations that arise as the women attempt to come to terms with the impossibility of their ever getting to be their father's "one and only." If a woman had already encountered difficulties feeling nurtured by her mother, she is likely to feel that it is imperative that she win her father's affections to compensate for her felt lack of maternal caring.* Because of this heightened need to win over the father's affections, these women are more likely to need their relationship with a married man to make up for what they had lost during both the oedipal and the preoedipal periods. If such women do find themselves unduly gratified by their fathers, they will subsequently form more stable adaptations in life than if they are doubly frustrated in their attempts to form relations with both their mothers and fathers.

---

*I am not referring to what actually happened during these patients' childhoods. This felt lack of maternal caring could either be the result of an actual failing on the part of the maternal object, a relative failing due to the girl's heightened needs, which the maternal object's reasonable ministrations failed to satisfy, or a projection of hostility into the mother by the daughter. Whichever the case may be, the resultant felt lack of maternal caring places a premium on winning father's love, with which women who had experienced reasonable maternal provision would not have to contend.

As satisfyingly simple as the above scheme seems to be, it should not be taken completely seriously since nothing so clear-cut could possibly be correct. I do feel, however, that this scheme may generally capture some real differences among the types of experiences that single women have with married men.

Now that we have examined the phenomenology of the other woman from behavioral and developmental perspectives, we can go on to speculate about some of the deeper psychological issues that account for such affairs.

THE MASOCHISTIC DIMENSION OF THE SINGLE WOMAN–MARRIED MAN SYNDROME

At some point in her relationship with the married man, the single woman becomes painfully aware of just how low a priority her needs are in comparison to the needs of the man's wife. This sometimes becomes abundantly clear when the single woman's need to have the married man by her side momentarily intensifies due to particular circumstances. Richardson (1985) writes, "Life's major passages—deaths, weddings, pregnancies—are especially destabilizing for the Other Woman because they cannot be processed in a socially normal way. She is alone, and more intensely so than she would be if she had no relationship at all, because there is the hope, the hidden expectation, that he will 'be there' for her in major crises at least" (p. 129). Even when no such clarifying event arises in the course of their relationship together, the single woman still finds herself waiting in the wings, year after year, playing the part of the understudy, hoping that one day she will be called upon to play the lead role in the married man's life. Though the single woman tries to remain patient, at some point hope begins to fade, and frustration comes to define her life with the married man.

In the single woman–married man syndrome, the chances of a married man leaving his wife for the other woman are quite slim. If the married man does ultimately leave his wife, he rarely marries the single woman with whom he had been having the affair (Spanier and Margolis 1983). Richardson (1985) quotes one woman, who had met her lover before he had even married:

> The night he got married, I really cracked up. I was a mess. But we kept seeing each other for five years more. Then his marriage was disintegrating, which was raising my hopes again. Well, I go out there for a vacation as I always do, and at one point he props me in front of the fireplace and tells me he's going to get divorced and marry his old high school sweetheart. But he wants us to keep our relationship going! Incredible. I cried and cried. [p. 120]

In Hollander's study, about a quarter of the men who had been having affairs ended up divorced, yet only half of those men subsequently sought a closer relationship with the other woman, and in each instance they were rebuffed by her.

In the single woman–married man syndrome, the single woman may justify her present lot in life as a means to an end, as something that she has to put up with until the married man, once and for all, leaves his wife as he had implied or promised he would do. It is only natural for others to wonder how long it will take the single woman to realize he never will. But until the single woman opens her eyes and recognizes that the relationship is all it is ever going to be, it could be argued that she is *not* engaging in masochistic behavior. Her perpetual waiting, hoping, and praying may be seen, by her and by others, as the result of naiveté rather than true masochism. Such explanations, while appealing in their simplicity, serve to hide the woman's unconscious reasons for having pursued a married man in the first place. In fact, as we shall see, the situation is a good deal more complicated than surface appearances might suggest.

The situation the other woman finds herself in could be described as masochistic in that she elects to remain in a perpetually frustrating relationship. The single woman would most likely object to this reasoning, and would argue that she is looking at the big picture, taking into account a time in the future when her needs for the married man's undivided devotion will be completely satisfied. In the meantime, she would argue, she is biding her time.

When I speak of the single woman–married man syndrome as masochistic I am not saying, as the term might suggest, that the single women is consciously seeking to suffer frustration in her attempts to make the married man hers. It is only to acknowledge the fact that while their arrangement undeniably frustrates certain of the single woman's stated needs, she nevertheless remains in the situation. Hope aside, the relationship is what it is. This much the woman cannot deny. Yet she continues to pursue the relationship, and even contributes to the maintenance of the status quo, all the while denying, to herself and to others, that she has anything to do with the way things have turned out. She may portray herself as a victim of circumstances, having had the bad luck to fall in love with a man who is already taken. Or she may portray herself as a victim of the man's refusal to fulfill his promise to leave his wife and marry her. But she remains blind to her own unconscious motives for wishing to keep the situation just the way it is.

People can be said to be masochistic when they unconsciously engineer situations that frustrate their consciously avowed wishes, all the while creating the appearance that they are the hapless victims of fate. As Reik (1941) put it:

> In the majority of cases it appears to the casual observer as if the misfortune and the bad luck in the lives of these people came from the outer world, as if they had to struggle continually against unlucky events and afflictions which kept interfering with their destiny. It seems as if a hostile fate had cursed them, as if they were the victims of a trick played on them by everyone and everything with which they came in contact. Analytic observation, however, justifies the assertion that these

people, quite unconsciously, stage a predominant part of their disasters and misery or turn events to their own disadvantage. Yet they make it appear as though destiny or some malevolent god had assigned them the blank in the lottery of life. [p. 10]

Hollander's (1975) study lent partial support to the hypothesis that single women who pursue romantic relationships with married men exhibit masochistic traits. The women in her study who had pursued affairs with married men tended to score higher on the female masochism scale of the Minnesota Multiphasic Personality Inventory (MMPI) and they tended to harbor more guilt feelings than women in the control group. They exhibited less of a capacity, and were less willing, to express aggression openly and directly, as measured by the Thematic Apperception Test (TAT), and, as a result, exhibited a passive-aggressive style in their dealings with others ($p < .01$). In addition, these single women exhibited less self-acceptance, felt more shame ($p < .05$), and were more socially introverted and withdrawn ($p < .05$), when compared with women in the control group, all of which corroborates the assertion that these women are, in fact, masochistic.

If masochism is simply thought of as pleasure in pain, or is equated with sexual masochism, the complexity of the condition will be lost. Freud (1924) differentiated three forms of masochism: (1) "erotogenic masochism," mistreatment as a necessary prerequisite for sexual excitement; (2) "feminine masochism," in which "the masochist wants to be treated like a small and helpless child, but, particularly like a naughty child" (p. 162) and adopts a castrated (hence, feminine) position vis-à-vis the powerful figure to whom he or she must submit; and (3) "moral masochism" (playing the part of the martyr), in which "the suffering itself is what matters; whether it is decreed by someone who is loved or by someone who is indifferent is of no importance. It may even be caused by impersonal powers or by circumstances" (p. 165). It is these latter two forms of masochism, a tendency to adopt a submissive position vis-à-vis others combined with a felt need to suffer as evidenced by self-sacrifices and by self-arranged punishments, that I propose to be often at work in the single woman–married man syndrome. The sexual dimension of such relationships need not be sadomasochistic since staged mistreatments need not be a requisite part of the sexual act.

Central to the dynamic of moral masochism is the question of what the moral masochist feels guilty about, what it is he thinks he or she has done that is now deserving of punishment. Freud (1924) felt that the answer to this question lay in the masochist's "temptation to perform 'sinful' actions, which must then be expiated by the reproaches of the sadistic conscience or by chastisement from the great parental power of Destiny" (p. 169). By invoking a powerful, threatening authority, masochists create an external power upon which, or upon whom, they can then rely to help them resist acting out their "sinful" fantasies. In this way, masochists attempt to keep in check their potentially destructive impulses or wishes. Keeping such impulses in check reassures masochists that their relations have been safeguarded from the destructive effects of these impulses, thus assuring that their relationship, along with the love they derive from it, remains intact.

While Freud (1924) had speculated about a form of primary masochism that derived from the fusion of the life instinct and death instinct, the type of masochism described in the preceding paragraph has been termed *secondary masochism*, since it derives from an original sadistic impulse that is secondarily turned upon the self, thus generating masochism. This brings us to the question of why an individual would feel it necessary to turn his aggressions inward, toward himself, rather than expressing it outward, toward the external objects for whom such aggression was originally targeted. To explore this dynamic, we turn to case material.

A Clinical Illustration

Lester (1957) presents the case of a 28-year-old, hard-working career woman who sought psychoanalysis because she felt as if life was passing her by. At the time she started her analysis, she was romantically involved with yet another in a series of married men. She felt that she was of no importance to him and "longed for joy and happiness but felt enmeshed in circumstances that denied her these" (p. 23).

The patient painted a dismal picture of her family life, about which she only had unhappy memories. She was the second of four children. The family was poor and lived in a crowded apartment. Her mother continually complained that she felt "overworked and unappreciated" and she reproached the patient for being lazy and neglecting her household duties. The mother considered the patient to be a "bad, worthless, disloyal daughter" (p. 23). Feeling abused by her mother's disregard for her, the patient passive-aggressively acted out by refusing to do what was expected of her at home. This behavior only served to perpetuate the mother's verbal attacks. Her father would slap the patient whenever she was disobedient or insolent. In response, she would run off, hide in the closet, and cry, "feeling abandoned, injured, and righteously defiant" (p. 23). When she did try to lend a hand, such as when her mother was hospitalized after giving birth to her younger brother, she felt her efforts went unrecognized. She felt that both parents hated her and considered her worthless and bad.

Lester describes a pattern the patient developed as an adult:

After leaving her parents' home, she had several love affairs, all similar in pattern. She was always attracted to an older, married man. She would assure herself that his marriage must have been unhappy before she had ever met him. Soon after their sexual relations began, she would suspect that he was using her as easy solace for his marital discord. Convinced that she really meant little to him, she would become withdrawn and unresponsive to his overtures and sit silently before him with head averted and tears tumbling down her cheeks. He would become impatient and sharp, and she would feel stricken by his callousness. They would see each other less and less, and she would feel hurt and abandoned. [p. 24]

The patient felt powerless in her personal life, though she proved to be an effective advocate for others' needs in her capacity as a trade union representative. She worked hard to avoid feeling criticized by others and, as a result, could be exploited by overbearing personalities. Her wish to please others often led to her agreeing to situations that proved personally unsatisfying. When the patient seemed justified in her feeling that others had taken advantage of her, she was unable to express indignation or anger, and instead suffered quietly, as she once had in the closet.

While the patient presented the image of a meek woman, she slowly began to share sadistic impulses and fantasies. She imagined cleaving a woman friend's skull with an axe and, when she would sleep with a boyfriend, she would be frightened that she might kill him in her sleep. Lester helped the patient become aware of both her hostile impulses and her underlying guilt about these impulses. Portraying herself as "the innocent" who suffered at the cruel hands of others, rather than accepting her role as potential perpetrator, helped the patient defend against these unacceptable impulses. It was the other person, not she, who was hostile. Once she had convinced herself of this construct, she no longer had to feel guilty and, instead, could experience righteous indignation. "If anyone spoke crisply to her, he was being rough and scornful. If a friend greeted her with insufficient enthusiasm, he was showing contempt. If a colleague demurred from her opinion, he was being dictatorial" (p. 25).

These revelations opened the patient's mind to Lester's suggestion that she may have played a more active role than she had ever imagined in making her childhood as grim as it had been. At first, the patient was skeptical about what Lester was suggesting. But when she happened upon a picture of herself at the age of 5, before her younger siblings had arrived, she burst into tears upon realizing that those had been the happiest times of her life— times when she had felt like a princess. The patient "recalled her parents' adoring approval of her childish preening and gay dancing. It had seemed to her that her mother and father, while fond of one another, each reserved his deepest affection for her, and she considered herself the beloved centre of the family" (p. 26). The patient was amazed that she could have forgotten so pleasurable a time as that. "With these recollections, she became fearful that her entire view of her life was being shaken" (p. 26).

These memories led the way to the patient's remembering how much she had hated the two younger siblings, whom she viewed as intruders, for having destroyed her paradise. She also recalled that when she had cared for the household while her mother was away giving birth to her younger brother, she had fancied herself the mistress of the house, making her father proud of her by looking after his needs.

In the transference, the patient's fantasies of being mistreated by the analyst gave way to fantasies of his sexually attacking her. In turn, this led her to realize that, as a child, she had wanted her father to hit her. The patient gradually became aware of her own aggressive impulses toward the analyst and her rage toward him when he appeared less involved with her than she wished he would be. She also became aware of a wish that he see no patients but her, since any time he gave to them she viewed as time taken away from her. She became aware of how possessive she could be, how she wanted to be every friend's favorite, and how, in her affairs with men, she relished winning over another woman.

Lester ultimately interpreted to the patient how her playing the role of exploited, injured child helped her deny her competitive, destructive impulses toward women and her sexual interest in men. By seeing herself as the injured party, the patient had also "forestalled acknowledging the reality of her oedipal defeat and the necessity of relinquishing her oedipal attachment" (p. 22). The patient ultimately realized that since she could not arrange to have her father love her sexually, she could manage to feel beaten by him and so preserve an illusion of physical intimacy between them. She concluded that "it's better to be beaten than ignored" (p. 29).

Before Lester had uncovered a time when this patient had been the apple of her parents' eyes, her case seemed to be an example of the malignant form of the single woman–married man syndrome in that she seemed to have had difficult, abusive relationships with both parents. But as I noted above, the scheme I offered with regard to a typology of single women was bound to prove somewhat simplistic, particularly given the fact that it is based on what subjects say about their childhoods before much has been psychoanalytically uncovered about their earliest experiences.

ALTERNATE PSYCHOANALYTIC FORMULATIONS OF MASOCHISM

Lester's psychodynamic formulation exemplifies the classic psychoanalytic explanation of masochism as resulting from children's innate aggressive reaction to the inevitable frustrations of the oedipal period combined with their narcissistic rage over having felt disappointed, rejected, and humiliated for failing to win over the oedipal object. Children react to their rage with the felt need to protect their objects from being destroyed by it. Anger turned against one's self (secondary masochism) defends against the prospect of object loss.

This formulation, which emphasizes the intrapsychic dimension of masochism, runs counter to how some analysts think masochism develops. These analysts offer a competing formulation that suggests that masochism is a function of actual, rather than perceived, environmental deprivation, and they are inclined to take exception to any formulation that relies exclusively on the intrapsychic explanations of masochism, seeing the intrapsychic stance as tantamount to blaming the victim for the mistreatment suffered at the hands of others. For instance, Socarides (1958) stated:

> It is now generally assumed from the reports of numerous writers that the masochist has undergone a most considerable degree of traumatization in very early life. With great frequency, we uncover severe periods of emotional deprivation, absence of the loving care of the parents, actual prolonged lack of satisfaction of physical needs, and early demands that the infant manage for himself owing to other pressing interests of the parents, including the early birth of additional siblings. . . . Often it becomes clear that the mother actually hated, resented, or chronically mistreated the child. [p. 588]

This view suggests that, often, masochism is the product of hostile parents who only have rejection, humiliation, and punishment to offer the child. Brenner (1959) stated, "Such a child comes to seek similar treatment in later life from other persons as a substitute for love. One might say it is the only kind of love he knows" (p. 203). Along similar lines, Berliner (1947) stated:

> The dependent child, in order not to lose the vitally needed love object, submits and accepts the suffering which the object imposes as if it were love, and is not conscious of the difference. The child introjects the pain-giving object because of an oral need for its love. Simultaneously it represses any hostile reaction against the love object because that also would cause its loss. The child does not love suffering or ill-treatment—nobody does—but because it loves the person who gives it, the ill-treatment is libidinalized. [p. 461]

It is interesting to note that while parental mistreatment initially appeared to be the genetic root of the masochistic traits of Lester's patient, just as this competing formation of masochism would suggest, a more thorough analysis revealed that beneath the supposed environmental deprivation lay the patient's own denied sadistic impulses. However, the fact that this proved so in this particular case should not lead one to conclude that environmental deprivation never plays a role in the genesis of masochism.

A third formulation offered to account for the development of a masochistic adaptation to life suggests that masochism is the result of the child's sense of having failed his parents by disappointing them or otherwise causing them pain. Markson (1993) writes, "Hostility and guilt are the consequences of these conditions—guilt for having caused the parental suffering, guilt for failing to relieve it, and guilt for all the hostility that has been generated towards a vulnerable, self-sacrificing parent" (p. 936). This formulation differs from the previously described formations in that it addresses the parents' narcissistic needs for their child to be a particular way. This formulation hinges on the proposition that it is incumbent upon the child to project an image that reflects positively on the parents, thus reinforcing the parents' sense of worth, either in the parents' own eyes or in the eyes of the community. If a child feels that he has been "unenjoyed" or "under-enjoyed" by his parents, as Markson puts it, that feeling will substantially impact the child's view of himself. Summing up the collected opinions of Berliner (1947, 1958), Menaker (1953), Loewenstein (1957), and Socarides (1958), Stolorow (1975) states, "In such circumstances, the child creates a debased and depreciated perception of his own self in order to sustain the image of an idealized, all-good, all-powerful maternal object on whom he can depend for nurture and protection. . . . Masochistic self-debasement in the service of object-aggrandizement functions to maintain an illusory but vitally needed dependent or symbiotic object relationship" (p. 444).

When such children grow to become adults, they will seek acceptance from idealized objects to help bolster their sense of themselves as worthy. Being romantically involved with a married man may, in the beginning, serve to help a woman feel worthwhile. Only later does it tend to reinforce, rather than refute, the woman's deprecated perception of herself.

Self-Deprecation, Hostility, and Covert Control: Defining Traits of the Masochist

As can be seen in the preceding section, there are a number of psychoanalytic explanations offered to account for the genesis of masochism. A masochistic adaptation to life has been thought to result from a child's (1) having failed to come to terms with the inevitable frustrations and narcissistic injuries that emerge during the oedipal phase of development (the intrapsychic explanation), (2) having been treated cruelly by one's parents (the environmental explanation), or (3) having been used by one's parents to satisfy the parents' narcissistic needs (a second type of environmental explanation). To these three formulations I would add a fourth, which combines intrapsychic and environmental causes of masochism. If a child's environment has actively interfered with, or otherwise failed to provide, adequate support to see him through a successful resolution of his oedipal frustrations, such hindrances could contribute to the development of a masochistic orientation to life. This could happen either because the parent had alternately treated the child seductively and rejectingly, thus heightening the child's level of frustration and aggression, or because the parents communicated to the child their intolerance for his expressed aggression, thus necessitating the repression of his aggression.

Whichever the presumed cause of masochism might be, masochistic patients tend to share in common a deprecated view of themselves. Hollander (1976) demonstrated that single women involved with married men thought less of themselves than women in the control group. But it cannot be determined whether this is the cause or the effect of a single woman's becoming involved with a married man. The women involved with married men saw themselves as less physically attractive and were less able to initiate conversations with men than women in the control group. Paradoxically, this occurred even though the study-group women felt unusually close to, and loved by, their fathers.

Masochistic patients do not believe they can ever count on getting the love they desire. They may see themselves as unworthy of love, presuming that their hostile impulses are destructive to those they depend on. Or they may have learned through experience that others treat them hostilely, use them to satisfy their own narcissistic needs, or utterly disregard them. Such experiences may lead masochists to believe that such mistreatment defines them, and accordingly predicts how all others will treat them. They will gravitate toward relationships that conform to these expectations, even though they suffer on account of the choices they make. Yet, by denying that they are in fact making choices, and instead picturing themselves as the victims of fate, they succeed in obscuring the masochistic nature of their experience. If mistreatment is what they have come to know, it may be secondarily libidinalized, thus providing an added dimension to the relationship.

If the single woman comes to idealize the married man (partly because he has already been chosen by another woman, thus attesting to his desirability), she may then experience a heightening of her own self-esteem by virtue of his willingness to become involved with her. As noted above, Richardson (1985) describes how the married man's willingness to reveal himself to the single woman provides her with a sense of importance. Akhtar (1985) describes how narcissistically gratifying the married man's interest is to the single woman who suffers with low self-esteem:

These men pour their complicated and often tragic life histories during hours and hours of intense conversation with these women. They seek warmth, empathy, and understanding. All this leads to a sort of transference idealization of the other woman in which she is viewed as a savior, friend, mother, therapist, and lover— in essence, someone badly needed to depend upon. It is this feeling of being needed that may be intoxicatingly pleasurable to women with low self-esteem and cause them to get more deeply involved in such relationships. [pp. 223–224]

Even though the single woman's self-esteem does tend to improve in the beginning stages of such a relationship, it is not long before the married man's behavior causes this process to backfire. Before long, the single woman realizes how much of a second-class citizen she is when compared with the man's wife and family. What had begun as an uplifting relationship ends up being nothing but a drag, ultimately causing the woman to feel worse about herself than she had felt before the relationship began. Hoping to recoup her loses, to regain the sense of importance and self-worth she had initially experienced in the affair's earliest days, the single woman redoubles her efforts to make the man hers. The single woman ultimately finds herself engaged in what almost always turns out to be a losing battle.

Hostility inevitably emerges in reaction to the ongoing frustrations of the affair. Socarides (1958) notes that masochistic patients are characterized "by an intense, imperative infantile craving for love, a fear of abandonment, and violent, destructive, hostile impulses" (p. 588). Hostility threatens to upset the precariously balanced relationship the single woman is having with the married man. She must find ways of coping with this hostility if she has any hope of holding the relationship together.

There are two chief ways that masochistic patients may deal with their heightened level of hostility and aggression. One way is to turn the aggression back on themselves (secondary masochism), thus leading them not only to invite others to treat them sadistically, but to accept such treatment as the best that can be expected, given the fact that by definition they are people others mistreat (illustrated in Lester's patient presented above). The other way in which masochists express their aggression is through the covert control exerted over others, control they are likely to steadfastly deny exerting. This leads to what Kernberg (1988) refers to as the masochist's enslavement of the unavailable object.

A joke that highlights the control the masochist exerts over the sadist describes an interaction between a masochist and a sadist: "Beat me! Hurt me! Punish me mercilessly! Mistreat me in the most despicable way you can imagine!" pleads the masochist, to which the sadist responds: 'No." Unlike the way in which the masochist is portrayed in this joke, in real life masochists have to make it appear as if they are submitting to treatment that is abhorrent to them. The sadist is not supposed to catch on to the fact that masochists manipulate the situation to their advantage by ensuring that the sadist treats them in ways that correspond to their unconscious needs.

At an unconscious level, the sadist enters willingly into a contract with the masochist that ensures that both of their needs are met. Were the sadist to truly be sadistic, he would not yield to the masochist invitation to mistreat the masochist. However, refusing the masochist this need to be mistreated is not the type of mistreatment the sadist has in mind. The sadist accepts the masochist's suffering at face value. It never occurs to him that the masochist might be paradoxically asking for it and actually wanting it. Instead, the sadist assumes that *he* is the one imposing mistreatment on the hapless masochist. In fact, nothing could be further from the truth! (Keiser 1949).

Reik (1941) alerted us to the fact that masochists are not nearly as powerless as they may seem. Though he writes in terms of the male personal pronoun when describing masochists, it should be understood that the same would apply for female masochists:

According to Dr. Horney the essential purpose of the masochist is to give up his whole personality completely and to be submerged in others. All his striving is said to be directed towards redemption of his self, towards losing his ego. Obviously the opinion as represented here is the opposite one: by a peculiar detour the masochist attempts to maintain his ego, to enforce his will. The masochist is a revolutionist of self-surrender. The lambskin he wears hides the wolf. His yielding includes defiance, his submissive opposition. Beneath his softness there is hardness; behind his obsequiousness rebellion is concealed. [p. 156]

Variations on the Repetition-Compulsion Theme

If one thinks in terms of masochists repeating as an adult a situation they suffered passively (without choice) as a child, one begins to see that triumph may come from the masochist's turning the situation around: subliminally "forcing" the sadist into the position of treating the masochist in ways the masochist claims to abhor but covertly desires. If the masochist is causing the mistreatment/rejection this time around, maybe the same can be said for the initial trauma. Maybe masochists had not originally been victimized as children, but, instead, had subtly seduced their caregivers into mistreating or rejecting them. Such reasoning could justify a belief that one had not, in fact, been mistreated or rejected as a child, since the child had ultimately been responsible for the mistreatment or rejection (Bernstein 1957, Eidelberg 1959, Loewenstein 1957).

The chief appeal of turning passively experienced mistreatments during childhood into ones that children appear to have actively provoked is that, by so doing, victims succeed in avoiding one of the most difficult aspects of the original mistreatment: the fact that they could do nothing whatsoever to escape such a fate, that they had been rendered utterly powerless in the process of being abused. This form of repetition compulsion differs from the one that usually comes to mind when that term is used. Freud's original concept of repetition compulsion relied on the concept of fixation. If a child fails to successfully traverse a particular developmental stage he may become fixated at that stage. As an adult, such an individual may end up repeating the specifics of that particular phase, with the help of his closest relations, in an effort to successfully resolve the issues he had failed to resolve as a child. For instance, were a young girl to fail to come to terms with the impossibility of ever becoming her father's bride, she might be on the lookout, as an adult, for situations that might provide her an opportunity to, once and for all, become the "oedipal victor" by getting a married man to leave his wife for her. Such a girl may have become fixated because of (1) the innate intensity of her needs for closeness, which the father's reasonable ministrations had failed to satisfy; (2) the frustration she had suffered on account of her father's having been emotionally distant; or (3) the frustration occasioned by her father's having been unusually emotionally close, which served to heighten the girl's expectations that she would ultimately become the father's lover.

In the case of the classic form of repetition compulsion, guilt and fear of the mother/wife's retaliation leads the woman to be sure not to succeed at winning over the married man. She wants, and does not want, to be the oedipal victor. The outcome of such a conflict leads to what on the surface appears to be yet another defeat. The closer the woman comes to winning over the man, the more inclined she will be to undermine her ultimate victory. She arranges to be punished for having dared to want what she knows she should not, and cannot possibly, have. In this way, she lessens the guilt she feels while simultaneously protecting herself from retaliation were she to succeed at stealing another woman's man.

The masochistic form of repetition compulsion provides an additional defense that helps the child cope with the frustrations that inevitably accompany the oedipal phase of development. By unconsciously portraying the oedipal situation as one the girl had complete control over, she succeeds at making it appear as if she had not truly been rejected after all, but had, instead, chosen to have her father turn down her seductive advances. When the child grows to be an adult, she may again arrange for just such a provoked rejection as a way of reassuring herself that she has always been in control of the men in her life. Of course, all of this occurs unconsciously. By contrast, the conscious experience is one of frustration and longing for matters to be otherwise.

Freud's original concept of repetition compulsion could be summarized as follows: by repeating an unsatisfactory childhood experience, one hopes to effect a successful outcome this time around so as to be able to circumvent the task of ultimately coming to terms with the fact that the original experience had been not just frustrating, but *shamefully* frustrating given one's inclination to take the failure personally as an indication of one's inadequacy or worthlessness. One simultaneously (via compromise formation) ensures that no such success is actually achieved—so as to avoid the guilt that would result from succeeding. By contrast, the masochistic form of repetition compulsion operates differently. Rather than attempting to undo the past by succeeding in the present, masochism aims to recast the past in light of present-day realities. By turning a passively experienced situation into an experience that one actively controls, one can look back on the original experience and view it as an experience one had also been in complete control over, as if one possessed an adult-like ability to control others even as a young child.

In certain instances, the classic and the masochistic forms of repetition compulsion work synergistically to help children cope with the rage, fear, guilt, and narcissistic mortification that may result in response to their having failed to satisfy their oedipal strivings. The classic form of repetition compulsion is better suited to help children cope with (1) the rage born of frustration when the oedipal wishes are not met, (2) the fear of the destructive potential of that rage, (3) the fear of precipitating retaliation from those with whom one is in competition, and (4) the guilt over coveting what belongs to others. By contrast, the narcissistic mortification is better handled by the masochistic form of repetition compulsion that operates by creating an illusion that the individual had always been in control of how he had been treated, so he would accordingly have no reason to feel hurt or injured by the rejection or mistreatment of others.

The suffering of the female masochist leads her to feel self-righteous, which, in turn, helps her justify taking whatever steps she feels necessary to achieve her goal. She may elect to portray herself as the victim in the hopes that by so doing she may be able to cause the man to feel guilty over how he had taken advantage of her. She may launch into a diatribe about how she has sacrificed the best years of her life by putting her life on hold while she waited patiently for him. Such a harangue may extract promises and concessions from the man, thus momentarily giving her the upper hand. This is one of the ways single women can influence married men to give them more of what they claim to want.

While the power relationship between the single woman and the married man is, in many ways, skewed in favor of the man, by the woman's continuing to portray herself as if she is perpetually in the "one down" position, she is paradoxically able to gain the upper hand, if only momentarily. This is a classic masochistic ploy, permitting the sadist to feel as if he is the one calling the shots when nothing could be further from the truth!

9

Treatment Implications

There is occasions and causes why and wherefore in all things.
William Shakespeare, *Henry V*, V, i, 3

It is with some reluctance that I now address the question of how one might approach working with single women or married men who have become involved in relationships that conform to the single woman–married man syndrome. My reluctance stems from a discomfort that spelling out a treatment approach could be misunderstood by some as constituting *the* way one ought to treat such cases. Nothing limits a therapist's creativity more than a how-to outline for treatment. A "cookbook" guide threatens the therapist's spontaneity, which is the last thing I would want this book to do. I believe that what therapists need most is an appreciation of the syndrome's existence and some ideas about how one might think about it. Everything else flows from these two elements. As a concession to those who may clamor for some direction about how to treat these cases, I will summarize what I have said in the preceding chapters that has bearing on treatment.

There are three issues that must be kept in mind when treating patients who are engaged in relationships that conform to the single woman–married man syndrome. The first is the fact that such a syndrome exists. Being alert to the existence of this syndrome should lead to the early recognition of such cases. This saves time by making it unnecessary for the patient to educate the therapist about this pattern, which often proves to be a lengthy process. The second is the therapeutic stance one adopts toward the material presented. Certain stances have a better chance of furthering the work of therapy than others. Accordingly, it is critical to examine the attitudes one has toward extramarital affairs, since these attitudes may play a role in unconsciously determining how one approaches such cases. Finally, there is the matter of appreciating the fact that the behaviors defined by this syndrome are driven by unconscious forces. It behooves the therapist to know about the underlying dynamics that may contribute to such behavior.

RECOGNIZING THE SYNDROME

Some may remain skeptical about the existence of the single woman–married man syndrome, believing that I have failed to prove my case. I have presented a few case histories in detail that I believe are illustrative of this syndrome and I have supplemented these case histories with vignettes from my own practice. As I mentioned in the beginning pages of this book, collecting and publishing such case material is problematic on a number of counts. To begin with, this material is highly confidential, given the potential problems it would create were a wife to discover her husband's indiscretions. Accordingly, very few case reports have appeared that might already have established the existence of this syndrome. Furthermore, the nature of clinical practice does not lend itself to the discovery of such a syndrome. Any therapist who treats cases in intensive therapy is unlikely to see enough patients engaged in this syndrome to be able to say anything statistically significant about it. Those therapists who see large numbers of patients in less intensive treatment for shorter periods of time may be in a position to have culled enough cases to say something about it. But they would be in no position to speak authoritatively about the underlying dynamics that drive such behavior or to offer something that is meaningful about this pattern. Besides, it is common for this syndrome to be subordinate to the chief reason the patient seeks treatment, so it may fail to become the focus of less intensive treatments. Finally, relatively few therapists make a practice of treating extramarital affairs. Frank Pittman (1989), a psychiatrist who practices in Atlanta, Georgia, is an exception. He reports having treated over 100 cases of extramarital affairs, and his work supports what I have proposed in this book.

It is customary for scientists to present their findings in peer-review journals rather than publish them first in book form. While this precedent makes sense and generally proves to be good practice, I believe that the limitations placed on the length of scientific journal articles preclude the type of detailed reporting needed to delineate the syndrome I have proposed in this book. I could have presented a single case report. But as much as can be gained from an in-depth presentation of one case, there are serious questions about whether a particular case says anything about people in general. Now that I have proposed criteria that define this syndrome, it may be possible for others to test my hypothesis to see whether it is replicable. Clinicians who have read this book stand ready to do their own research into the question of whether this theory is valid and clinically useful.

There are advantages and disadvantages to alerting clinicians about the existence of a behavior pattern that is believed to constitute a syndrome. The advantages are obvious and amount to saving therapists from having to reinvent the wheel. Understanding how this syndrome unfolds—the course it runs and how it typically ends—helps inoculate therapists from becoming swept up in the patient's explanatory system or enthusiastic hopefulness about the relationship's prospects. The therapist's continuing to encourage a single woman patient to "hang in," remain hopeful, and persevere, is the last thing such a patient needs. But the same can be said for the adoption of an attitude that attacks the relationship as hopeless. Like all interventions, tact and timing are everything. One must not rush a patient to accept what the therapist thinks to be correct about the relationship. The therapist may ultimately prove to be right, but there may be disadvantages to presenting one's theories to patients before they are ready to hear them. The patient's maintaining hopefulness is so central to this syndrome that the therapist may have to wait for the patient to catch up to him.

The disadvantages of becoming savvy about the existence of a syndrome lies in the danger of being too quick to assume that the case under consideration neatly fits into that mold. Jumping to conclusions is as much a problem as remaining oblivious to the existence of the syndrome. As important as it is to be knowledgeable about human behavioral patterns, it is just as important to remain skeptical about one's urge to reach a quick understanding of any given case. The single woman–married man syndrome should remain a hypothetical possibility until such time as the mounting evidence becomes strong enough to make the case that this syndrome does, in fact, apply to the particular patient under consideration.

The single woman–married man syndrome is neither a disease nor a disorder. Though I have dedicated the latter part of this book to speculations about the developmental backgrounds and unconscious motives that might lead a single woman and a married man to pair up, it cannot be said that all such pairings resulting in relationships that conform to the single woman–married man syndrome are the product of such backgrounds and motives. It would be a mistake to conclude that every individual who becomes involved in this type of relationship shares in common certain personality traits with others who are similarly involved. But it would be just as preposterous to think that there might not be subgroups of individuals engaged in such relationships that do bear certain similarities with others so engaged.

I was careful, in the beginning of this book, to make clear that this syndrome could be reactive in nature, that the behavioral pattern defined by the syndrome could be the *result* of having fallen into a troubling relationship rather than the determining force that brought the couple together in the first place. The narcissistically gratifying aspect that is so apparent early in the course of the relationship gradually pales in comparison to the emerging feelings of frustration and powerlessness. As a result, the relationship typically follows an emotionally tumultuous course that proves hellish for both participants. Both suffer on account of what the relationship ultimately puts them through. Such a relationship may be upsetting to experience, yet not necessarily indicative of underlying psychopathology that led the patient to seek out such a masochistic experience.

THE THERAPEUTIC STANCE

The optimal attitude for a therapist to adopt when treating such cases is that of empathic inquisitiveness. As mentioned in Chapter 1, attitudes about extramarital affairs run the gamut from moralistic, to blame seeking, to dismissive, to prurient. Adopting any one of these attitudes will undoubtedly limit the success of treatment. If, for instance, a therapist sees a man's extramarital affairs as little more than the manifestation of a healthy sexual urge coming into conflict with society's unrealistic demand of monogamy, treatment is not likely to help the patient reach any deeper understanding about his underlying motives.

While therapists are used to adopting a nonjudgmental stance toward the situations they are presented with, certain types of case material are more likely than others to stimulate countertransference reactions in therapists. This is particularly true of the single woman–married man syndrome. Extramarital affairs are a par-

ticularly charged topic that is likely to challenge the therapist's
dedication and ability to remain neutral.

Empathic inquisitiveness proves particularly valuable when
treating women and men engaged in the single woman–married
man syndrome. This stance is defined by an attitude of curious,
naïve, compassionate open-mindedness toward the material presented. Though some may think it so, it is not synonymous with
taking the patient's side or confirming the patient's beliefs about
why he acts as he does or why certain things happen to him as
they do. It is particularly important not to side with patients in
their portrayal of themselves as victims in this relationship. This
is not to say that one should turn a deaf ear to how the patient
experiences himself as a victim. It is only to say that being understanding about the fact that this is how the patient experiences
things does not mean that the therapist necessarily sees them the
same way. I understand that this may be a difficult line to walk.
But failing to maintain a degree of objectivity toward the material can threaten the entire treatment enterprise. Reinforcing the
patient's view that he is nothing more than a hapless victim who
is being controlled by his partner promises to lead the therapy
in circles. Agreeing with the patient's point of view does not constitute empathy.

Just as one might side with the patient's experience of him-
or herself as victim, it is just as easy for therapists to err in the
opposite direction. Anger toward patients whom the therapist
views as predators may lead a therapist to blame the patients for
having coerced or manipulated their seemingly innocent partner
into such a relationship. More often than not, it is the male patient who stimulates the therapist's protectiveness toward the
partner who is viewed as the patient's prey. But women can also
be viewed as having manipulated the man in ways that the therapist views as shameful.

An appreciation for the intersubjectivity of this type of relationship saves one from lapsing into blaming one of the parties
for bearing the lion's share of the responsibility for how things
have turned out. The single woman–married man syndrome is a

type of dance that is choreographed by the unconscious psyches of the dancers. To believe otherwise is to lapse into simplistic thinking about this matter. Though it may appear as if one of the partners has, in fact, been rendered helpless by the actions of the other, it is really the unconscious needs of each party that play the largest role in keeping the individuals involved in a relationship that, on the surface, appears to have ceased to be satisfying.

UNCONSCIOUS DYNAMICS

Another challenge encountered when treating such cases is determined by the therapist's ability to appreciate just how out of control these men and women feel in terms of coming to some sort of resolution of the relationship. Some therapists may question the validity of patients' self-portrayal as powerless to extricate themselves from such a relationship. Some may further question the validity of referring to a behavioral pattern as a syndrome when that behavior appears to be under the individual's volitional control. I consider such thinking psychologically unsophisticated. For instance, most therapists would never regard the behavior of those suffering from bulimarexia, a condition characterized by self-induced vomiting and self-imposed dietary restrictions, to be unworthy of being considered and treated as a bona fide psychological condition just because some believe the core problem to be failed will power. It is a throwback to the dark ages to regard such psychological conditions as nothing more than bad behavior. Just as is the case with bulimarexia, unconscious thoughts and fantasies play a large role in determining the behavior of those engaged in the single woman–married man syndrome. It is critical that therapists who undertake the treatment of such cases appreciate this fact and be on the lookout for the unconscious motivations that are driving the behavior.

But while I believe in calling the behaviors that constitute the subject of this book a syndrome, I am not dismissing the individual's responsibility for acting as he or she does. When individuals find themselves acting out of control, at least from a conscious standpoint, they have a responsibility to come to terms with what is driving such behavior. The problem often encountered when treating women and men engaged in the single woman–married man syndrome is that both parties may initially be unwilling to accept the fact that their behavior is being determined by factors that lie outside of their conscious awareness. Treating such cases requires an unusual amount of patience, since the level of resistance to think psychologically about their situation runs particularly high. Helping such patients accept a degree of responsibility for having unconsciously gotten themselves into such a jam can prove to be a frustrating task for therapists.

The biggest challenge a therapist faces when attempting to treat patients engaged in the single woman–married man syndrome is the addictive-like nature of such relationships. What makes drugs or activities such as gambling or promiscuity so addicting is their ability to create sudden, dramatic changes in how one feels inside. An external cure for an internal state is the essence of an addiction. It is much like a light switch you can turn on and off at will. Nothing works as well as an addictive substance or circumstance, which is why it is so difficult to give up. This proves particularly true when in comes to the single woman–married man syndrome.

The initial attraction of such a relationship lies in the narcissistic gratification provided early in its course. The intensity of this gratification leads the participants to feel that they are not just in love, but in love in a way that no one has ever been before. This narcissistic gratification is a kind of high. While there is some degree of narcissistic gratification whenever anyone falls in love, the intensity of the need for such gratification is greater in individuals who become involved in the single woman–married man syndrome. This is why the relationship proves so hard to give up. Even when it proves more than either individual can bear, the moments when it provides intense narcissistic gratification keep the two involved. For a therapist to attempt to undo such a relationship is as difficult as when a policeman becomes involved in a domestic dispute. It takes considerable time and energy for the relationship with the therapist to offer the narcissistic gratification to the patient that helps provide the therapist with some of the leverage he needs to make progress with the patient.

Patients may only offer therapists an opening when they are temporarily on the downslope of the relationship. When it has momentarily ceased to provide the same type of gratification and instead is proving frustrating, the therapist may be invited to work with patients on why they have been unable to extricate themselves from so difficult a relationship. This is akin to how alcoholics or drug-dependent patients become open to change when they hit bottom.

Apart from the deep narcissistic gratification each derives from the relationship, single women and married men have their own unique dynamics that require addressing in the course of treatment. The most prominent problem that men tend to present with is an inability to decide whether to leave their wife for the other woman. These men always think in terms of leaving one for the other. They never see it as two independent decisions because, in their mind, it is not. Having to decide between two is a luxury that these men unconsciously enjoy no matter how consciously conflicted they appear to be. Such a situation is very reassuring to the man's "ego" since it not only proves his worth, it also reassures him that he can't lose. There is always one waiting in the wings. It is critical that therapists keep this in mind. Such a man's greatest fear is that he will decide to stay with one woman, who then leaves him.

These men are highly ambivalent and seem genuinely confused about what they want. Therapists must resist the urge that wells up in them in response to such incessant fence sitting to take a stand about what would be in the patient's best interest. Though a man in such a situation literally begs the therapist to make up his mind for him, it is obviously pointless to accede to such wishes. The man isn't going to listen anyway. He is not helped by a list of the pros and cons for staying with versus leaving the wife. It is best if the therapist avoids being seduced into buying into the patient's contention that he needs the therapist to help him decide, once and for all, which woman he would rather be with. It is more productive to help the patient explore the roots of his ambivalence and the nature of his conflict about permitting himself to become truly intimate with any one woman than to become sidetracked trying to invent ways for the patient to resolve the question of how to make a decision he won't later regret. There is no direct way to help patients decide how to make the "right" decision because they take refuge in their confusion.

What is typically at the core of the married man's problem is his intolerance of emotional vulnerability, which limits his ability to be emotionally intimate. In particular, these men are phobic about becoming vulnerable to women by virtue of their needing them. Such men have a way of always keeping one foot out the door. Historically, many of them had trouble not only deciding between the two women in their lives, but deciding whether to marry their wives in the first place. Sometimes it took the wife's forcing the issue by giving the man an ultimatum in order for the man to agree to wed. Though the wife may believe that the man's agreeing to marry indicates that he has finally overcome his resistance to commit, this often proves not to be so. Unbeknownst to her, the man has his own secret emotional prenuptial agreement—one that limits his emotional liability.

It is important to avoid focusing exclusively on the man's relationship with the single woman when treating a man engaged in the single woman–married man syndrome, since his problems relating to her are typically symptomatic of a larger problem, one having to do with his inability to permit himself to be intimate and vulnerable with any woman. For this reason, it is useful to help the man explore the nature of his relationships with women in general, as well as his relationship with his wife, including the role his feelings toward his wife play in the pursuit of the extramarital affair.

These men never reveal enough of themselves to be truly vulnerable to the women they become involved with. By revealing only select aspects of themselves to these women, the men ensure that no one woman ever comes to know him well enough for her to constitute an emotional threat. But in the process, no woman ever satisfies him to the degree she otherwise might were he to risk being known completely by her.

When it comes to treating single women engaged in this type of relationship, there are other issues that must be addressed. Such women must be helped to begin to turn their attention to what is going on in their own minds as opposed to what is going on in the man's mind. These women usually believe that all it will take to wrest the man from his wife's control—for they are often inclined to see the man as unavailable through no fault of his own—is for them to try harder or be better in some specified way. The woman's low self-esteem is readily apparent. Much rides on the relationship, for it is seen as capable of validating the woman the way nothing else can. The woman's masochistic tendencies are also readily apparent and in need of attention. But in order to treat such women, it is important for the therapist to have an appreciation of the complexity of masochism rather than thinking of it simply as "pleasure in pain." These issues must ultimately be addressed in the course of therapy.

Much can be gained by an in-depth exploration of the woman's earliest relationships since this usually proves to be where the problem originated. In her mind, the relationship with the married man promises to compensate for what she missed out on as a child. Accordingly, it is essential that some work be done on this period of her life.

It is particularly important that therapists not buy the woman's claim that she wholeheartedly wants the married man all to herself, since this usually proves not to be the case. Though she complains that the relationship is going nowhere, she nevertheless tolerates this situation, sometimes for years, representing her continued involvement as reflecting only her hopefulness when it may actually reflect her conflict about having things any other way.

In order to treat the men and women who become involved in these types of affairs, it is necessary that the therapist have a sophisticated appreciation of the factors that permit individuals to develop the ability to fall in love and remain in love. It is also important to understand the role that control, submission, and surrender play in love. These issues are the topic of the book's next, and final, chapter.

10

On the Nature
of Love

My crown is in my heart, not on my head;
Not deck'd with diamonds and Indian stones,
Nor to be seen. My crown is called content;
A crown it is that seldom kings enjoy.
William Shakespeare, *Henry VI*, Part Three, III, I, 62

Attempting to say anything about the nature of love might strike
the reader as a presumptuous task. Philosophers have grappled
with this issue for centuries, so what more is left to say about the
subject? I do not pretend to understand anything so deep, transcendent, and divine as love. But several aspects of love touch on
the subject of the single woman–married man syndrome.

This chapter discusses the processes involved in an adult's
developing the capacity to love another adult sexually; the relationship between power and love, with a special emphasis on a
comparison between the act of submission and that of surrender; the psychological effects of losing a love relation, as has been

described by Freud (1917) in his paper "Mourning and Melancholia"; and a comparison of romantic love with what Kernberg refers to as "mature love."

THE DEVELOPING CAPACITY
TO LOVE ANOTHER SEXUALLY

The psychosexual development of boys and girls leads to significant differences in the ways that men and women love one another. The original love object for boys and girls is the same. Through her ministrations, the mother is the primary object of attachment and of the child's affections. But while boys retain a primary investment in their mother, this is not the case with girls, who come to a point in development where they switch partners, making the father their chief love interest.

These developmental differences cannot be overstated, for they help account for a host of differences in the way in which men and women approach loving someone of the opposite sex. Remaining libidinally focused on their mother results in boys having to contend with the frustrations of never succeeding at attaining their goal—to eliminate all competitors, that is, father and siblings, and be the mother's "one and only." Girls, on the other hand, are developmentally forced to renounce their primary interest in mother, and, as a result, cope with frustration in an entirely different fashion.

Dealing with the frustration of never getting to be mother's primary love interest is one of the central organizing experiences of boyhood. The frustration and narcissistic injury a boy experiences in response to this perceived rejection/failure is so intense that it becomes emotionally taxing for him to remember this painful experience. This parallels the way many children younger than the age of 6 deal with the experience of losing a parent, a loss so unbearable that it is often coped with by the complete elimination of the parent from the child's memory. With regard to a boy's oedipal wishes, infantile amnesia, which leads to an inability to remember much from before the age of 4, helps the boy forget what it was he so desperately desired. While a woman can remain "Daddy's little girl" her entire life, a man is not likely to appreciate being seen as "Mommy's little boy" much past latency age. This expression is tantamount to pouring salt into the wound of a boy's painful realization that he never had what it took to win mother over.

Because a man remains unconsciously invested in his mother throughout his life, frustration and narcissistic vulnerability play key roles in all of his subsequent relations with women, all of which tend to echo his first experience with his mother. This frustration begets aggression, thus making aggression a factor in all men's love relationships with women. How a man contends with the undeniable existence of his aggression toward women plays a key role in how he loves, and whether he can love, women. My characterizing aggression as the product of frustration should not be understood as a complete accounting of the origins of aggression. Aggression can arise as a primary drive, just as it can develop as a result of environmental deprivation. But for simplicity's sake, I have used the reactive form of aggression to make my point.

The relationship between "fucking" a woman, that is, an aggressive, even hostile act, and "making love" to her reflects one of the chief, unresolvable conflicts in male–female sexual relations. As a term, *fuck* contains all the elements of aggression. The idea of "fucking a woman's brains out" is, at times, considered the ideal sexual experience for men. There is no hiding the intense aggression behind such impulses. Yet wishing to use a woman in this way need not preclude the man's capacity to love her in the most complete and affectionate way possible at other points in their relationship. Some might consider this an odd assertion. But it is just this task—to somehow blend affection, which derives from one's earliest years, with innate aggression and aggression born of frustration and narcissistic injury, with the pubertally intensified sexual drive—that constitutes one of the culminating achievements of a man's sexual life.

Freud (1912) addressed these issues:

> There are only a very few educated people in whom the two currents of affection and sensuality have become properly fused; the man almost always feels his respect for the woman acting as a restriction on his sexual activity, and only develops full potency when he is with a debased sexual object. . . . It sounds not only disagreeable but also paradoxical, yet it must nevertheless be said that anyone who is to be really free and happy in love must have surmounted his respect for women and have come to terms with the idea of incest with his mother or sister. Anyone who subjects himself to serious self-examination on the subject of this requirement will be sure to find that he regards the sexual act basically as something degrading, which defiles and pollutes not only the body. The origin of this low opinion, which he will certainly not willingly acknowledge, must be looked for in the period of his youth in which the sensual current in him was already strongly developed but its satisfaction with an object outside the family was almost completely prohibited as it was with an incestuous one. [pp. 185–186]

To be sure, this statement is both disagreeable and controversial. The idea that a man must have surmounted his respect for a woman in order to be free to love her completely seems, at first glance, to be outrageous. But a more careful reading of the complete text yields a different sense of what Freud meant by "respect." It was his opinion that men tend to overvalue women. If this tendency is taken to an extreme, as happens when men are unable to feel tenderness (affection) toward the women they sexually desire, this results in the feeling that women deserve men to be "perfect gentlemen" who would never even think about having sex with women because gentlemen recognize sex for what it is: the slightly repugnant, anally tinged act that the latency boy envisioned it to be, and an aggressive, hostile act driven by the wish to retaliate for the narcissistic injury of having been rejected by mother as a boy ("Fuck you for rejecting me!!!"). Such sentiments naturally contribute to fantasizing the sexual act as *meaning* to defile and degrade according to the talion principle—in retaliation for the boy having felt that he had been treated cruelly by his mother when she rejected him by refusing to accept him as her sole love object.

Given how complex and conflicted the sexual act tends to be, it is no wonder that Freud (1912) stated, "Something in the nature of the sexual instinct itself is unfavorable to the realization of complete satisfaction" (pp. 188–189). In the end, Freud saw this conflict as emanating not solely from intrapsychic causes, but as the product of the individual's need to bow to the demands placed upon him or her by society: "We may perhaps be forced to become reconciled to the idea that it is quite impossible to adjust the claims of the sexual instinct to the demands of civilization" (p. 190).

POWER AND LOVE: SUBMISSION AND THE ACT OF SURRENDER

A romantic view of love leaves no room for any consideration of the role that power plays in love relations. The sheer power of love itself is seen as setting everything right—with each partner tripping over the other in a mad dash to see who can more selflessly satisfy the other's need. This is not, however, what actually happens over the long haul. Every relationship has its power dimension, and love relations are no exception.

The need to exert control over one's partner stems both from an active desire to ensure that one's needs are met and a defensive reaction to the fear that if one ceases to look out for oneself, it is unlikely that others will accept that responsibility. Control maneuvers may be relatively transparent and benign, in which case they may not be deemed objectionable by the other. At times, however, control maneuvers can be ruthless, devious, and ultimately undermining of the couple's ability to feel safely intimate.

Ethel Person (1988) writes that "the ultimate balance of power often resides in the partner who is least fearful of losing the relationship" (p. 183). I would amend that by substituting the word *appears* for *is*, since it is often a power ploy to convince the other that one is not all that invested in the relationship. Only by calling the partner's bluff is one able to ultimately determine the veracity of such a claim. And if one is too scared to test the relationship in this way, then one is at risk for losing power in the process. Many men claim not to care whether a relationship continues, yet completely fall apart once a breakup occurs.

In Chapter 2, we saw how Monica Lewinsky gradually lost any sense of power over what was happening between her and President Clinton. The same was true for Edwin Gottesman, described in Chapter 3, who became hopelessly addicted to his relationship with Jennifer Scott. It is not always the woman who feels a loss of power as the relationship unfolds. But in most instances of the single woman–married man syndrome, the sense of loss of control shifts back and forth between the two partners.

Seduction, domination, and submission are three strategies employed to exert control over others. Of these, seduction is the most benign and acceptable form, since it acknowledges the role of the other as active agent who can go along with, or resist, the seduction. Seducers are permitted by the seducee to think of themselves as the ones who are making it all happen, but this is purely an illusion. Seducers may be the first to let their wishes be known; they may even be masterful in persuading the seducee to go along with the plan by wearing away at the seducee's resistance; but at no point do seducers truly act as a Svengali whose magnetism overpowers the seducee's will. The seducee may be in denial of his or her wish to go along with the seducer's plan, and the seducer may play upon the unconscious part of the seducee that is "game for such action," but the ultimate responsibility for the consensual act rests on the shoulders of both the seducer and the seducee.

Domination is quite a different story. It is the most overt means by which one person attempts to control another. Domineering behavior operates by forcefully asserting one's needs or one's beliefs while simultaneously undermining the other's position (beliefs, needs, etc.). The behavior of the domineering individual is often coercive and threatening, on the one hand, and mocking and derisive, on the other. Attempting to possess one's lover in these ways works to ensure that the domineering partner never has to admit needing anything from his lover, since his bullying behavior has so broken the lover's spirit and self-confidence that it is highly unlikely that she can muster the emotional wherewithal to leave him. But it is an empty victory, since attempting to possess another's love in this way throws doubt on the genuineness of that love, given the fact that it is no longer freely given.

While submission may appear to be a response to the other's need to dominate, as is seen in the animal kingdom, where alpha males prove their dominance and are thereafter accorded status by virtue of the deference paid them, in humans, submission can be a ploy or strategy by which to manipulate the one who is supposedly dominant. At first glance, submission appears to have everything to do with being controlled by another. Yet in its own covert way, submission can be employed as an effective means to exert control over others. Submission subtly manipulates while domination overtly coerces. According to Person (1988), submission is a ploy used more by females than by males. By catering to the man's needs, the woman makes herself indispensable to him, thus making it hard for him either to leave or act freely in the relationship. The guilt produced in the man by the woman's portrayal of herself as a martyr furthers the covert power she has over him, all the while leaving him believing that he is the one who is, in fact, in control. Permitting the man to believe he is dominating is a time-honored female ploy that aims to protect the man's "ego" while ensuring that the woman's needs are met.

In the single woman–married man syndrome, the woman's claim that she is forever submitting to the married man's wishes without due regard for her own begins to look spurious when one considers how submission can be an unconscious ploy to control the other. The parallels with sadomasochistic relationships are worth noting. In such relationships, the masochist creates an illusion that he or she is controlled by the sadist, yet, behind the scenes, the masochist is covertly manipulating the sadist every bit as much as the sadist is overtly manipulating the masochist, maybe more so. There are other times, however, when submission is more a reaction to domination than a ploy in its own right. When this is the case, the effect of submission can be devastating. Person (1988) writes: "This mode of relating to the beloved necessarily carries with it a sense of self-impoverishment. The lover sacrifices himself to the security of the relationship. Unlike the impulse to surrender, where the aim is transcendence, the motivation here is not so grand. The lover does not seek . . . to be reborn, or enlarged, but seeks to secure the truncated self. Subordination is deeply damaging to self-esteem" (p. 176).

Since it is rarely consciously clear to the individual involved when his or her submitting is an unconscious ploy and when it is the result of being emotionally overpowered by another's attempts to dominate (or one's own tendencies to regress to a state of passivity), it can be argued that submission generally has a detrimental effect on the individual along the lines outlined by Person. I would suggest that man's fear of being drawn into a submissive position oftentimes accounts for his need to dominate. And, as I will explain below, this fear of finding himself in the submissive position may interfere with his feeling free to surrender to a love relation, since surrender and submission are sometimes mistaken as equivalent. And, if the man's ego is fragile and prone to regression, his fears may turn out to be founded.

Sex between a man and a woman offers the promise of "sweet surrender": the transcendent experience of momentarily losing one's self, one's sense of separate distinctness, in the experience of "we-ness." Surrender results in fleeting moments when the boundaries between self and other as separate psychic entities become temporarily blurred. It is the realization of the myth of Aristophanes (see Plato's *Symposium*), which tells of how all humans had once been alike until Zeus severed them into the two sexes as punishment for their insolence and arrogance. Ever since, men and women have searched for their lost halves: "since their original nature had been cut in two, each one longed for its own other half and stayed with it. They threw their arms round each other, weaving themselves together, wanting to form a single living thing" (Plato 1999, p. 24). Through such moments of imagined merger, each individual transcends for a time the lonely isolation defined by his distinct uniqueness, in Aldous Huxley's words (quoted in Person 1988), "To get out of themselves, to pass beyond the limits of that tiny island universe, within which each individual finds himself confined" (p. 138).

While some confuse surrender with a more regressive type of merger, one that creates the illusion that the psychic distinction between self and other has been completely obliterated, there is a critical difference between these two phenomena. Kernberg (1974b) writes, "In contrast to the primitive fusion of self- and object images during the symbiotic phase of development (Mahler 1968), the higher level fusion of orgasm is based upon and reconfirms one's own individuality, and particularly a mature sexual identification" (p. 751). Kernberg (1977) elaborates:

There is a basic, intrinsic, contradiction in the combination of these two crucial features of sexual love; the precondition of firm boundaries of the self with the constant awareness of the indissoluble separateness of individuals, and the sense of transcendence, of becoming one with the loved person. The separateness brings about loneliness and longing and fear for the frailty of all relations; the transcendence in the couple's union brings about the sense of oneness with the world, of permanence and new creation. Loneliness, one might say, is a precondition for transcendency. . . . Sexual passion integrates the simultaneous crossing of boundaries of the self into awareness of biological functioning beyond the control of the self and the crossing of boundaries in a sophisticated identification with the loved object while yet maintaining the sense of separate identity. [pp. 95–98]

By surrender, I do not mean defeat. Surrender takes on that meaning only in situations that are adversarial, where surrender is more akin to submitting to another. Dictionary definitions of "surrender" attribute two distinct meanings to the term. One is synonymous with submission or capitulation: "to yield to the power, control, or possession of another upon compulsion or demand" (*Webster's New Collegiate Dictionary*). The other definition of surrender is impersonal: "to give (oneself) over to something (as an influence or course of action)." Emanuel Ghent (1990) contrasts surrender with submission: (1) "One may surrender 'in the presence of another,' not 'to another" as in the case of submission." (2) "Surrender is not a voluntary activity. One cannot choose to surrender, though one can choose to submit. One can provide facilitative conditions for surrender but cannot make it happen." (3) "[Surrender] may be accompanied by a feeling of dread and death, and/or clarity, relief, even ecstasy." (4) "Its ultimate direction is the discovery of one's identity, one's sense of self, one's sense of wholeness, even one's sense of unity with other living beings. This is quite unlike submission in which the reverse happens: one feels one's self a puppet in the power of another; one's sense of identity atrophies." (p. 111). Unlike surrender, which provides the individual with a momentary reprieve from the awareness of his distinctive isolation, thus enhancing and enriching his sense of self, submission holds out the hope of redemption only to disappoint in the end.

When falling in love is the result of mutual surrender, what results clearly enriches each of the parties involved. But what happens when falling in love is, instead, the result of mutual submission? This concept will strike some as odd. The very nature of submission seems to preclude any such configuration since, like sadomasochism, submission is always relative to someone who is dominant. Nevertheless, I believe that in certain types of love relations, specifically those encountered in the single woman–married man syndrome, both parties adopt submissive positions vis-à-vis the other, just not at the same time. The partners jockey for the position of submissive victim. The woman's claim to the title is the most obvious given how little she seems to be getting in return for the sacrifices she makes. But the man often is left feeling utterly powerless in the process, as was evident in the case of Edwin Gottesman, described in Chapter 3. A man in such a position feels manipulated by the woman's covert threat to reveal the affair, and in many ways finds himself submitting to her when she momentarily gains the upper hand.

COPING WITH THE LOSS OF
A TRANSFORMING OBJECT

Therapists frequently see patients who are distraught over the loss of a particular type of love relationship. Prior to coming to therapy, such patients have typically gone to great lengths trying to win back the affections of a lover they claim they cannot live without. For such patients, losing this lover is like losing a piece of themselves. They are desperate to get this piece back so they can feel complete and whole again. In fact, these patients are, in many respects, the epitome of desperation. They may even go so far as to ask the therapist to speak to their ex-lover on their behalf, to put in a good word for them or to inform the one who left them about how they are suffering: they cannot eat or sleep, and have ceased to be able to function since they are spending every waking moment thinking only of the ex-lover.

This type of breakup differs from others, which, while upsetting and psychologically disruptive, bears none of the hallmarks of the type of breakup described above. What are the chief differences between these two types of breakups? What has been lost in each? And why does the mourner react to each situation differently?

In the preceding chapters, we have seen numerous examples of just how desperate some people become when separated from the one upon whom they have grown dependent. In the case of Monica Lewinsky (Chapter 2), we saw a woman who, by the accounts of those who knew her at the time, had become completely obsessed with her relationship with President Clinton. She felt as if she was going out of her mind whenever it appeared that her relationship with the president was in jeopardy. She would adopt extreme measures, employ subtle threats, become hysterical to the point of "going ballistic," and would act in ways that worried the president's secretary. Edwin Gottesman (Chapter 3) was no less "crazed" when Jennifer Scott suddenly and unexpectedly disappeared. He panicked and felt as if he was nearly going out of his mind. He could not eat, sleep, or attend to his business affairs. He shamelessly lied, feeling that such actions were justified given how desperate he felt. As he put it, "It's amazing what a man will do under those circumstances" (Hunt 1969, p. 201).

Why were Monica Lewinsky and Edwin Gottesman so desperate to get their lovers back? Is this the sign of "true love"? Or, is it the by-product of an aspect of these relationships that goes beyond mere love? And, in such instances, what *is* being mourned: the loss of the one who is loved, or the loss of who one had become by virtue of having been loved by that individual?

Love relations offer participants a host of different benefits: (1) a chance to share one's life with another, to not have to live in lonely isolation; (2) a chance to feel part of something larger than oneself, to be a partner in an entity; (3) a chance to be emotionally and physically intimate with another, to be able to experience the loosening of boundaries that demarcate one's physical existence from others; (4) a chance to feel loved and valued by another, to feel as if one's existence matters to someone other than oneself; (5) a chance to love another, to have another toward whom one can direct one's loving feelings, thus providing an opportunity to feel like a loving person. Taken together, these benefits amount to the reasons humans willingly bond with others humans for extended periods of time, including "forever."

Above and beyond these listed benefits are others that provide an additional dimension to love relations. Sometimes love transforms individuals, tapping potential they had no idea lay latent within them. Suddenly, as a result of being loved by another, one experiences oneself as a completely different person. This was dramatically illustrated in the case of Edwin Gottesman, who, after beginning a relationship with Jennifer Scott, suddenly found himself acting quite uncharacteristically generous, carefree, gallant, and passionate.

If these changes become autonomous and no longer require that one remain attached to the lover who had facilitated the transformation, then that individual's continuing commitment to that relationship is freed from the contaminating thought that one must remain in the relationship if one hopes to be able to remain transformed. If this is not the case, then the relationship is at risk of becoming primarily about maintaining this transformation. This is not to say that the transforming lover is not loved for his or her own right; it is only to note that this dimension of love is overshadowed by the love of what another has permitted one to become.

Upon the dissolution of such a relationship, individuals whose transformation had depended upon a continuing connection with the transforming other typically fall apart. They show signs of suffering from what Freud (1917) called "melancholia," a condition that shares in common most of the features of mourning save for one, "the lowering of the self-regarding feelings" (p. 244). Freud elaborated: "The patient represents his ego to us as worthless, incapable of achievement and morally despicable. . . . He is not of the opinion that a change has taken place in him, but extends his self-criticism back over the past; he declares that he was never any better . . . [and he believes that his] sole aim has been to hide the weakness of his own nature" (p. 246).

Both mourning and melancholia are triggered by the loss of someone who or something that was critically important to the individual. But, in the case of melancholia, "the patient is aware of the loss which has given rise to his melancholia, but only in the sense of *whom* he has lost but not *what* he has lost in him" (Freud 1917, p. 245). The melancholic individual remains unaware of what the loss meant to him in that he fails to recognize the critical function that individual served in his or her life. "The analogy with mourning led us to conclude that he has suffered a loss in regard to an object; what he tells us points to a loss in regard to his ego" (p. 247).

Freud's psychological explanation of the psychogenesis of melancholia is as intricate as it is convoluted. Rather than gradually abandoning most of his emotional connection to the lost object (save for a trace element that subtly enters the ego as happens in the case of mourning), the melancholic instead identifies with the lost object, introjects aspects of that object, and then wages an internal war between the critical agency of his own psyche (the superego) and another aspect of his psyche (the ego), which has been altered via the identification and introjection. All of the anger one felt toward the original object, which had been ambivalently held, comes to attack one's own ego that has become identified with the lost object. "We perceive that the self-reproaches are reproaches against the loved object which have been shifted away from it on to the patient's own ego" (p. 248).

Freud's psychological explanation about melancholia was determined, in part, by his then current beliefs about the nature of relationships between people. He felt that melancholia was the product of narcissistic relationships, which, along with "anaclitic-type" relationships, make up the universe of possible relationships. He defined a narcissistic object choice as one in which an individual loves another whom he sees as either being like he is, like he once was, or like he wishes to be. By contrast an object who is chosen because he or she bears certain similarities to the original caregiving (need-satisfying) individual is referred to as an "anaclitic-type object choice."

Though Freud was careful to note that relationships typically show signs of containing elements of both types of object choice, many other types of relationships have been discovered since he first penned his theory on narcissism in 1914. For instance, Heinz Kohut (1971), the father of self psychology, offered case material illustrating what he referred to as "selfobjects," which are functions that can be served by individuals capable of satisfying a host of different needs, such as the need to be "mirrored," to have one's self affirmed, which had gone unaddressed by Freud. One might even choose an object based on a sense that that object seems a likely candidate to provide the facilitating environment necessary for the individual to psychologically develop. Christopher Bollas (1979) describes just such an object:

> The infant's first experience of the object is as a process, rather than a thing in itself, but he perceptually identifies his experience of the object (an experience of psychosomatic transformation) with the maternal object. . . . I want to identify [this] first object as a *transformational object*. The mother is not yet identified as an object but is experienced as a process of transformation, and this feature remains in the trace of this object-seeking adult. . . . Thus, in adult life, the quest is not to possess the object; it is sought in order to surrender to it as a process that alters the self, where the subject-as-supplicant now feels himself to be the recipient of enviro-somatic caring, identified with metamorphoses of the self. [p. 98]

I would suggest that melancholia can be explained as a reaction to the loss of a relationship one has had with a transformational object, as defined by Bollas. The desperation that follows the breakup of such a relationship is understandable if one assumes that the loss is tantamount to the loss of an individual's ability to maintain an aspect of himself that was spawned by, and remains dependent on, a continuing relationship with this transforming other. Since these dynamics remain unconscious, the individual is only aware of having lost someone who offered him an opportunity to love and be loved, to experience intimacy, and have someone with whom to share his life. But he does not recognize what else has been lost in the process. To restate Freud's thesis: the patient knows whom he lost, but he does not know what he lost in himself.

ROMANTIC VS. "MATURE" LOVE

Romantic love is often the driving force behind the single woman–married man syndrome, which, to a certain extent, accounts for both the powerful attraction each partner feels toward the other and the difficulty each experiences trying to break free of the attraction's grasp. Falling in love is a rejuvenating experience, particularly for those who have lapsed into the doldrums of mid-life, or who are either incapable of achieving mature love, or incapable of deriving sufficient satisfaction from its more subtle rewards. The excitement of an affair is a fountain of youth, a restorer of one's narcissistic investment in oneself, and, as such, it often proves nearly impossible to resist. But it can also be a snake pit into which one drops. Clawing one's way out of a hopelessly entangled romantic extramarital affair is a challenge for those who succumb to the charms of romance.

Historically, attitudes about romantic love have been mixed. It is currently regarded as an ideal state, particularly in the Western world, where it is considered a prerequisite to marriage. But this was not always the case. In past centuries the state of falling in love was considered a malady, akin to a bout of temporary insanity. It was the duty of society to ensure that one not base a

life decision on so fickle a feeling as romantic love. The univer-
sality of romantic love has been questioned by Lawrence Stone
(1988), a professor of history at Princeton University, who notes
that historians and anthropologists are "less certain whether or
not romantic love is merely a culture-induced sublimated
psychological overlay on top of the biological drive for sex, or
whether it has biochemical roots which operate quite independently from the libido. Would anyone in fact 'fall in love' if they
had not read about it or heard it talked about? Did poetry invent
love, or love poetry?" (p. 16).

The romantic tradition, which began in the twelfth and thir-
teenth centuries, was "made fashionable by a group of poets and
troubadours . . . culture dictated that it should occur between
an unmarried male and a married woman, and that it should
either go sexually unconsummated or should be adulterous"
(Stone 1988, p. 17). Hence, romantic love, as originally conceived, was unrequited or tragic. Gaylin and Person (1988) note
that "only late in the Arthurian tradition of courtly love did marriage come to be seen as the end toward which love should
strive" (p. xii). But while Shakespeare's works indicated that
romantic love was a familiar concept to his audience, Stone
(1988) notes that it was not widely accepted as a legitimate cause
to wed.

> It was not, therefore, until the romantic movement and
> the rise of the novel, especially the pulp novel, in the
> nineteenth century, that society at large accepted a new
> idea—that it was normal and indeed praiseworthy for
> young men and women to fall passionately in love, and
> that there must be something wrong with those who
> have failed to have such an overwhelming experience
> sometime in late adolescence or early manhood. Once
> this new idea was publicly accepted, the dictation of
> marriage by parents came to be regarded as intolerable
> and immoral. [p. 19]

The most romantic relationships are those that give little consideration to practical matters. The idea that one would choose the least probable mate, at least by conventional standards, is an uplifting testament to the romantic nature of the human spirit. In the 1970s cult classic movie *Harold and Maude*, one sees a previously sullen and suicidal teenager transformed by a high-spirited "youth" in her late seventies, whom, by the movie's end, he has fallen in love with and wishes to marry. The movie illustrates the triumph of the romantic spirit over the deadening influences of society that had only served to drive Harold closer to the brink.

Some consider it an affront to the romantic spirit for a couple to consider such practical matters as whether they can get along well enough, operate as a team, and truly be partners over time. Romanticism has no patience for a consideration of practicalities. While nonpassionate relationships seem not to hold a candle to ones that are all about consuming passion, relationships that are the most passionate—so passionate that it seems impossible to forgo the experience—nevertheless often prove to be untenable over the long haul. One might think to look to the sky and ask, "Why, God, would you make it be that the most romantic relationships are the very ones that are not workable?"

The idea that true love ought to prevail over all other considerations is a romantic vision. It holds that the most improbable pairings (Harold and Maude/Edwin Gottesman and Jennifer Scott), if infused with passionate love, *must* find ways to work out. But time and again this proves not to be the case. Sometimes the very issues that make the relationship so damned exciting are the ones that make it impossible for a couple to be able to live together. As they say: "Can't live with 'em, can't live without 'em."

Some may take offense at my seeming to malign so noble and distinguished an institution as romantic love. In particular, they may object to my efforts to place romance under the microscope in an effort to dissect its workings. Romance is all about illusion, so the romantic is likely to want to derail any attempt to look too closely at the love relationship by insisting that I "pay no attention to the man behind the curtain." I think there is a time and a place in each person's life for romantic love. But the romantic view would accept no such limitations, and would elevate romance to a position above all else. In my view, romantic love is not the product of happenstance as the myth of Cupid would have us believe. Rather, a person who suddenly finds himself in the grip of romantic love was already unconsciously primed to be looking for just such an opportunity. Romantic love can just as easily be worth it as not.

Ethel Person (1988) would surely take issue with this view of romantic love, since she has been critical of how certain psychoanalysts understand love. For instance, she points out that some analysts seem to regard romantic love as a manifestation of immaturity:

Rationalists regard romantic love as a foolish if not downright dangerous illusion which creates impossible expectations in people and makes them unable to just accept the good that *is* possible in relationships. . . . They generally denigrate the experience of falling in love. In essence they downgrade romantic love and endorse some version of nonpassionate 'love' which is based on a rational decision to commit oneself to a person or situation. They counsel a kind of love stripped of "excess"— mature, as it were—and based on mutual respect, shared values, and common interests. Duty and responsibility are valued above emotional pleasure and sexual passion. [pp. 15–17]

Kernberg is most likely the rationalist Person had in mind when she wrote the above passage. Over the span of twenty-five years, Kernberg (1974a,b, 1977, 1980, 1988, 1991, 1995) has elaborated a theory of love that endeavors to explain how individuals develop the ability to fall in love and achieve "mature love." Kernberg (1977) defines mature sexual love as "a complex emotional disposition which integrates sexual excitement, tenderness, genital identification, a mature form of idealization, and a deep commitment to an object relation" (p. 94). Kernberg (1974b) underscores Freud's belief that love requires that one have developed an ability to blend or fuse one's tender regard for a woman (care and concern for the woman one "makes love to") with the wish to use the woman as a "pure sexual object" (even to the point of aggressively or hostilely "fucking" her). Kernberg asserts that the ability to tolerate such ambivalent feelings toward one's love object is the result of an individual having outgrown an earlier tendency to primitively split objects by either idealizing them (seeing them as all good) or devaluing them (seeing them as all bad). Mature love includes the ability to experience tender, loving feelings as well as hostile, aggressive feelings toward the same person, sometimes even at the same time, without experiencing a major shift in how one regards that individual. By comparison, individuals who employ primitive splitting mechanisms experience their tender and hostile feelings either alternately or, simultaneously, toward different objects. Fusing one's loving feelings with one's hateful feelings results in a diminution of both feelings when compared to how intensely these feelings are experienced by those inclined to idealize or completely devalue their objects.

Genital identification is another one of Kernberg's requirements for mature love. Kernberg (1974b) writes of how the achievement of the capacity to relate to whole objects, as opposed to part objects "results in a deepening awareness of the self and others, the beginning of the capacity for empathy and for higher level identifications" (p. 748). For individuals who are capable of mature love, the personal validation that comes from having been proven man enough to bring one's partner to orgasm is not nearly as important as the pleasure that comes from identifying with the excitement and gratification one's mate is experiencing through orgasm. In other words, the narcissistic gratification one derives from having been instrumental in causing another to feel such pleasure, is, for the narcissist, proof of his or her own worth and power.

Higher level identifications, as Kernberg calls them, account for an individual's ability to be empathic with the experiences of his lover. How far this might be expected to extend is illustrated in the writings of Cavell (1988), who suggests that one current-day expectation of marriage is that it "bear the brunt of one another's subjectivity . . . as providing (or sustaining the) proof of one another's existence" (p. 91). Being able to bear the brunt of another's subjectivity may be about the best definition of intimacy we have. This entails more than the mere tolerance of the partner's unique ways of experiencing and interpreting life. It includes true empathy for the way one's partner relates to the world. While romantic love may appear more intense than other forms of love, it is not clear whether the romantic affair derives its intensity from true intimacy (bearing the brunt of another's subjectivity) or from the intense narcissistic gratification that results from such an exchange.

Kernberg (1974b) also insists that mature love include a mature idealization of one's mate, which contrasts with the type of idealization typically encountered as a result of primitive splitting operations, such as one sees in patients suffering from borderline personality organizations. Kernberg believes that the evolution of one's idealizations is largely a function of super-ego developments. He cites Chasseguet-Smirgel (1973), who suggests

> that in mature love, in contrast to transitory adolescent falling in love, there is a limited projection of a toned-down ego ideal on the idealized love object. . . . Normal idealization constitutes an advanced developmental level of this mechanism by which infantile and childhood morality are transformed into adult ethical

systems. Idealization, thus conceived, is a normal function of the love relationship, establishing continuity between "romantic" adolescent and mature love. Under normal conditions, it is not the ego ideal that is projected, but ideals that stem from advanced structural development within the superego (including the ego ideal). [pp. 86–87]

Kernberg (1974b) states:

A mature selection of the person one loves and with whom one wants to live one's life involves mature ideals, value judgments, and goals, which, in addition to the satisfaction of the need for love and intimacy, give a broader meaning to life. It may be questioned whether the term "idealization" still applies here, but insofar as a person is selected who corresponds to an ideal to be striven for, there is an element of transcendence in such a selection, a commitment to a person that comes naturally because it is the commitment to a certain type of life as represented by what the relationship with that person might or will be. [p. 750]

Mature love, as Kernberg has described it, contrasts with the falling in love with love that is so characteristic of those in constant search for romantic love. Romantic love has the capacity to satisfy deep narcissistic needs, particularly in a relationship's earliest stages, before the affair begins to take on the characteristics of a marriage, which so often happens over the course of time. Men whose characters are chiefly structured along narcissistic lines, or who have entered a period of narcissistic vulnerability, are more prone to both fall in love with women other than their wives, and to find it excruciatingly hard to end such affairs, given the narcissistic gratifications they derive from such relationships. Such men are also more likely to be unable to maintain enough of a sense of themselves to permit themselves to surrender to the relationship without fearing that they may be in jeopardy of losing themselves in the process, as noted earlier in this chapter.

Judith Viorst (1968, p. 71) offers these concluding thoughts at the end of her book entitled *It's Hard to Be Hip Over Thirty and Other Tragedies of Married Life*:

It's true love because
I put on eyeliner and a concerto and make pungent
observations about the great issues of the day
Even when there's no one here but him,
And because
I do not resent watching the Green Bay Packers
Even though I am philosophically opposed to football,
And because
When he is late for dinner and I know he must be either
having an affair or lying dead in the middle of the
street,
I always hope he's dead.
It's true love because
If he said quit drinking martinis but I kept drinking them
and the next morning I couldn't get out of bed,
He wouldn't tell me he told me,
And because,
If his mother was drowning and I was drowning and he
had to choose one of us to save,
He says he'd save me.
It's true love because,
When he went to San Francisco on business while I had
to stay home with the painters and the
exterminators and the baby who was
getting the chicken pox,
He understood why I hated him,
And because,
When I said that playing the stock market was juvenile
and irresponsible and then the stock I wouldn't let
him buy went up twenty-six points,

I understood why he hated me,
And because,
Despite cigarette cough, tooth decay, acid indigestion,
    dandruff, and other features of married life that
    tend to dampen the fires of passion,
We still feel something
We can call
True Love.

References

Akhtar, S. (1985). The other woman: phenomenological, psycho-dynamic, and therapeutic considerations. In *Contemporary Marriage: Special Issues in Couples Therapy*, ed. D. Goldberg, pp. 215–240. Homewood, IL: Dorsey.

Akhtar, S., and Kramer, S., eds. (1996). *Intimacy and Infidelity: Separation-Individuation Perspectives*. Northvale, NJ: Jason Aronson.

Alexander, R. (1987). *The Biology of Moral Systems*. Hawthorne, NY: de Gruyter.

Altman, I., and Ginat, J. (1996). *Polygamous Families in Contemporary Society*. Cambridge, UK: Cambridge University Press.

Altman, L. (1977). Some vicissitudes of love. *Journal of the American Psychoanalytic Association* 25: 35–52.

Aries, E. (1976). Interaction patterns and themes of male, female, and mixed groups. *Small Group Behavior* 7:7–18.

Asperger, H. (1944). "Autistic psychopathy" in childhood. In *Autism and Asperger Syndrome*, ed. U. Frith, pp. 37–92. Cambridge, UK: Cambridge University Press.

Atwood, G., and Stolorow, R. (1984). *Structures of Subjectivity*. Hillsdale, NJ: Analytic Press.

Barkow, J., Cosmides, L., and Tooby, J. (1992). *The Adapted Mind: Evolutionary Psychology and the Generation of Culture*. New York: Oxford University Press.

Berliner, B. (1947). On some psychodynamics of masochism. *Psychoanalytic Quarterly* 16:459–471.

——— (1958). The role of object relations in moral masochism. *Psychoanalytic Quarterly* 27:38–56.

Berne, E. (1964). *Games People Play*. New York: Ballantine.

Bernstein, I. (1957). The role of narcissism in moral masochism. *Psychoanalytic Quarterly* 26:358–377.

——— (1983). Masochistic pathology and feminine development. *Journal of the American Psychoanalytic Association* 31:467–486.

Billy, J. O. G., Tanfer, K., Grady, W. R., and Kelpinger, D. H. (1993). The sexual behavior of men in the United States. *Family Planning Perspectives* 25:52–60.

Blum, H. (1976). Masochism, the ego ideal, and the psychology of women. *Journal of the American Psychoanalytic Association* 24:157–191.

Bollas, C. (1979). The transformational object. *International Journal of Psycho-Analysis* 60:97–107.

Braunschweig, D., and Fain, M. (1971). *Eros et Anteros*. Paris: Payot.

——— (1975). *La Nuit, le Jour: Essai Psychoanalytique sur le Fonctionnement Mental*. Paris: Payot.

Brenner, C. (1959). The masochistic character: genesis and treatment. *Journal of the American Psychoanalytic Association* 7:197–226.

Burke, R., Weiser, T., and Harrison, D. (1976). Disclosure of problems and tensions experienced by mental patients. *Psychological Reports* 38:531–542.

Buss, D., and Shackelford, T. (1997). Susceptibility to infidelity in the first year of marriage. *Journal of Research in Personality* 31:193–221.

Cato, L. (1996). *The Other Woman*. Atlanta, GA: Longstreet.

Cavell, S. (1988). Two cheers for romance. In *Passionate Attachments*, ed. W. Gaylin and E. Person, pp. 85–100. New York: Free Press.

Chasseguet-Smirgel, J. (1973). *Essai sur L'ideal du Moi*. Paris: Presses Universitaires de France.

Cloud, J. (1999). Monica's makeover. *Time*, March 15, pp. 38–40.

Eidelberg, L. (1959). Humiliation in masochism. *Journal of the American Psychoanalytic Association* 7:274–283.

Fitzpatrick, M. (1984). A typological approach to marital interaction: recent theory and research. *Advances in Experimental Social Psychology* 18:1–47.

———— (1988). *Between Husbands and Wives: Communication in Marriage*. Beverly Hills, CA: Sage.

Freud, S. (1909). Analysis of a phobia in a five-year-old boy. *Standard Edition* 10:3–249.

———— (1910). A special type of choice of object made by men (contributions to the psychology of love I). *Standard Edition* 11: 164–175.

———— (1912). On the universal tendency to debasement in the sphere of love (contributions to the psychology of love II). *Standard Edition* 11:179–190.

———— (1914). On narcissism: an introduction. *Standard Edition* 14:69–102.

———— (1917). Mourning and melancholia. *Standard Edition* 14:239–258.

———— (1924). The economic problem of masochism. *Standard Edition* 19:157–170.

Frith, U. (1991). *Autism and Asperger Syndrome*. Cambridge, UK: Cambridge University Press.

Gaylin, W., and Person, E. (1988). Introduction: thinking about love. In *Passionate Attachments: Thinking About Love*, ed. W. Gaylin and E. Person pp. ix–xiii, New York: Free Press.

Ghent, E. (1990). Masochism, submission, surrender—masochism as a perversion of surrender. *Contemporary Psychoanalysis* 26:108–136.

Ginsberg, D., and Gottman, J. (1986). The conversation of college roommates. In *Conversation of Friends: Speculation on*

Effective Development, ed. J. Gottman and J. Parker. New York: Cambridge University Press.

Glasgow, E. (1923). The difference. In *The Other Woman: Stories of Two Women and a Man*, ed. S. Koppelman, pp. 167–189. Old Westbury, NY: Feminist Press.

Glass, S., and Marano, H. (1998). Shattered vows. *Psychology Today,* July/August, 31, p. 34.

Glass, S., and Wright, T. (1977). The relationship of extramarital sex, length of marriage, and sex differences on marital satisfaction and romanticism: Athanasiou's data reanalyzed. *Journal of Marriage and the Family* 39:691–703.

—— (1985). Sex differences in type of extramarital involvement and marital dissatisfaction. *Sex Roles* 12:1101–1120.

—— (1988). Clinical implications of research on extramarital involvement. In *Treatment of Sexual Problems in Individual and Couples therapy*, ed. R. Brown and J. Field, pp. 301–346. Costa Mesa, CA: PMA Publishing.

—— (1992). Justification for extramarital relationships: the association between attitudes, behaviors, and gender. *Journal of Sex Research* 29:361–387.

Gottman, J. (1979). *Marital Interaction: Experimental Investigation.* New York: Academic Press.

—— (1994). *What Predicts Divorce? The Relationship between Marital Processes and Marital Outcomes.* Hillsdale, NJ: Lawrence Erlbaum.

Gottman, J., and Krokoff, L. (1989). The relationship between marital interaction and marital satisfaction: a longitudinal view. *Journal of Consulting and Clinical Psychology* 57:47–52.

Gottman, J., and Levenson, R. (1985). A valid procedure for obtaining self-respect of affect in marital interaction. *Journal of Consulting and Clinical Psychology* 53:151–160.

—— (1988). The social psychophysiology of marriage. In *Perspectives on Marital Interaction*, ed. P. Noller and M. Fitzpatrick, pp. 182–200. Clevedon, UK: Multilingual Matters.

Gottman, J., and Porterfield, A. (1981). Communicative competence in the nonverbal behavior of married couples. *Journal of Marriage and the Family* 43:817–824.

Green, A. (1986). *On Private Madness*. London: Hogarth.

—— (1993). *Le travail du regatif*. Paris: Minuit.

Greene, B., Lee, R., and Lustig, N. (1974). Conscious and unconscious factors in marital infidelity. *Medical Aspects of Human Sexuality* 8:97–105.

Hollander, I. (1976). The other woman: personality characteristics and parent–child relationships of single women repeatedly involved with married men. *Dissertation Abstracts International* 12:1–152.

Horney, K. (1966). The dread of women. In *Psychoanalysis and Male Sexuality*, ed. H. Roitenbeek, pp. 83–96. New Haven, CT: College and University Press.

Howitt, P. (1995). *Sliding Doors*. Beverly Hills, CA: Intermedia Film Equities and Mirage Enterprises.

Humphrey, F. (1982). Extramarital affairs: clinical approaches in marital therapy. *Psychiatric Clinics of North America* 5: 581–593.

Hunt, M. (1969). *The Affair: A Portrait of Extramarital Love in Contemporary America*. New York: World.

—— (1974). *Sexual Behavior in the 1970s*. Chicago: Playboy Press.

Huston, T., and Ashmore, R. (1986). Women and men in personal relationships. In *The Social Psychology of Female–Male Relations*, ed. R. O. Ashmore and F. Del Boco, pp. 167–210. New York: Academic Press.

Keiser, S. (1949). The fear of sexual passivity in the masochist. *International Journal of Psycho-Analysis* 30:162–171.

Kelley, H., Cunningham, J., Chrisham, J., et al. (1978). Sex differences in comments made during conflict within close heterosexual pairs. *Sex Roles* 4:473–492.

Kernberg, O. (1974a). Barriers to falling and remaining in love. *Journal of the American Psychoanalytic Association* 22:486–511.

—— (1974b). Mature love: prerequisites and characteristics. *Journal of the American Psychoanalytic Association* 22:743–768.

—— (1977). Boundaries and structure in love relations. *Journal of the American Psychoanalytic Association* 25:81–114.

—— (1980). Love, the couple, and the group: a psychoanalytic frame. *Psychoanalytic Quarterly* 49:78–108.

—— (1988) Between conventionality and aggression: the boundaries of passion. In *Passionate Attachments: Thinking about Love*, ed. W. Gaylin and E. Person, pp. 63–83. New York: Free Press.

—— (1991). Aggression and love in the relationship of the couple. *Journal of the American Psychoanalytic Association* 39:45–80.

—— (1995). *Love Relations: Normality and Pathology*. New Haven, CT: Yale University Press.

Kinsey, A., Pomeroy, W., and Martin, C. (1948). *Sexual Behavior in the Human Male*. Philadelphia: Saunders.

Kinsey, A., Pomeroy, W., Martin, C., and Gebhard, P. (1953). *Sexual Behavior in the Human Female*. Philadelphia: Saunders.

Kohut, H. (1971). *The Analysis of the Self: A Systematic Approach to the Psychoanalytic Treatment of Narcissistic Personalities*. New York: International Universities Press.

Komarovsky, M. (1962). *Blue-Collar Marriage*. New York: Random House.

—— (1976). *Dilemmas of Masculinity*. New York: Norton.

Koppelman, S., ed. (1984). *The Other Woman: Stories of Two Women and a Man*. Old Westbury, NY: Feminist Press.

Laumann, E. O., Gagnon, J. H., Michael, R. T., and Michaels, S. (1994). *The Social Organization of Sexuality: Sexual Practices in the United States*. Chicago: University of Chicago Press.

Lester, M. (1957). The analysis of an unconscious beating fantasy in women. *International Journal of Psycho-Analysis* 38:22–31.

Levenson, R., and Gottman, J. (1983). Marital interaction: physiological linkage and affective exchange. *Journal of Personality and Social Psychology* 45:587–597.

Locke, H. (1951). *Predicting Adjustments in Marriage: A Comparison of a Divorced and a Happily Married Group*. New York: Holt.

Loewenstein, R. (1957). A contribution to the psychoanalytic theory of masochism. *Journal of the American Psychoanalytic Association* 5:197–234.

Los Angeles Times (1998). The Clinton testimony: details: Lewinsky seen in another light, September 22.

Mahler, M. (1968). *On Human Symbiosis and the Vicissitudes of Individuation. Volume I: Infantile Psychosis*. New York: International Universities Press.

Markson, E. (1993). Depression and moral masochism. *International Journal of Psycho-Analysis* 74:931–940.

Marx, E. (1987). Relations between spouses among Negev Bedouin. *Ethnos* 1–2:156–179.

Maykovich, M. (1976). Attitudes versus behavior in extramarital sexual relations. *Journal of Marriage and the Family* 38:693–699.

Menaker, E. (1953). Masochism—a defense reaction of the ego. *Psychoanalytic Quarterly* 22: 205–220.

Morgan, M. (1973). *The Total Woman*. New York: Pocket Books.

Morton, A. (1999). *Monica's Story*. New York: St. Martin's.

Person, E. (1988). *Dreams of Love and Fateful Encounters: The Power of Romantic Passion*. New York: Penguin.

Petersen, J. (1983). The *Playboy* readers' sex survey. *Playboy*, 30(3): 9off.

Phelps, E. (1865). No news. In *The Other Woman: Stories of Two Women and a Man*, ed. S. Koppelman, pp. 13–40. Old Westbury, NY: Feminist Press.

Pioneer Log (1999). Bliss leaves LC to reveal the truth about Monica Lewinsky, March 12, vol. 63, #48.

Pittman, F. (1989). *Private Lies: Infidelity and the Betrayal of Intimacy*. New York: Norton.

Plato (1999). *The Symposium*, trans. C. Gill. London: Penguin.

Raush, H., Barry, W., Hertel, W., and Swain, M. (1974). *Communication, Conflict, and Marriage*. San Francisco: Jossey-Bass.

Reik, T. (1941). *Masochism in Modern Man*. New York: Farrar & Straus.

Richardson, L. (1979). The "other woman": the end of the long affair. *Alternative Lifestyles* 2:397–414.

—— (1985). *The New Other Woman: Contemporary Single Women in Affairs with Married Men*. New York: Free Press.

—— (1988). Sexual freedom and sexual constraint: the paradox for single women in liaisons with married men. *Gender and Society* 2:368–384.

Rickman, J. (1951). Number and the human sciences. In *Selected Contributions to Psycho-Analysis*, ed. Anonymous. London: Hogarth.

Ross, J. (1996). Male infidelity in long marriages: second adolescences and fourth individuations. In *Intimacy and Infidelity: Separation-Individuation Perspectives*, ed. S. Akhtar and S. Kramer, pp. 109–130. Northvale, NJ: Jason Aronson.

Rubin, L. (1976). *Worlds of Pain*. New York: Basic Books.

Schaap, C. (1982). *Communication and Adjustment in Marriage*. The Netherlands: Swets and Feitlinger.

Smith, T. W. (1991). Adult sexual behavior in 1989: number of partners, frequency of intercourse and risk of AIDS. *Family Planning Perspectives* 22:102–107.

Socarides, C. (1958). The function of moral masochism: with special reference to the defence processes. *International Journal of Psycho-Analysis* 39:587–597.

Spanier, G., and Margolis, R. (1983). Marital separation and extramarital behavior. *Journal of Sex Research* 19:23–48.

Starr, K. (1998). *The Starr Report*. New York: toExcel.

Stoller, R. (1979). *Sexual Excitement: Dynamics of Erotic Life*. New York: Pantheon.

Stolorow, R. (1975). The narcissistic function of masochism (and sadism). *International Journal of Psycho-Analysis* 56:444–448.

Stolorow, R., and Atwood, G. (1992). *Contexts of Being: The Intersubjective Foundations of Psychological Life.* Hillsdale, NJ: Analytic Press.

Stone, L. (1988). Passionate attachments in the west in historical perspective. In *Passionate Attachments*, ed. W. Gaylin and E. Person, pp. 15–26. New York: Free Press.

Terman, L., Buttenweiser, P., Ferguson, L., et al. (1938). *Psychological Factors in Marital Happiness.* New York: McGraw-Hill.

Thompson, A. (1983). Extramarital sex: a review of the research literature. *Journal of Sex Research* 19:1–22.

Tuch, R. (1975). Relationship of a woman's menstrual status and her response to illness in her children. *Psychosomatic Medicine* 37(6): 388–394.

Viorst, J. (1968). *It's Hard to Be Hip Over Thirty and Other Tragedies of Married Life.* New York: World.

Ware, H. (1979). Polygamy: women's views in transitional society, Nigeria, 1975. *Journal of Marriage and Family* 41:185–195.

Webster's New Collegiate Dictionary. (1975). Springfield, MA: Merriam.

Weiss, S. (1987). The two-woman phenomenon. *Psychoanalytic Quarterly* 56:271–331.

Whitehurst, R. (1969). Alienation or extension of normal behavior. In *Extra-marital Relations*, ed. G. Nubeck, pp. 129–145. Englewood Cliffs, NJ: Prentice Hall.

Wiederman, M. (1997). Extramarital sex: prevalence and correlates in a national survey. *Journal of Sex Research* 34: 167–174.

Wills, T., Weiss, R., and Patterson, G. (1974). A behavioral analysis of the determinants of marital satisfaction. *Journal of Consulting and Clinical Psychology* 42:802–811.

Credits

The author gratefully acknowledges permission to reprint material from the following sources:

"The 'Other Woman': The End of the Long Affair," by Laurel Richardson, in *Alternative Lifestyles* 2:397–414. Copyright © 1979 and used with permission of Plenum Publishing Corporation.

The New Other Woman: Contemporary Single Women in Affairs with Married Men, by Laurel Richardson. Copyright © 1985 by Laurel Richardson. Reprinted with the permission of The Free Press, a Division of Simon & Schuster, Inc.

Monica's Story, by Andrew Morton. Copyright © 1999 by Andrew Morton and Prufrock LLC. Reprinted by permission of St. Martin's Press, LLC and Michael O'Mara Books, Ltd.

The Affair, by Morton Hunt. Copyright © 1969, 1971 by Morton Hunt. This usage granted by Lescher & Lescher, Ltd.

"True Love," by Judith Viorst, from *It's Hard to Be Hip Over Thirty and Other Tragedies of Married Life*. Copyright © 1968, renewed 1996, by Judith Viorst. This usage granted by Lescher & Lescher, Ltd.

Index

ABOUT THE AUTHOR

Richard Tuch, M.D., is a Training and Supervising Analyst with the Los Angeles Psychoanalytic Society and Institute, Assistant Clinical Professor of Psychiatry at the University of California at Los Angeles, and Attending Psychiatrist at the Cedar-Sinai Medical Center. He has written numerous articles on such subjects as writer's block, the limits of empathy as a therapeutic tool, and the role of social cognition in personal relationships. A frequent presenter at meetings of the American Psychoanalytic Association, Dr. Tuch is the recipient of the 1995 Karl A. Menninger Memorial Award for Psychoanalytic Writing. He maintains a private practice in West Los Angeles. This is his first book.